MUSIC LITERATURE OUTLINES

SERIES II

MUSIC IN THE BAROQUE

by

Harold Gleason and Warren Becker

Third Edition

Frangipani Press

Division of T.I.S. Publications

THIRD EDITION
COPYRIGHT   1980

FRANGIPANI PRESS - TIS PUBLICATIONS
P.O. Box 1998
Bloomington, Indiana 47402

Library of Congress Catalogue Card Number: 79-66417
ISBN 0-89917-016-1

Johann Sebastian Bach
1685 - 1750

CONTENTS

MUSIC IN THE BAROQUE

ILLUSTRATIONS

PREFACE TO THE THIRD EDITION

This edition of *Music Literature Outlines, Series II, Music in the Baroque,* is a complete revision of the second edition. The unique outline form of the earlier editions has remained essentially unchanged. The bibliographies of books, articles and music at the end of each *Outline* have been revised and brought up to date, and considerable new material has been added.

The authors hope that the systematic organization of information in the *Outlines* will afford the student, teacher and performer a resource whereby a comprehensive understanding of the music in the Baroque may be obtained. This understanding should be enlarged by performing the music, listening to records with scores and consulting the bibliographies. The bibliographies of books and articles have been chosen with care and, with few exceptions, limited to the English language. The bibliographies of music have been selected from reliable or critical editions and include monumental editions, complete or authoritative editions of composers works and easily accessible anthologies.

The authors are indebted to Verne W. Thompson, Catharine Crozier Gleason, and Ruth Watanabe, Librarian of the Sibley Music Library of the Eastman School of Music, Rochester, New York, for help in the preparation of the earlier editions of the *Outlines*, and to the librarians and staffs of the Central Library, University of California, San Diego, the San Diego State University Library, and the Music Materials Center, Andrews University, Michigan, for their assistance in making valuable materials available.

September 1, 1979
San Diego, California

Harold Gleason
Warren Becker

MUSIC IN THE BAROQUE

OUTLINE I

INTRODUCTION

The Baroque — Features of the Italian Baroque Style before 1600
Characteristics of the Baroque Style
A Brief Summary of the Baroque

I. **The Baroque**

    A.   The term "baroque," used to designate a historical period and style in music, art, and architecture, may have been derived from *barrôco,* a Portuguese word which described an irregularly shaped pearl.

        1.   Eighteenth-century French critics applied the term in a derogatory sense and considered baroque music to be "extravagant," "bizarre," "grotesque," and "unnatural."

    B.   The usual dates assigned to the Baroque period, 1600–1750, are only approximate and mark the period from the rise of monody with the Italian Camerata to the death of **J. S. Bach.**

        1.   The Baroque has also been divided arbitrarily into Early (*c.* 1580–*c.* 1640), Middle (*c.* 1640–*c.* 1690), and Late or High Baroque (*c.* 1690–*c.* 1740). The first date marks the beginning of Baroque traits in Italy. The dates overlap, vary in different countries, and by 1740 a new style known as "rococo" made its appearance, particularly in France and Germany.

II. **Features of the Italian Baroque Style before 1600**

    A.   The changes in style from Renaissance to Baroque began gradually in Italy during the second half of the 16th century with a reaction against polyphony. The following are some of the important developments:

        1.   The splendor of the Venetian School of **Giovanni Gabrieli** with the use of homophony, double chorus, and opposing instrumental and vocal groups (*concertato* style).

        2.   Madrigals which portrayed the text (text-painting) through the use of chromaticism, and the dramatic and expressive use of dissonance.

        3.   The breaking down of modality and intervallic harmony, and the gradual appearance of major and minor tonalities.

        4.   The prominence of the upper voice in homophonic, rhythmic dance-songs.

III. **Characteristics of the Baroque**

    A.   Composers of the Baroque introduced many new forms, types, techniques, and stylistic innovations which continued to expand the many different forms of musical expression.

    B.   Texture

        1.   A new texture in vocal and instrumental music resulted from the invention of the *basso continuo,* which continued to be used in vocal and ensemble music for at least two decades after 1750.

            a.   The similar and equal voices of polyphony were reduced to a melody and bass. The inner part was filled in with chords played on a lute or keyboard instrument.

C. Styles of compositions
1. *Stile antico* (*prima prattica*). The "old style" or "first practice" of polyphonic church music of the Renaissance was preserved along with the new *stile moderno*, and composers wrote in both styles.
2. *Stile moderno* (*seconda prattica*). In the "modern style" or "second practice" the text dominated the music.
3. In the late 17th century music was classified as church, chamber, or theatre, sometimes without a clear distinction in style.
D. Affections and figures
1. During the entire Baroque, composers endeavored to make the music represent the feeling or mood (affection) of the text.
2. Musical figures (motifs) were later classified, particularly in Germany, and used to represent certain affections.
3. Singers, through the recitative, expressed the meaning of the text with extreme, and often violent, realism.
E. Harmony and dissonance
1. Tonality emerged as chords became functional, and by 1650 a new treatment of dissonance was possible.
2. Dissonant notes could be used with the chords and resolved upward or downward.
    a. Fast harmonic rhythm with dissonant chords became possible, and altered and unprepared sevenths appeared.
F. Idiomatic writing
1. The difference between vocal and instrumental styles became more pronounced.
    a. Vocal and instrumental idioms were sometimes exchanged, especially in Late Baroque music, and music for specific instruments was exploited.
G. Rhythm
1. There was a new rhythmic flexibility from the completely free, unmeasured rhythm of the recitative and early toccata to strict metrical strong and weak beats which became a characteristic of the later Baroque style.
H. Melody
1. Melody became expressive, more free, with wide ranges and chromatic, augmented, and diminished intervals. Virtuoso singing developed.
I. Improvisation and ornamentation
1. Keyboard players improvised extended pieces as well as continuo parts, and improvisation was a part of the musician's equipment.
2. Singers and string players improvised embellishments based on the written notes, and extemporizing "divisions on a ground" was a popular diversion in England.

IV. A Brief Summary of the Baroque

A. The influence of Italian music was strong throughout the entire Baroque. At the beginning of the 17th century, Florence was the center of the Camerata who initiated the new style of monody.
B. Venice was an important center for music during the entire 17th century which saw the rise of vocal, instrumental, and keyboard forms.
1. These forms include the recitative, aria, opera, oratorio, cantata, ensemble canzona, concerto, *sonata da camera, sonata da chiesa, concerto grosso,* and the keyboard ricercar, canzona, and toccata.
C. Rome was a center for church music which preserved to some extent the Renaissance *a cappella* tradition and made use of the Venetian polychoral style.
1. Opera was performed in Rome for a time during the 17th century, and in the 18th century the Neapolitan School came into prominence.
D. French music in the Baroque was under the patronage of the royal courts during the

reigns of Louis XIII (1610-1643) and Louis XIV (1643-1715), and by 1650 a national style had evolved. Emphasis was on the ballet and opera. However, organ, clavecin, and instrumental ensemble music played an important part.

1. The "rococo" style began in France in the early 18th century with **François Couperin** (1668-1733) as its chief representative, in Germany with **Georg Philipp Telemann** (1681-1767), and in Italy with **Domenico Scarlatti** (1685-1757).

E. The final development of the English madrigal school took place in the early 17th century during the reigns of Elizabeth and James I, and reached its height with the music of **William Byrd** (1543-1623). The court masque was a popular form of entertainment during the Early Baroque.

1. The music showed characteristic Italian and French influence in the continuo song with lute accompaniment, and instrumental ensemble music for ballets.

2. During the Civil War and Commonwealth (1642-1660), the development of vocal and keyboard music declined. After the Restoration, which began in 1660, new Italian Baroque styles and forms appeared, culminating in the music of **Henry Purcell** (*c.* 1659-1695).

3. In the Late Baroque, music in England was generally imported from Italy, France, and Germany.

F. German composers, following the devastating Thirty Years War (1618-1648), were active in almost all fields of music except opera. The Italian techniques of monody and *concertato* style influenced the composers of vocal and instrumental music from early in the 17th century.

1. The tradition of **Sweelinck** and **Scheidt** brought the organ chorale to the north and central German composers, and **Frescobaldi's** influence was felt in south Germany.

2. The fusion of Italian and German styles by **Heinrich Schütz** (1585-1672) became the principal characteristic of German music. It remained for **Johann Sebastian Bach** to achieve a complete synthesis of the Italian, French, and German styles.

3. The contributions of the German-born, Italian-trained **George Frideric Handel**, who became a British subject in 1726, anticipated in many ways the new harmonic and melodic style of the next period.

G. Baroque music has continued to be a source of inspiration throughout succeeding generations. The significance of this, as expressed by Manfred Bukofzer, "should not be explained as the result of a freak coincidence, nor by the fact that industrious musicologists have happened to unearth such music," but rather "that modern composers, consciously and unconsciously, return to formal and technical devices of the baroque style and make them serve a new function in modern music."

The following standard references will be used in these *Outlines.* They will not be included in the Bibliographies. A list of abbreviations will be found on page 170.

Apel, Willi. *Harvard Dictionary of Music,* 2nd edition, revised and enlarged. Cambridge: Harvard University Press, 1972.

Bukofzer, Manfred. *Music in the Baroque Era.* New York: W. W. Norton, 1947.

Grout, Donald J. *A History of Western Music.* New York: W. W. Norton, 1960.

————————*A Short History of Opera.* New York: Columbia University Press, 1947.

Lang, Paul Henry. *Music in Western Civilization.* New York: W. W. Norton, 1941.

Palisca, Claude V. *Baroque Music* (*BM*). Englewood Cliffs, NJ: Prentice-Hall, 1968.

OUTLINE II

MUSIC IN ITALY

EARLY BAROQUE

Introduction — Monody — Madrigals — Emilio de' Cavalieri
Opera in Florence and Mantua — Opera in Rome — Opera in Venice
Church Music — Instrumental Music
Bibliography of Books — Articles — Music

I. Introduction

A. The key to the beginning of the Baroque style was the introduction of the *basso continuo* with emphasis on the upper and lower voice and an instrumental accompaniment. This was evident in the solo and polyphonic madrigals with continuo bass and the beginnings of opera.

B. The major musical characteristics of the Early Italian Baroque include a strong reaction to polyphony, dramatically expressive recitative in free rhythm, new treatment of dissonance, experimental non-functional (pre-tonal) harmony, small forms, and sectional treatment. Idiomatic instrumental ensembles and keyboard music began their developments. Church music was relatively unimportant.

II. Monody

A. Monody is a type of solo song, known as recitative, with a chordal accompaniment "realized" from a *basso continuo* (continuous bass).

1. Monody was used in the aria, solo madrigal, opera, cantata, and oratorio.

2. Recitative (*stile recitativo*), the new melodic style, used music to "recite" or declaim a text with the inflections of speech.

3. The chordal accompaniment was improvised from the continuo bass on a harpsichord, small organ, lute, or harp. The bass line was usually strengthened by the use of a viola da gamba, violone, violoncello, or bassoon.

   a. Figures were used to indicate the intervals above the bass note, except for common chords in root position. Chromatic alterations were indicated by a sharp, flat, or natural placed with the figure. A diagonal line through a figure usually indicated a sharp.

B. Unifying devices of monody

1. Strophic variations (arias)

   a. The same bass line and harmony, with some alterations, were used for each stanza and the melody was usually varied more or less.

2. Repetitions and repeated refrain sections.

3. Brief imitations between bass and melody.

4. The separation of recurring arias and scenes by instrumental sinfonias or ritornellos.

C. The Florentine Camerata (*c.* 1573-*c.* 1592)   (*SR,* 290, 352, 363)

1. The Camerata was a group of musical and literary intellectuals who were led by Count **Giovanni de' Bardi** (1534-1612) and **Jacopo Corsi** (*c.* 1560-1604). Included in the group were **Girolamo Mei** (1519-1594), a student of Greek music; **Vincenzo Galilei** (*c.* 1520-1591), a theoretician and father of the astronomer; **Giulio Caccini** and **Jacopo Peri**, singers-composers; **Emilio de' Cavalieri**, a Roman nobleman and composer; and the poets **Ottavio Rinuccini** (1562-1621) and

4

Torquato Tasso (1544-1595).

a.   The Camerata met at the palace of **Count Bardi** in Florence to discuss a new musical style. This style was derived from what they knew of the lyrical qualities of ancient Greek tragedy and its use of monophonic music.

1)   In order to express a phrase of poetry perfectly, the Camerata suggested that there could be only one unique succession of tones and rhythm, rather than four or five polyphonic lines of music contradicting each other. Thus, with the text predominant, the Camerata exploited the accompanied recitative as a kind of "harmonic speech" in which the words were to be sung as they would be spoken. The words must be clearly understood and also "represent" the true sentiment of the text (*stile rappresentativo*).

D.   **Giulio Caccini** (*c.* 1546-1618)

1.   *Le Nuove Musiche,* 1602 (1601, Florentine calendar)   (*RRMB,* v. 9; *AM,* v. 31, p. 35; v. 45, p. 29; *M* 2ab)

a.   This "new music" was published in Florence. It is a collection of twelve through-composed "madrigals" and ten "arias," mostly strophic variations, in monodic style for solo voice. There is continuo accompaniment for *chitarrone,* a long archlute with bass strings. These are the earliest surviving compositions in the Florentine monodic style.

1)   *Nuove musiche e nuova maniera di scriverle* (New pieces of music and a new way of writing them out) is another important collection by **Caccini**. It was published in Florence in 1614 and contains 36 songs for solo voice and continuo.

b.   In the important Preface to *Le Nuove Musiche* (*SR,* 377), **Caccini** explains vocal embellishments (*gorgia*) and tempo rubato (*spezzatura*). Also in the Preface, his advice on vocal style and technique includes singing an even scale, proper breath support, and not sliding to the pitch nor singing falsetto. Crescendos and diminuendos were added to vocal lines, and even to single notes.

c.   Solo madrigals

1)   **Caccini's** through-composed solo madrigals for voice and continuo mark the beginning of the new Baroque style. More than the arias, the solo madrigals were capable of the most intense feeling as the vocal line was completely free to illustrate the text, even individual words.

2)   *Amarilli mia bella* (My lovely Amaryllis)   (*RRMB,* v. 9, p, 85; *GMB,* No. 173; *MSO,* 68; *AM,* v. 32, p. 32; *ICDMI,* v. 4)

a)   This is an example of the use of text-painting, harmonic and melodic dissonance, chromaticism, change of meter and rhythm, and ornamentation.

3)   *Dovrò dunque morire* (I must die, then?)   (*RRMB,* v. 9, p. 95; *MM,* 122; *AM,* v. 45, p. 29; *M* 2c)

a)   The continuo part for the above two solo madrigals was "realized" for lute by Robert Dowland (*c.* 1586-1641), son of John.

d.   Aria

1)   *Sfogava con le stelle* (Under the night sky he vented his grief)   (*HAM,* No. 184; *ICDMI,* v. 4)

2)   *Ard' il mio petto* (My unhappy breast burns)   (*GMB,* No. 172; *AM,* v. 32, p. 29)

III .   Madrigals

A.   In the Early Baroque, the continuo madrigal flourished in Florence, Venice, Mantua, Ferrara, and Rome, the musical centers of Italy. Foremost among composers of continuo songs was Claudio Monteverdi.

B.   **Claudio Monteverdi** (1567-1643)

1.   **Monteverdi** was born in Cremona and died in Venice. He studied counterpoint with

Ingegneri, head of the music at the Cremona cathedral, and learned to play the viol and organ. In 1590 he entered the service of the Duke of Mantua as a string player and singer, and was appointed chapel master in 1602. From 1613 to his death, he held the position of greatest prestige in Italy, *maestro di cappella* at St. Mark's in Venice.

2. Monteverdi's compositions comprise a wide variety of styles and forms from Renaissance *a cappella* madrigals for five voices to his masterpiece, the opera *L'incoronazione di Poppea*.

3. Monteverdi's principal works include nine books of madrigals, stage ballets and dance plays, church music, and four operas of which one is lost. His earliest works comprise a series of three-voice *a cappella* motets published in Venice in 1582. Among the poets whose texts are used in these madrigals are **Gabrielo Chiabrera, Giambattista Guarini, Giambattista Marino, Francesco Petrarch, Ottavio Rinuccini,** and **Torquato Tasso.**

4. *Book I, 1587; Book II, 1590; Book III, 1592; Book IV, 1603* (CE, vols. 1-4)
   a. **Monteverdi's** first four books of madrigals were all in five parts and represent his transition from the homophonic-contrapuntal *a cappella* style of the Late Renaissance (*prima prattica*) to the new freedom of expression of the Baroque found in his continuo madrigals beginning in *Book V. Books I* and *II* contain 21 madrigals each, and *Books III* and *IV* contain 20 madrigals each.
   b. *Ohimè, se tanto amate* (CE, v. 4, p. 54; HAM, No. 188)
      1) This five-part madrigal from *Book IV* represents the culmination of the Italian *a cappella* madrigal. The text begins, "Alas, if you like so much to hear me say 'Alas,' why do you cause him to die who says 'Alas'? . . . But if you wish my heart to have life from you, then you will have from me thousands and thousands of sweet Alas's."

5. *Book V, 1605* (CE, v. 5)
   a. **Monteverdi** planned to publish this collection of 19 madrigals under the title which reads in translation "Second Practice, or On the Perfection of Modern Music." In the last six madrigals the new style is represented by **Monteverdi's** first use of a continuo part.
      1. The madrigals using continuo became less contrapuntal and the voices took on greater freedom in concertato style.
      2. There are four madrigals for five voices, one for six, and one for nine voices which is divided into two choruses. Elements of the concertato style which **Monteverdi** uses include solo passages, solo ensembles, choruses, and intervening instrumental sinfonias.
   b. *Cruda Amarilli* (Cruel Amaryllis) (CE, v. 5, p. 1; MSO, v. 1, p. 69)
      1. Opening the collection was the madrigal which was the basis of **Giovanni Artusi's** violent attack on the "imperfections of modern music" (SR, 393, 405).
   c. *Ahi come a un vago sol* (Alas, like a lovely sun) (CE, v. 5)
      1. This madrigal is the first of the continuo madrigals and shows **Monteverdi's** use of refrain, trio, highly ornamented solo passages, duet in parallel thirds, and short motif imitation. All these techniques are characteristic of the fully developed *stile concertato.*

6. *Book VI, 1614* (CE, v. 6)
   a. Among the 18 madrigals in *Book VI* there are many in concertato style with contrasting solo (monodic) and ensemble groups of voices and/or instruments.
      1. The first madrigal is a five-voice arrangement of *Lamento d' Arianni* (CE, v. 6, p. l). It is used as a solo madrigal in **Monteverdi's** second opera, *Arianna*, and is the only surviving part of the opera (CE, v. 11; GMB, No. 177).
         a) A "spiritualized" version of the lament, *Pianto della Madonna* (Weeping of the Madonna), closes the last book published under **Monteverdi's** super-

vision, *Selva Morale e Spirituale*, 1640-1641 (*CE*, v. 15; p, 757).

    2)   *Zefiro torno e'bel tempo rimena* (The west wind returns) (*CE*, v. 6, p. 22)

      a)   Triple meter and repetition mark the influence of the dance in this five-voice madrigal on a Petrarch poem. Changes in rhythm and tempo support the meaning of the text.

7.   *Book VII, 1619* (*CE*, v. 7)

  a.   This book of 35 madrigals, entitled *Concerto* includes "madrigals and other kinds of songs," and is the high point of the madrigals.

    1)   There is great variety in **Monteverdi's** use of the concertato style including duets, trios, quartets, a sextet, and a few songs for solo voice.

    2)   All the madrigals have an accompaniment with the continuo alone or with a small ensemble of two violins and two flutes, which also is used for sinfonias and ritornellos between strophes.

  b.   Concertato madrigals

    1)   *Tempro la cetra* (Vigor of the harp) (*CE*, v. 7, p. 2)

      a)   Basically of strophic structure, this sectional solo madrigal has elements of variation in the melody and recitative and arioso styles are hardly distinguishable. Part of the opening sinfonia is later incorporated into the recurring ritornellos and the closing sinfonia.

    2)   *Se i languidi miei sguardi* (If my listless glance) (*CE*, v. 7, p. 160)

      a)   *Book VII* includes the two famous *Lettera amoroso* for soprano although the poem calls for a bass voice. This "letter" is a recitative written in highly expressive, theatre style (*stile rappresentativo*) and is to be sung without strict rhythmic beat (*senza battuta*).

    3)   *Con che soavità* (With what sweetness) (*CE*, v. 7, p. 137)

      a)   In this work **Monteverdi** arrives at one of his highest artistic achievements. Limited range of intensive declamation, moments of instrumental and vocal interplay, and simple melody accompanied by three continuo groups of instruments is characteristic of **Monteverdi's** mature concertato style.

    4)   *Ohimè dov'è il mio ben?* (Alas, where is my treasure?) (*CE*, v. 8, p. 152)

      a)   This continuo madrigal for two sopranos, set to a poem by **Bernardo Tasso**, includes recitative, arioso, and polyphonic madrigal style in the form of variations on the traditional *romanesca* melody which appears in the bass (see *Romanesca*, p. 15).

    5)   *A quest' olmo* (Either this elm) (*CE*, v. 7, p. 14)

      a)   A small orchestra of two violins and two flutes accompanies this sextet and demonstrates the maturity of **Monteverdi's** concertato style.

  c.   Stage ballet

    1)   *Tirsi e Clori* (*CE*, v. 7, p. 191)

      a)   **Monteverdi**, while at St. Mark's in Venice, was still called upon by the Mantuan court to furnish music for state occasions. This stage ballet was probably written for the coronation on January 5, 1616, of Duke Ferdinand, **Monteverdi's** former employer.

      b)   **Monteverdi** gave instructions for the performance of this work. Tirsi and Clori first sing a pastoral dialogue, each with his own continuo instruments (chitarrone and clavicembalo). Tirsi's part is in triple rhythm of a *balletto*, and Clori's part is in aria style in duple meter. Strophes one and three are Tirsi's dance song, and Clori's arioso alternates in strophes two and four. The fifth strophe is a duet with borrowed material from strophe three, Tirsi's dance song. They then join in the *ballo* sung by a five-part chorus and accompanied with an orchestra of eight *viole da braccio*, a *contrabasso*, a spinet (square form of the *cembalo*), and two small lutes.

8. *Book VIII* (*CE*, v. 8)
   a. The *Madrigali Guerrieri at Amorosi* (Madrigals of War and Love) is a large comprehensive collection of madrigals which includes a great variety of forms and styles. The book is divided into two sections: 1) "Madrigals of War" and *Il Combattimento di Tancredi e Clorinda,* followed by a *ballo,* and 2) "Songs of Love," two madrigals *alla francese* and the *Ballo dell' Ingrate* (Dance of the ungrateful).
      1) Included are madrigals requiring a large chorus combined with various soloists and a small orchestra, solo madrigals with continuo, duets, trios, and five-part madrigals.
   b. Appearing for the first time is the *stile concitato* (agitated or excited style). In the preface **Monteverdi** explains the rationale and characteristics of this new style (*SR*, 413).
   c. *Il Combattimento di Tancredi e Clorinda,* 1624 (*CE*, v. 8, p. 133; *HAM,* No. 189; *AMI*, v. 6, p. 135; *ICDMI*, v. 19)
      1) This dramatic cantata with narrator (*testo*) is intended to be sung in costume, with the singers using gestures and stepping in rhythm. Parlando in *stile rappresentativo* is used at highly dramatic moments.
      2) The text is based on part of **Torquato Tasso's** *Gerusalemme Liberata* (Jerusalem delivered), which recounts in an epic manner the capture of Jerusalem during the first crusade (1096-1099). Tancred, a Norman leader, falls in love with an infidel girl, Clorinda. Tancred meets her one night and, failing to recognize her, slays her.
      3) The orchestra consists of four different sizes of *viole de braccio, contrabasso da gamba* and *clavicembalo.* Unique techniques, turned to dramatic effects for the first time, include the string tremolo to depict combat and pizzicato.
   d. *Il Ballo dell' Ingrate* (*CE*, v. 8, p. 314; *AMI*, v. 6, p. 197)
      1) Composed in very expressive theatrical style, this dramatic *balletto* "moved the listeners to tears, touched their hearts, and created a highly emotional state in the audience."
         a) The setting is the entrance to Hades where Amor and his mother, Venus, implore Pluto to extricate from Hades eight ungrateful souls of maids who refused the favors of Amor.
         b) For the narrative **Monteverdi** uses recitative but frequently breaks over into arioso style, and some unusual dissonance intensifies the plot.
         c) The instrumental compositions include sinfonias for changes of scenes, entratas to introduce and accompany the ballet, and ritornellos used after each strophe in Pluto's recitative. The orchestra, which consists of five *viole de braccio* with harpsichord and chitarrone, may be doubled for a large hall.
9. *Book IX* (*CE*, v. 9)
   a. A collection of 21 strophic songs, *Madrigali e canzonette a due, e tre, voci,* was published posthumously by Alessandro Vincenti in 1651 in Venice. It contains compositions of various styles and some of rather early date. Included are strophic dance songs patterned after the *balletto* and *canzonetta.*
      1) *Di far sempre gioire* (*CE*, v. 9, p. 50)
         a) Each variation of this set of solo strophic variations alternates with a refrain sung by a trio.
      2) *Ohimè ch' io cado* (*CE*, v. 9, p. 111)
         a) This is a highly developed monodic song with six stanzas over the same bass, with melodic variations and ritornellos.
      3) *Zefiro torno e di soavi* (*CE*, v. 9, p. 9; *NS*, 49)
         a) Not to be confused with the madrigal of the same name in *Book VI,* this

one, written on a Rinuccini text for two tenors, has a chaconne bass two
measures in length repeated 56 times and, after a recitative section, is repeated another 5 times. Throughout the work, Monteverdi effectively
sets the text with realistic imagination.

10. Other continuo songs (*CE*, v. 10)

    a.   In addition to the nine books of madrigals there are three other collections of
songs mostly based on the dance: 1) the early *Canzonette a 3 voci*, first issued
in 1584, in the Renaissance tradition, 2) *Scherzi musicali a 3 voci*, edited by
Monteverdi's brother, Giulio Cesare, in 1607, and 3) *Scherzi Musicali Cioè Arie,
& Madrigali in stile recitativo, con una Ciaccona A 1 & 2 voci*, edited by
Bartholomeo Magni in 1632.

C.   In addition to Caccini and Monteverdi, many other composers adapted similar
techniques and published many collections of continuo songs.

    1.   Luzzasco Luzzaschi (1545-1607) demonstrates the transition from polyphony to
monody in his *Madrigale per cantare e sonare*, 1601, for one to three voices with a
written-out continuo part (*GMB*, No. 166; *AM*, v. 31, p. 16).

    2.   Felice Anerio (1560-1614) published several books of varied-voice madrigals from
1585 to 1611 (*AM*, v. 31, p. 45).

    3.   Agostino Agazzari (1578-1640) published many madrigals from 1596 to 1608 and in
in 1607 published his views on playing figured bass in his *Del sonare sopra'l basso*
(*SR*, 424).

    4.   Paolo Quagliati (1555-1628) published monodies and concertato ensemble com-
positions up to five voices in *La sfera armoniosa* (The harmonic sphere), 1608
(*SCMA*, v. 13).

    5.   Alessandro Grandi (*c.* 1570-1630) published his *Cantade ed Arie* in 1620 (*CW*, v. 40).

        a.   The *Cantade,* which were strophic variations, foreshadowed the chamber cantata.
Grandi's *arie* were strophic continuo songs in contrast to the *arie* of Caccini which
generally were strophic variations.

    6.   Salomone Rossi (1587-1628) includes continuo madrigals in his five books of mad-
rigals, 1600 to 1622.

I V.   Emilio de' Cavalieri (*c.* **1550-1602**)

A.   Cavalieri, a Roman nobleman, was a member of the Florentine Camerata and "In-
spector General of Arts and Artists at the Tuscany Court."

B.   *Rappresentazione di Anima e di Corpo*, Rome, 1600 (*M* 3a; *BMB*, v. 1; *ICDMI*, v. 10;
HAM, No. 183; *GMB*, No. 169; *TEM*, 211; *AM*, v. 45, p. 28; v. 37, p. 17)

    1.   The "Spectacle of the Soul and the Body" is an opera with sacred words and al-
legorical characters, and is related to the earlier morality plays. It was first presented as a devotional service at the Oratorio della Vallicella of St. Filippo Neri's
Church in Rome. The allegorical characters include Soul, Body, Life, Time, World,
Heaven, Earth, Hell, Intellect, and Pleasure.

    2.   There are 90 short numbers including a spoken dialogue, recitatives, homophonic
choruses, solo songs, instrumental ritornellos, sinfonias, and dances (galliard, can-
ary, and corrente).

    3.   The accompaniment is for *lira doppio* (two violins), *gravicembalo* (large harpsi-
chord), *chitarrone,* and two flutes.

V.   Opera in Florence and Mantua

A.   Secular and sacred dramatic entertainments from early times included music during
their performances, although much of the music has been lost.

1. *Intermedii* were light and often elaborate theatrical entertainments including music for soloists, choruses, and instrumental ensembles. They were introduced between the acts of stage plays. An *entr'acte* is an interlude for instruments alone.

2. The pastoral drama librettos of the 16th century were suitable for the setting of continuous music and were a strong influence on the development of early opera.

B. **Jacopo Peri** (1561-1633)

  1. *Dafne*

    a. In 1594 Peri began to work on his first opera, *Dafne,* a dramatic pastorale by **Ottavio Rinuccini,** but only a few airs and a recitative survive.

  2. *L'Euridice,* 1600 (published in 1601)   (*ICDMI,* v. 24; *GMB,* No. 171; *HAM,* No. 182; *AMI,* v. 6, p. 1; *MMF,* Ser. 1, v. 28; *BMB,* v. 2; *AM,* v. 31, p. 33; v. 45, p. 26; *SR,* 373; *BM,* 31; *SHO,* 5; *Outline,* p. 24)

    a. This opera, the earliest surviving dramatic work set entirely to music, was performed at the Pitti Palace in Florence to celebrate the marriage of Henry IV, King of France, and Marie de' Medici. **Giulio Caccini** contributed some numbers to this performance and also published his own complete setting in 1601, just prior to that of **Peri** (*AM,* v. 45, p. 27; *SR,* 370).

      1) Comparing the scores of **Caccini's** *Euridice,* **Cavalieri's** *Rappresentazione* and **Peri's** *Euridice,* all three include arias, choruses, dances, and recitatives, but **Peri's** makes use most significantly of the new monodic style.

    b. The classic myth tells of the rescue of Euridice from Hades by Orpheus on condition that he not look back or speak to her until they reach the upper world. He does look back, and Euridice is returned to death forever. In **Rinuccini's** version, however, there is no condition and Euridice is restored to life.

    c. The work is a chamber opera with the action carried on by solo voices in *stile rappresentativo* over a slow-moving continuo. The melody follows the natural inflections, rhythms, and accents of the text in a "representative" or theatre style.

    d. The Prologue by "Tragedy" is in the form of a strophic aria of seven stanzas. The choruses are short and may be homophonic or mildly polyphonic (*M* 9, pp. 7, 20), monophonic (voices in unison) (*M* 9, pp. 2-4), and used to accompany the ballets (*M* 9, p. 50).

    e. The continuo was realized by a *gravicembalo, chitarrone, liuto grosso* (large lute), or *lira grande* (a large many-stringed bowed instrument). These were probably used in various combinations. There are short ritornellos for three flutes (*M* 9, pp, 11, 12; *AMI,* v. 6m pp. 25, 28).

C. **Claudio Monteverdi** (1567-1643)

  1. *Orfeo,* Mantua, 1607 (*CE,* v. 9; *M* 6d; *BMB,* v. 6 [facsimile]; *PAM,* v, 10; *ICMI,* v. 9; *GMB,* No. 176; *HAM,* No. 187; *MM,* 126; *AM,* v. 45, p. 35; *BM,* 36)

    a. In this masterpiece set to a poem of **Alessandro Striggio, Monteverdi** realized the full dramatic power of the text. In general, the plot follows that of **Rinuccini.** However, in the **Striggio** version, when Orfeo rescues Euridice from death, Orfeo looks back and Euridice is returned again to death. Orfeo sings his lament and is then transported to heaven.

    b. The opera is in five acts with a Prologue sung by "Music" rather than by "Tragedy" as in **Rinuccini's** version. The first and second acts are pastoral in character, the third and fourth infernal, and the fifth shows Orfeo ascending to heaven and the sudden appearance of Apollo.

      1) *Castrati* (male sopranos) were used for the first time in opera. Their voices had an unusually wide range, a special timbre, and great power.

    c. **Monteverdi** achieved variety and flexibility by the use of various forms for dramatic effect and unity through structural balance.

      1) Vocal forms include the strophic variation, strophic song, dance song, chamber duet, and madrigal. The recitative is used for highly dramatic situations. The

many choruses are in concertato style, in madrigal style, or are used to accompany dancing. They are rarely part of the dramatic action.

  2) The 26 instrumental pieces include sinfonias, ritornellos, interludes, and the first operatic overture, which is in the style of a fanfare entitled "Toccata."

    a) *Sinfonia* is a term loosely used to designate an introductory instrumental piece. A variety of forms and styles may be noted.

  d. The nearly 40 instruments listed in the score may be divided into three categories:

    1) *Fundament* instruments: those capable of playing chords, which include harp, cither, chitarrone, clavicembalo, and small organ.

    2) String instruments: violin, viola, violoncello, and contrabass viol.

    3) Wind instruments: trumpet, trombone, recorder, and cornett, which is a wood instrument with finger holes and a cup-shaped mouthpiece.

  e. Specific instrumentation is rarely given, except for a definite type of dramatic situation. Two of these ensembles are   1) "Underworld" ensemble: five trombones, two bass viols, one contrabass, regal, small organ, and two cornetts; and 2) "Heavenly orchestra:" ten violins of various sizes, two contrabass viols, two chamber organs, a regal, two chitarrones, two harps, two cithers, and two harpsichords.

  f. *Possente spirto* (*CE*, v. 11, p. 84; *MSO*, 72)

    1) This aria is sung by Orfeo in Act III and is the most elaborate aria in the opera. Each of the different strophes has a different melody. On a separate staff above the melody, **Monteverdi** has written out extraordinary virtuoso embellishments. Each strophe is accompanied in concertato style by different groups of instruments including continuo: strophe 1 — two violins; 2 — two cornetts; 3 — two harps; 4 — two violins; 5 — continuo alone; and 6 — three *viole da braccio*. Ritornellos occur after each of the first three strophes.

D. Other composers of early Florentine opera include **Francesca Caccini** (*from* 1588), daughter of **Giulio Caccini**, *La Liberazione di Ruggiero dall' isola d'Alcina* (The liberation of Ruggiero from the island of Alcina), 1625 (*B* 17, v. 1, p. 174); and **Marco da Gagliano** (*c.* 1575-1642), *La Flora* (The goddess of flowers), 1628 (*B* 17, v. 1, p. 180), composed in collaboration with **Jacopo Peri**, and *Dafne,* 1608 (*PAM*, v. 10).

VI. Opera in Rome

A. About 1630, Rome became the center of opera following the early 17th-century development of opera in Florence and Mantua. There it came under the patronage of the influential Barberini family, princes of the church. In Rome, emphasis shifted from the dramatic to a more spectacular display and singing took on a greater virtuosity. The librettos were often based on allegorical or moralizing rather than mythological and historical subjects.

  1. These operas marked the beginning of the separation of the recitative from the aria, and the establishment of a basic orchestra of strings and continuo. The chorus held a prominent position in the opera, but it gradually gave way to the solo song.

B. **Stefano Landi** (*c.* 1590-*c.* 1655)

  1. *Sant' Alessio,* Rome, 1632 (*B* 17, v. 1, p. 202; *BMB*, v. 11 [*facsimile*]; excerpts in *AMI*, v. 5, pp. 43, 47, 51, 55; *AM*, v. 31, p. 40)

    a. *Sant' Alessio* was first performed in 1632 at the opening of the new theatre seating 3000 in the Palazzo Barberini. The sets were made by the famous architect and sculptor **Giovanni Lorenzo Bernini** (1598-1680).

    b. It is based on the legend of Saint Alexis (5th century) with a libretto by **Giulio Rospigliosi** (1600-1669), the future **Pope Clemens IX** (1667).

    c. The opera is in three acts and includes recitatives, arias, duos, trios, ensembles, eight-voice choruses, and use of comic episodes. The part of Alessio is sung by a soprano castrato.

      d.   The two extended sinfonias (*canzone*) (*B* 17, v. 1, pp. 202, 252; *AM.* v. 45, p. 45) represent an important development toward the operatic overture. The sinfonia to Act I (slow–fast–slow) anticipates the French overture of **Lully** and the sinfonia to Act II is fast–slow–fast; it resembles somewhat the later Italian overture. The instrumentation includes three violins, harp, lute, theorbo, contrabass, and continuo (*gravicembalo*).

      e.   *Poca voglia di far bene* (Little desire to do good) (*HAM*, No. 209; *AMI*, v. 5, p. 47; *B* 17, v. 1, p. 210)

          1.   A comic duet by two pages who spend their time making merry and celebrating every day as a holiday.

    2.   *La morte d'Orfeo,* 1619 (*B* 17, v. 1, p. 188)

      a.   This tragic comedy pastorale in five acts includes the first use of comic episodes in serious opera.

  C.   Other opera composers of Rome, some associated with the Barberinis, were **Michelangelo Rossi** (born *c.* 1600), *Erminia sul Giordano* (Erminia at the Jordan), Rome, 1637 (*B* 17, v. 1, p. 258; *BMB*, v. 12; *AM*, v. 31, p. 56); **Marco Marazzoli** (d. 1662), *Il trionfo della pietà ossia la Vita humana* (The triumph of piety or The Life of Man), 1656; **Loreto Vittori** (*c.* 1590-1670), *La Galatea*, Rome, 1639 (*B* 17, v. 1, p. 273; *AM*, v. 31, p. 31); and **Luigi Rossi** (1597-1653), *L'Orfeo*, Paris, 1647 (*B* 17, v. 1, p. 295).

VII. Opera in Venice

  A.   The first public opera house, Teatro di San Cassiano, was opened in Venice in 1637 and two others were opened in 1639. Opera was formerly performed in private homes for invited guests. With the opening of other theatres, opera remained tremendously popular throughout the century.

    1.   Opera under **Monteverdi** developed a new style designed for public appeal.

      a.   Choruses were largely replaced by ensembles for solo voices, and songs for virtuoso singers were added. The melodies became more tuneful and rhythmic, with major and minor harmonies. Orchestras after *Orfeo* were mainly strings and continuo.

  B.   Claudio Monteverdi (1567-1643)

    1.   *Il Ritorno d'Ulisse in patria* (The return of Ulysses to his country), Venice, 1641 (*CE*, v. 12; *DTÖ*, v. 57)

      a.   *Il Ritorno* was first produced at the oldest theatre, S. Cassiano. The libretto was written by **Giacomo Badoaro** and is based on an epic by **Homer**. It is not only partly mythological and partly historical, but allegorical characters also figure in it.

      b.   It marks a definite change in **Monteverdi's** style. Recitatives are developed with the use of sequence, imitation between melody and bass, arioso-like sections, tone repetition, and *parlando* (spoken music). Several arias are based on short chaconne-like basses and in strophic variation form. Comic (*CE*, v. 12, p. 53; *DTÖ*, v. 57, p. 30), serious, and spectacular scenes are contrasted.

      c.   The instrumental music consists mostly of sinfonias which are used as ritornellos. The combat between Ulysses and the suitors in Act II (*CE*, v. 12, p. 167) is portrayed in a *sinfonia da guerra* (sinfonia of war).

      d.   Penelope's lament in Act I, scene I (*CE*, v. 12, p. 13) and Ulysses' monologue in Act I, scene 7 (*CE*, v. 12, p. 48) are the great moments of the opera.

    2.   *L'incoronazione de Poppea* (The coronation of Poppea), Venice, 1642 (*CE*, v. 12; *M* 6c; *BMB*, v. 81; *B* 17, v. 2, pp. 65-203; *Outline p.* 23)

      a.   **Monteverdi's** last opera, written at the age of 75, is one of the outstanding masterpieces of operatic literature. The libretto, written by **Francesco Busenello**, is based on the story of Nero and his ardent love for Poppea, the wife of Ottone.

      b.   The music is a remarkable portrayal of conflicting passions and all-powerful love.

A wide variety of forms and styles have been adapted to the dramatic situations with complete mastery.

  c.   The opera is preceded by a Prologue in which allegorical characters reveal the power of Love over men. Included are parlando sections in *stile concitato* (p. 81), realistic recitatives (p. 229), strophic variations (p. 95), monologues (pp. 49, 229), duets (pp. 9, 141), ostinato-type basses (pp. 9, 146, 222), canonic writing (p. 9), arias (pp. 188-191), duet in da capo form with a chaconne bass (p. 246; *GMB*, No. 178), a trio (p. 128), and comic scenes. (The page references refer to *CE*, v. 13)

VIII. **Church Music**

  A.   Composers of the Early Italian Baroque wrote church music in the "old" conservative polyphonic style as well as in the "new" progressive style. In addition to monody and the concertato style for few or many voices, the "new" style included the "colossal" style which took advantage of multiple vocal and instrumental ensembles in vast acoustical areas.

  B.   **Orazio Benevoli** (1605-1672) (*M* 1)
    1.   After early experience in Rome, **Benevoli** was employed by the Austrian court in Vienna, 1643-1645. He was then appointed director of music at the Vatican in 1646 and remained there until his death. His later works, mostly written for St. Peter's in Rome, include Masses, solo cantatas (*CS*, v. 22), Psalms, motets (*AM*, v. 47, p. 96), and anthems for from 12 to 48 voices in 4 to 12 choirs.
    2.   *Festival Mass* (*DTÖ*, v. 20)
      a.   A 53-part Mass, written for the consecration of the Cathedral of Salzburg, 1628, is in the "colossal" style. It includes solos, solo ensembles, two eight-part choruses, each accompanied with a continuo and three instrumental ensembles: two string, one woodwind, and three brass ensembles.

  C.   **Lodovico Grossi da Viadana** (1564-1645)
    1.   **Viadana** took the name of his birthplace near Mantua. He served as chapel master at the cathedrals of Mantua and Fano and entered the Franciscan order in 1596.
    2.   *Canto Concerti Ecclesiastici a 1, 2, 3, 4, Voci con il Basso Continuo per sonar dell' Organo*, 1602 (*AM*, v. 31, p. 19; v. 45, p. 31; *SR*, 419; *BM*, 66)
      a.   **Viadana** composed these "100 Church Concertos" for one to four voices to replace the practice of one or two singers using a few parts from a five to eight voice motet and letting the remaining parts be supplied by the organ. In his preface, **Viadana** states that this "imperfect, or wearisome, or ugly" practice was not only difficult for the singers but "far from pleasing to the listeners" because it is "full of long and repeated pauses; closes are missing; there is a lack of melody, and, in short, very little continuity and meaning." This use of *basso continuo* may antedate that by **Peri** and **Caccini** since **Viadana** states in his preface that some of the "Concerti" had been "composed five or six years ago when in Rome." Some instruction for the organist who plays the continuo is given.
        1)   *Salve regina* (*GMB*, No. 168)
          a)   In the form of a duet, this "concerto" for tenor and soprano is a setting of the odd-numbered verses and the final verse of the antiphon for the Blessed Virgin Mary. Imitation between soprano and tenor is common and the bass part on the organ doubles the tenor part.
        2)   *Exaudi me, Domine* (Hear me, O Lord) (*HAM*, No. 185)
          a)   This solo concerto is a setting of two verses from Psalm 69. **Viadana** makes use of descriptive coloraturas and a kind of imitation between the solo voice and the bass.
    3.   *Geistliche Konzerte* (*CS*, vols. 5, 40, 51); *Masses* (*MD*, vols. 10, 19)

D. **Claudio Monteverdi** (1567-1643)
   1. The main body of **Monteverdi's** church music is published in three large collections listed below.
      a. *Sanctissimae Virgini Missa senis vocibus Ad Ecclesiarum Choros Ac Vespere . . . ,* 1610 (*CE,* v. 14, p. 123)
         1) Included in this collection is the *a cappella* "Mass for the Blessed Virgin Mary for six voices for church choirs and Vespers for many voices, together with some sacred harmonies suitable for chapels or princes' chambers."
            a) The Mass, in fugal texture, is modeled on the old *stile prima prattica.*
            b) *Vespere* is a large concertato work in which choruses are accompanied with an orchestra, soloists sing with an orchestra, single and double choirs sing with organ accompaniment, and single and double choirs and solo voices alternate in strophic variations on a harmonized plainsong melody.
               (1) *Domine ad adiuvandum* (Lord, with Thy assistance) (*CE,* v. 14, p. 123; *GSS,* 430); *Laetatus sum* (I rejoice) (*CE,* v. 14; *CMA,* 284; *M* 6f, v. 6)
      b. *Selva Morale e Spirituale,* 1641 (*CE,* v. 15)
         1) The music of this collection was written for services at St. Mark's in Venice where **Monteverdi** had 30 singers and 20 instrumentalists. It contains 29 compositions in addition to a complete Mass and a Gloria in seven voices with four trombones and strings.
      c. *Messa a quattro Voci et Salmi,* 1650 (*CE,* v. 16; *M* 6f, v. 9; *CS,* vols, 7, 23, 58, 65)
         1) Published posthumously by **Alessandro Vincenti,** this collection contains a four-voice Mass and Psalms from one to eight voices in concertato style.

IX. **Instrumental Music**

A. Instruments
   1. Under the influence of the expressive *stile rappresentativo* the quieter and more flexible instruments became popular. These include the viols, violins built by **Gasparo da Salò** (1540-1609; **Giovanni Paolo Maggini,** 1580-1632; the **Amati** family, *c.* 1535-1684; lutes, guitars, *cornetti,* recorders, flutes, oboes, bassoons, and keyboard instruments (clavichords, harpsichords, small organs). Brass instruments were used more frequently after 1700, especially in Germany.
   2. An independent repertory of idiomatic instrumental music gradually developed from the late 16th century into the early 17th century. Possible devices in common use were rapid scale passages, figurations, wide leaps, and points of imitation. With the advancement of the violin family, techniques unique to string instruments include double stops, harmonics, tremolo (repeated notes), pizzicato, *col legno* (use of the bow stick), *scordatura* (unusual tuning), and positions as high as the sixth position.
B. Forms and types
   1. There is much use of the variation idea, especially the *basso ostinato* (ground bass). Continuous variations on a dance bass are *basso ostinato* variations. Sectional harmonic variations on a dance bass are dance variations. The term "partita" was often applied to this type of variation (*AMI,* v. 3, pp. 207, 211).
      a. A new texture, with the upper and lower parts prominent, resulted from the use of the continuo in ensemble music.
   2. Popular songs (*romanesca, ruggiero*) and dance tunes (*folia, passamezzo, bergamasca*) were used as the basis for variations for many types and combinations of instruments.
      a. Early dances were generally performed in pairs (*passamesso* and *saltarello, pavane* and *galliarde*).
         1) The melody of the second dance became a rhythmic variation of the first, a practice that suggests the beginning of the variation suite. Variations of single

dances were often written for keyboard instruments.

b.   Variations were usually constructed on the basses associated with the tunes. Sometimes the melody, and sometimes both the melody and the bass were used (*romanesca, folia, bergamasca*).

1)   The bass theme was varied, but the successive notes of the theme appeared on the first beat of the measure and outlined the harmonic scheme. Each variation also varied the melody.

c.   *Romanesca* bass

1)   The *romanesca* tune in the following example from the *prima parte* of the Frescobaldi variations is indicated in half notes. Although not shown here, the second half of the tune is repeated (*ripresa*).

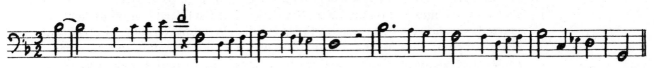

a)   **Girolamo Frescobaldi.** *Partite sopra l'aria della Romanesca* (*HAM*, No. 192; *M* 4e, v. 3, p. 46), an aria with 13 variations.

d.   *Ruggiero* bass

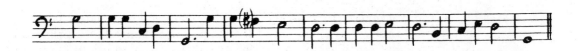

1)   **Girolamo Frescobaldi.** *Partite sopra l'aria di Ruggiero* (*M* 4e, v. 3, p. 60; *AM*, v. 11, p. 68), an aria with 11 variations.

e.   *La Frescobalda* (*M* 4e, v. 4, p. 90), an aria with four variations.

3.   Chaconne (*ciacona*) and Passacaglia

a.   The chaconne and passacaglia were the most important types of *basso ostinato* (continuous) variations. They are related to the old dances only in the use of triple meter.

b.   The chaconne and passacaglia appeared as ground basses about 1600 in both vocal and instrumental music. Baroque composers used the two terms without any clear distinction, and writers of that time, as well as today, are often in disagreement. Some modern writers call variations on a ground bass a passacaglia and variations on *ostinato* harmonies a chaconne.

    c.   Early passacaglias were sometimes without a ground bass, but harmonies and/or rhythmic patterns were repeated.

        1)   **Girolamo Frescobaldi.** *Cento Partite sopra Passacagli* (M 4e, v. 3, p. 77)

    d.   Chaconne basses outlining a fourth were in common use, particularly the four-note series descending from tonic to dominant. The basses might be inverted, extended, or varied in rhythm or notes.

    4.   The Toccata (from *toccare,* "to touch" the keys or strings of the lute), Prelude (independent piece for church or home use), and *Intonazione* (short, introductory piece to give pitch to singers) were all free improvisatory forms and the earliest types of idiomatic keyboard music.

    a.   The early toccatas of **Andrea Gabrieli** and **Girolamo Diruta** consisted of chords and scale passages. **Merulo** (1533-1603) developed the toccata into a piece with alternate free and fugal sections.

    b.   **Giovanni Maria Trabaci** (1575-1647)   (M 10a; *AMI,* v. 3, p. 370)

        1)   **Trabaci** was a member of the Neapolitan school of keyboard composers which exerted considerable influence on **Frescobaldi.** He published two collections of keyboard compositions, the first in 1603 which contains mainly ricercars, canzonas, toccatas, some dances, and capriccios, and the second in Naples in 1615 which contains ricercars and capriccios.

    c.   **Girolamo Frescobaldi** (1583-1643)

        1)   **Frescobaldi** was born in Ferrara and died in Rome. A student of **Luzzasco Luzzaschi,** in 1604 he was elected a member of the St. Cecilia Academy. In 1608 he became organist of the Cappella Giulia of St. Peter's where he succeeded **Ercole Pasquini.** He was in Brussels in 1607, Mantua in 1615, and was court organist at Florence (1628-1633) while on leave from Rome. He was a teacher of **Froberger** and possibly **Kerll.**

        2)   **Frescobaldi's** style is rich, bold, and often dissonant and chromatic. His themes are generally short. The character of the toccata was changed into a rhapsodic piece with many varied sections, striking syncopations, suspensions, cross rhythms, and unusual 16th-century proportional "time signatures."

        a)   *Toccata IX* (*HAM,* No. 193; *M 4e,* v. 4, p. 34); *Toccatas* (*RGO,* v. 2, pp. 24, 27)

        3)   *Fiori Musicali,* Venice, 1635 (M 4e, v. 5)

        a)   The "Flowers of Music" is a valuable collection of organ music which was known to **Bach.** Included are three organ Masses and two secular pieces. The organ Masses are *della Domenica,* Mass XI (Feasts of the Lord); *delli Apostoli,* Mass IV (Feasts of the Saints); and *della Madonna,* Mass IX (Feasts of the Virgin). They differ from earlier organ Masses in that only the Kyries are taken from the Ordinary of the Mass. The remaining pieces are free compositions to be used during the Mass. The two secular pieces are *Bergamasca* (M 4e, v. 5, p. 61) and *Capriccio* (M 4e, v. 5, p. 66).

        b)   In the Preface **Frescobaldi** gives directions for the use of an expressive freedom in the performance of many of the pieces, particularly the *Toccata per l'Elevazione* to be played during the Elevation of the Host (M 4e, v. 5, pp. 18, 42, 60). *Toccatas* (M 4e, v. 5, pp. 4, 24, 34, 48, 56).

5. *Ricercar(e)* (to search or seek again)
   a. The polythematic ricercar from *c.*1500 was made up of short imitative sections in the style of a motet. The first theme often appeared later in augmentation or diminution. A free type was called "fantasia."
   b. The monothematic ricercar from *c.* 1600 was in variation style and often designated *sopra un soggetto* (upon a subject). Each variation might be an exposition of the theme varied melodically and rhythmically, or each variation might present the theme unvaried, but with a new counter-subject. This type led to the later Baroque fugue.
   c. The non-imitative ricercar was often in the style of the toccata, prelude, or *intonazione.*
   d. **Costanza Antegnati** (1549-1624)
      1) *L'Antegnata Intavolatura de Ricercare d'Organo,* 1608 (*CEKM,* Ser. 9; *AMI,* v. 3, p. 153)
         a) These 12 ricercars were first published as an addendum to **Antegnati's** important treatise on organ building, *L'Arte Organica,* 1608.
   e. **Girolamo Frescobaldi** (1583-1643) (*M* 4e, v. 5, pp. 16, 34, 38, 44, 54, 57; *MM,* 145; *MSO,* 100)

6. *Canzona* (plural is *canzone*) or *canzone* (plural is *canzoni*)
   a. The canzona is a keyboard or instrumental ensemble piece originally in the style of the 16th-century French chanson (*canzona francese*). Canzonas with special themes (cuckoo, hexachord, *ruggiero*) and a lively contrapuntal treatment were called "capriccios."
   b. **Girolamo Frescobaldi** (*M* 4e, v. 5, p. 66; *RGO,* v. 2, pp. 30, 32)
   c. The early *canzone,* although mainly imitative, alternate short homophonic and imitative sections with variations in tempo and texture. These multi-sectional *canzone* are called "patchwork" or "quilt" canzonas. The rhythm was more lively, ♩ ♪ ♪ was characteristic, note values were shorter, and counterpoint was more free than in the ricercar. During the 17th century the keyboard and ensemble canzonas were separated in form and style.
   d. Keyboard *canzona*
      1) The imitative keyboard canzonas published by **Trabaci** in 1603 and 1615 and others were precursors of the fugue. **Frescobaldi** in his publications of 1615, 1628, 1635, and 1645 established the "variation-canzona" which was based on one theme with free expressive sections. "Fugues" attributed to **Frescobaldi** are spurious.
      2) **Giovanni Maria Trabaci** (1575-1647)
         a) *Canzona francese* (*HAM,* No. 191)
      3) **Girolamo Frescobaldi** (1583-1643)
         a) *Canzone* (*M* 4e, v. 5, pp, 13, 20, 31, 46, 53; *HAM,* No. 194; *GMB,* No. 196; *AMI,* v. 3, p. 238; *RGO,* v. 2, p. 34; *AM,* v. 19, p. 45)
         b) **Bach** borrowed the theme from the *Canzon dopo l'Epistola* in **Frescobaldi's** *Fiori musicali* for his *Canzona in D minor* (*S.* 588).
      4) Anonymous, *Canzona per l'epistola* (*MM,* 98)
         a) This keyboard canzona in three fugal sections and contrasting meter was planned to take the place of the Gradual and Alleluia following the Epistle in the Mass.
   e. Ensemble *canzona* (*sinfonia, canzon da sonar, sonata*)
      1) Canzonas for solo instrumental ensembles, with or without continuo, were written in various styles: polythematic, monothematic, and in the free, multi-sectional style established by **Frescobaldi.** Early ensemble canzonas (**Gabrieli**) anticipated the concerto in the use of the echo and tutti and concertino effects.

7. Sonata
   a. The early few-voiced "sonatas" were one-movement pieces similar to the multi-sectional canzonas. After about 1630 the sections began to be decreased in number and increased in length, with greater contrast in style and tempo between sections. The many-voiced, imitative style of the canzona was then replaced by the continuo style of the Baroque sonata.
   b. Sonatas were identified by the number of parts, including the continuo. A sonata in one part without accompaniment (solo sonata) was marked *senza continuo*. *Sonata a due* indicated two written parts and continuo (three players), *a tre*, three written parts (four players), *a quattro*, four written parts (five players).
      1. The continuo part was realized by the organ or *cembalo* (harpsichord), with a gamba or cello reinforcing the bass line. The violin became the principal melody instrument with some use of the cornett (zink).
   c. A brilliant instrumental style developed, especially in the *sonata a due* as composed by **Fontana** and **Marini**. Idiomatic possibilities of the instruments used include rapid scale passages, figurations, wide skips, double stops, harmonics, tremolo (repeated notes), pizzicato, *col legno* (use of the bow stick), *scordatura* (unusual tuning), and positions as high as the sixth position.
   d. **Tarquinio Merula** (*c.* 1590-1655)
     1) *Canzoni overo Sonate concertate per chiesa e camera* (for "church and chamber"), Venice, 1637
      a) *Canzona "La Strada"* (*GMB*, No. 184)
     2) *Il secondo libro delle canzoni da suonare a tre, duoi violini, e basso, con il basso generale*, Venice, 1639
      a) *Canzon detta la Vesconta* (*HAM*, No. 210; *AIM*, No. 17), for two melody instruments and continuo. This is an early example of a trio sonata.
      b) *Canzon detta la Cancelliera* (*AIM*, No. 16)
     3) *Composizioni per organo e cembalo*, (*M 8*)
   e. **Salomone Rossi "Ebreo"** (1587-1628)
     1) *La Moderna "Varie Sonate, Sinfonie, Gagliarde, Brandi e Correnti per sonar due Viole da braccio et un Chitarrone o altro stromento simile,"* 1613
      a) This includes "sonatas" (variations) on the *Romanesca* and *Ruggiero* tunes for two melody instruments and continuo. There are also early examples of the trio sonata idea and the use of popular tunes in instrumental ensembles.
      b) *Sonata detta la Moderna*, 1613 (*HM*, v. 110) for two violins and continuo.
   f. **Giovanni Battista Fontana** (d. 1630)
     1) *Sonate a uno, due, tre per il violino o cornetto, fagotto, chitarrone, violoncino o simile altro instrumento,* Venice, 1641
      a) *Sonata a due* (*HAM*, No. 198); *Sonata a tre* (*AIM*, No. 12); *Sonata a due* (*AIM*, No. 13)
   g. **Biagio Marini** (1597-1665) (*HM*, vols. 129, 143)
     1) *Affetti musicali* (Musical affections), 1617, "for violins, cornetti, and other sorts of instruments."
      a) The term "affetti" emphasizes the emotional "affect" of the music, or indicates a type of ornamentation.
      b) *Sonata "La Gardana"* (*GMB*, No. 182)
      c) *Sinfonia "La Orlandina,"* for violin or cornett and continuo. The five sections use duple and triple meter, a variety of tempos, and restatement of material. The style of accompanied monody is adapted to instrumental writing.
     2) *Arie, madrigali, et corenti a 1, 2, 3*, Venice, 1620
      a) *La Martinenga, Corrente a 3* (*AIM*, No. 9a; *AMI*, v. 7, p. 1)

    b) *Il Priulino, Balleto & Corrente* (*AIM*, No. 9b; *AMI*, v. 7, p. 10)
    c) *Romanesca* (*HAM*, No. 199; *AIM*, No. 10; *AMI*, v. 7, p. 13; *AM*, v. 31)
      p. 61), variations for violin and continuo.
  3) *Sonate, symphonie, canzoni pass'emezzi, baletti, cornetti gagliarde, e ritornelli a 1-6 voci, per ogni sorte d'instrumenti. . . con altre curiose e moderne inventioni,* Venice, 1628
    a) *Sonata per il violino* (*GMB*, No. 183), use of double and triple stops, Lombard rhythm, short sections, changes in time and tempo.
  4) *Per ogni sorte d'instrumento musicale diversi generi di sonata da chiesa e da camera a due, & quattro,* Venice, 1655
    a) *Balletti e Correnti* (*AMI*, v. 7, pp. 19-41)
    b) *Sonata in D minor* (*HM*, v. 129; *AIM*, No. 22; *AMI*, v. 7, p. 49)
h. **Carlo Farina** (*c.* 1600-*c.* 1640)
  1) *Paduanen, Gagliarden, Couranten, Französichen Arien, benebenst einem kurzweiligen Quodlibet, von allerhand seltzamen Inventionen,* Dresden, 1627
    a) *Capriccio stravagante* (A fragment in *AIM*, No. 11), for four strings. In this *Capriccio* there are imitations of instruments and animals, and double stops, harmonics, and *col legno* are used.

SELECTED BIBLIOGRAPHY

Books

1. Aldrich Putnam. "The 'Authentic' Performance of Baroque Music," in *Essays on Music in Honor of Archibald Thompson Davison by His Associates.* Cambridge: Department of Music, Harvard University, 1957.

2. ————*Rhythm in Seventeenth Century Italian Monody.* New York: W. W. Norton, 1966.

3. Allen, Warren D. *Philosophies of Music History, a Study of General Histories of Music 1600-1960.* New York: Dover Publications, 1962.

4. *An Alphabetical Index to Claudio Monteverdi Tutte le Opere,* edited by the Bibliography Committee of the New York Chapter MLA. (Music Library Association Index Series I)

5. Arnold, Denis. *Monteverdi.* New York: Farrar, Straus, and Giroux, 1963.

6. Arnold, Denis and Nigel Fortune, eds. *The Monteverdi Companion.* London: Faber and Faber, 1968; New York: W. W. Norton, 1972.

7. Arnold Frank T. *The Art of Accompaniment from a Thorough-Bass.* London: Oxford University Press, 1931.

8. Blume, Friedrich. *Renaissance and Baroque Music: A Comprehensive Survey,* tr. by M. Herter from the article "Barock" in *MGG.* New York: W. W. Norton, 1967.

9. Borroff, Edith. *Music of the Baroque* (*MOB*). Dubuque, Iowa: Wm. C. Brown Co., 1970; reprint, New York: Da Capo Press, 1978.

10. Boyden, David D. "Dynamics in Seventeenth- and Eighteenth-Century Music," in *Essays in Music in Honor of Archibald Thompson Davison by His Associates.* Cambridge: Department of Music, Harvard University, 1957.

11. ————*The History of Violin Playing from its Origins to 1761 and its Relationship to the Violin and Violin Music.* London: Oxford University Press, 1965.

12. Dannreuther, Edward. *Musical Ornamentation.* London: Novello & Co., 1891. Reprint, Complete in One Volume, Edwin F. Kalmus. (Diruta, Caccini, Monteverdi, Carissimi, A. and G. Gabrieli, Merulo)

13. Dent, Edward J. "The Musical Form of the Madrigal," in *Twentieth Century Views of Music History,* ed. William Hays. New York: Charles Scribner's Sons, 1972.

14. Donington, Robert. *The Interpretation of Early Music,* revised ed. London: Faber and Faber, 1973.
15. Fraenkel, Gottfried S., ed. *Decorative Music Title Pages.* New York: Dover Publications, 1968. (201 examples from 1500-1800)
16. Gatatopoulos, Stelios. *Italian Opera; an Introduction.* London: Dent, 1971.
17. Goldschmidt, Hugo. *Studien zur Geschichte der italianische Oper im 17. Jahrhundert,* 2 volumes in one. Wiesbaden: Breitkopf & Härtel, 1901, 1904. Reprint in 1967.
18. Kerman, Joseph. *Opera as Drama.* New York: Alfred A. Knopf, 1956.
19. Landon, H. C. Robins, ed. *Studies in 18th-Century Music.* London: George Allen and Unwin, 1970.
20. Lang, Paul Henry. "The Doctrine of Temperaments and Affections," in *Twentieth Century Views of Music History,* ed. William Hays. New York: Charles Scribner's Sons, 1972.
21. Lewis, Anthony and Nigel Fortune, ed. *The New Oxford History of Music,* volume V. (*Opera and Church Music, 1630-1750*). London: Oxford University Press, 1975.
22. MacClintock, Carol. *The Solo Song, 1580-1730.* New York: W. W. Norton, 1973.
23. Marshall, Robert L., ed. *Studies in Renaissance and Baroque Music in Honor of Arthur Mendel.* Hackensack, NJ: J. Boonin, 1974.
24. Norman, Gertrude and Miriam Lubell Shrifte. *Letters of Composers: an Anthology, 1603-1945.* New York: Alfred A. Knopf, 1946. (Letters of Sweelinck, Monteverdi, Schütz, Scheidt, Rameau, Handel, Bach, and Tartini)
25. Palisca, Claude V., ed. *Girolamo Mei: Letters on Ancient and Modern Music to Vincenzo Galilei and Giovanni Bardi. Musicological Studies and Documents,* vol. 3. Rome: American Institute of Musicology, 1960.
26. Redlich, Hans F. *Claudio Monteverdi: Life and Works,* tr. by Kathleen Dale. London: Oxford University Press, 1949. Reprint, Westport, CT: Greenwood Press, 1952.
27. Salop, Arnold. "On Stylistic Unity in Renaissance-Baroque," in *Essays in Musicology: A Birthday Offering for Willi Apel,* ed. Hans Tischler. Bloomington, Indiana: Indiana University Press, 1968.
28. Schrade, Leo. *Monteverdi: Creator of Modern Music.* New York: W. W. Norton, 1950, 1969.
29. Smithers, Don L. *The Music and History of the Baroque Trumpet before 1721.* Syracuse: Syracuse University Press, 1973.
30. Stevens, Denis. *Monteverdi.* London: Dent, 1963.
31. Selfridge-Field, Eleanor. *Venetian Instrumental Music from Gabrieli to Vivaldi.* New York: Holt, Rinehart & Winston, 1975.
32. Wellesz, Egon. "The Beginning of Baroque in Music," tr. by Patricia Kean, in *Twentieth Century Views of Music History,* ed. William Hays. New York: Charles Scribner's Sons, 1972.
33. Williams, Peter F. *Figured Bass Accompaniment.* Edinburgh: University Press, 1970.
34. Worsthorne, Simon T. *Venetian Opera in the Seventeenth Century.* Oxford: Clarendon Press, 1954.

Articles

1. Allen, Warren D. "Baroque Histories of Music," *MQ* 25 (1939), p. 195.
2. Arnold, Denis. "Giovanni Croce and the *Concertato* Style," *MQ* 39 (1935), p. 37.
3. ——————"Alessandro Grandi, A Disciple of Monteverdi," *MQ* 43 (1957), p. 171.
4. Baron, John H. "Monody: A Study in Terminology," *MQ* 54 (1968), p. 462.
5. Bonta, Stephen. "Liturgical Problems in Monteverdi's Marian Vespers," *JAMS* 20 (1967), p. 87.
6. ——————"The Uses of the sonata da chiesa," *JAMS* 22 (1969), p. 54.
7. Brindle, Reginald Smith. "Monteverdi's G minor Mass: An Experiment in Construction," *MQ* 54 (1968), p. 352.

8.   Buelow, George J. "Music, Rhetoric, and the Concept of the Affections: a Selective Bibliography," *Notes* 3, No. 2 (1973), p. 250.

9.   Burkely, Francis. "Priest-Composers of the Baroque: A Sacred-Secular Conflict," *MQ* 54 (1969), p. 169.

10. Donington, Robert. "The choice of instruments in baroque music," *Early Music* 1 (1973), p. 131.

11. Fenlon, Iain. "The Monteverdi *Vespers*: suggested answers to some fundamental questions," *Early Music* 5 (1977), p. 380.

12. Gallico, Claudio. "Newly Discovered Documents Concerning Monteverdi," *MQ* 48 (1962), p. 68.

13. Ghisi, Federico. "Ballet Entertainments in the Pitti Palace, Florence, 1608-1625," *MQ* 25 (1939), p. 421.

14. ———————"An Early Seventeenth-Century MS with Unpublished Italian Monodic Music by Peri, Caccini and Marco da Gagliano," *Acta Mus* 20 (1948), p. 46.

15. Hitchcock, H. Wiley. "Caccini's'Other' *Nuove musiche*," *JAMS* 27 (1974), p. 438.

16. ———————"A New Biographical Source for Caccini," *JAMS* 26 (1973), p. 145.

17. ———————"Vocal Ornamentation in Caccini's *Nuove Musiche*," *MQ* 56 (1970), p. 389.

18. Johnson, Margaret F. "Agazzari's 'Eumelio,' a 'dramma pastorale'," *MQ* 57 (1971), p. 491.

19. Kenton, Egon F. "The Late Style of Giovanni Gabrieli," *MQ* 48 (1962), p. 427.

20. Maze, Nancy. "Tenbury MS. 1018: A Key to Caccini's Art of Embellishment," *JAMS* 9 (1956), p. 61.

21. Palisca, Claude V. "Girolamo Mei: Mentor in the Florentine Camerata," *MQ* 40 (1954), p. 1.

22. Pirrotta, Nino. "Temperaments and Tendencies in the Florentine Camerata," *MQ* 40 (1954), p. 169.

23. ———————"Commedia dell'Arte and Opera," *MQ* 41 (1955), p. 305.

24. Porter, William V. "Peri and Corsi's *Dafne*: Some New Discoveries and Observations," *JAMS* 18 (1965), p. 170.

25. Prunières, Henry. "Opera in Venice," *MQ* 17 (1931), p. 1.

26. ———————"Monteverdi's Venetian Operas," *MQ* 10 (1924), p. 178.

27. Redlich, Hans F. "Claudio Monteverdi: Some Problems of Textual Interpretation," *MQ* 41 (1955), p. 66.

28. Rose, Gloria. "Agazzari and the Improvising Orchestra," *JAMS* 18 (1965), p. 382.

29. Schott, H. "Early Music for Harpsichord: the 17th-century in Italy, France, England and Germany," *Early Music* 4 (1976), p. 281.

30. Schrade, Leo. "Monteverdi's *Il Ritorno d'Ulisse*," *MQ* 36 (1950), p. 422.

31. Selfridge-Field, Eleanor. "Addenda to Some Baroque Biographies," *JAMS* 25 (1972), p. 236.

32. Silva, Giulio. "Beginnings of the Art of Bel Canto," *MQ* 8 (1922), p. 53.

33. Stevens, Denis. "Where are the Vespers of Yesteryear?" *MQ* 47 (1961), p. 315.

34. Tomlinson, Gary A. "Ancora su Ottavio Rinuccini," *JAMS* 28 (1975), p. 351.

35. Walker, Frank. "Orazio: The History of a Pasticcio," *MQ* 38 (1952), pp. 3, 69.

36. Walker, Thomas. "Ciaconna and Passacaglia: Remarks of Their Origin and Early History," *JAMS* 21 (1968), p. 300.

37. Weaver, Robert L. "The Orchestra in Early Italian Opera," *JAMS* 17 (1964), p. 83.

38. Winzenburger, Walter P. "Meter and Tempo Indications in Music of the Early Baroque," *BACH* 3, No. 1 (Jan 1972), p. 13.

Music

1.   Benevoli, Orazio.
   a.   *Documenta liturgiae polychoralis Sanctae Ecclesiae Romanae*, vols. 1, 2, 3, 4, 5, 16, 17.

      b.   *Monumenta Liturgiae Polychoralis Sanctae Ecclesiae Romanae,* Ser. I A, vols. 1, 2, 3, 4, 8; Ser. IB, v. 1; Ser. I C, v. 1; Ser. II A, v. 1; Ser. II B, vols. 1, 2, 3, 4, 9; Ser. II C, v. 1; Ser. II D, v. 1.

      c.   *Opera omnia,* v. 1, Nos. 1, 2, 3; v. 2, Nos. 1, 3.

2.   Caccini, Giulio

      a.   *Le nuove musiche.* Facsimile reprint. Roma: Casa Editrice Claudio Monteverdi, 1930. (*Prime fioritura del melodramma italiano collezione diretta da Francesco Mantica.* Vol. 2)

      b.   *Le nuove musiche.* Facsimile reprint. Roma: Reale Accademia d'Italie, 1934.

      c.   Two songs from *Le nuove musiche* in Robert Dowland, *A Musicall Banquet,* 1610. London: J. & W. Chester, 1924 (*Tudor edition of Old Music,* Ser. B, No. 2, ed. Gerald M. Cooper)

3.   Cavalieri, Emilio del

      a.   *Rappresentazione de anima e di corpo.* Facsimile reprint. Roma: Casa editrice Claudio Monteverdi, 1912. (*Prime fioritura del melodramma italiano collezione diretta da Francesco Mantica.* Vol. 1) (Revised edition, Milan: Ricordi, 1956)

4.   Frescobaldi, Girolamo

      a.   (*CE*) New edition edited under the auspices of the Commune de Ferrara: the series is a sub-imprint of *Monumenti Musicali Italiani,* edited by the Societa Italiana di Musicologia.

      b.   *Arie musicale,* ed. Helga Spohr. *Musikalische Denkmäler,* v. 4.

      c.   *Arie musicale,* ed. Felice Boghen. Firenze: G. & P. Mignani, 1933.

      d.   *Ausgewählte Orgelsätze,* ed. F. X. Haberl. New revised edition by B. F. Richter. Leipzig: Breitkopf & Härtel, n. d.

      e.   *Orgel- und Klavierwerke,* ed. Pierre Pidoux, 5 vols. Kassel: Bärenreiter, 1949-71. (*Fiori musicali,* v. 5)

      f.   *Nove Toccate Inédite,* ed. Sandro dalla Libera. Kassel: Bärenreiter, 1962.

      g.   *Opere per organo e cembalo,* ed. Fernando Germani, 3 vols. Rome: Edizioni De Santis, 1951 (*Fiori musicali,* v. 3)

      h.   *Sei madrigali a cinque voci,* ed. Felice Boghen. Kassel: Bärenreiter, 1922.

5.   Jeppesen, Knud. *La Flora, Arie & Antiche Italiane.* Copenhagen: Hansen, 1949. (*Survey of Italian Bel Canto from c. 1600 until mid-18th C.* An Anthology including monodies by Caccini, Cavalli, Carissimi, Frescobaldi, Monteverdi, and Peri.)

6.   Monteverdi, Claudio

      a.   (*CE*) *Tutte le opere de Claudio Monteverdi,* ed. G. Francesco Malipiero, 16 vols. Asolo, 1926-1940. (Reprint by Universal, 1960's)

      b.   *Five Songs,* ed. George Hunter and Claude Palisca. Bryn Mawr, PA: Theodore Presser, 1963.

      c.   *L'incoronazione de Poppea,* Facsimile reprint. Milan: Fratelli Bocca, 1938.

      d.   *Orfeo,* Facsimile reprint of the first edition, 1609, ed. Adolf Sandberger. Augsburg, 1927.

      e.   *Sacre Cantiunculae. Istituzioni e monumenti dell'arte musicale Italiana,* Old series, v. 6.

      f.   *Musiche vocali e strumentali sacre e profane,* vols. 6, 9.

7.   Marini, Biagio. *Le lacrime d'Erminia in stile recitativo,* Parma, 1623. Facsimile (*BMB,* v. 8)

8.   Merula, Tarquinio. *Composizioni per organo e cembalo,* in *Monumenti di Musica Italiana,* Ser. 1, v. 1.

9.   Peri, Jacopo. *Euridice.* Facsimile of the 1601 edition. Roma: Reale Academie d'Italia, 1934, v. 3.

10.   Trabaci, Giovanni Maria. *Composizioni per organo e cembalo. Monumenti di Musica Italiana,* Ser. 1, v. 3.

      b.   *L'Oratorio de Filippini, Istituzioni e monumenti dell'arte musicale Italiana,* Old series, v. 5.

1.   The beginning of the solo madrigal *Amarilli mia bella*.
From the first edition of **Caccini's** *Le Nuove musiche* (1601).

2.   The beginning of the *Prologue*.
From the MS of *L'incoronazione di Poppea* by **Monteverdi**.

4. Recitative, sung by "Time," and chorus.
From the first edition of Cavalieri's *Rappresentazione* (1600).

3. Prologue, sung by "Tragedy."
From the first edition of Peri's *Euridice* (1601)

TOCCATA PRIMA

5.   A page from the first edition of **Frescobaldi's**
Toccate d'intavolatura di cembalo et di organo (1637).

OUTLINE III

MUSIC IN THE NETHERLANDS, GERMANY, AND AUSTRIA

EARLY AND MIDDLE BAROQUE

Introduction — The Netherlands
Protestant Church Music in Germany — Catholic Church Music
Continuo Song — Keyboard Music — Ensemble Music
Bibliography of Books — Articles — Music

I. Introduction

A. During the first half of the 17th century in Germany, the Thirty Years War (1618-1648) was a desperate political and religious struggle which had a devastating effect. The cultural life of the Netherlands and Germany was divided as tolerance between the north and south disintegrated.

B. The Protestant north Holland composers showed the influence of English virginalists and used the Calvinistic Psalm tune as a main vehicle of musical expression. Composers in north Germany used the Italian styles as the principal basis for their own music. They achieved unification by assimilating the "new" monodic (recitative and aria) and *concertato* (solo, chorus, and instruments) styles with the Lutheran chorale. Catholic composers in south Germany relied upon similar Italian models, but with little use of the chorale.

C. During the second half of the 17th century, violent controversies arose between the orthodox Lutherans and the Pietists. The orthodox Lutherans believed in the use of "figured" or elaborate music sung by a trained choir (*Kantorei*), while the Calvinistic Pietists believed in simple, often superficial, songs which could be sung by the congregation.

D. The principal composers of the Early and Middle Baroque were **Sweelinck** in Holland, and **Schein, Scheidt,** and **Schütz** in Germany.

II. The Netherlands

A. **Jan Pieterzoon Sweelinck** (1562-1621) (*M* 9 abc)
   1. **Sweelinck** was born in Deventer and came to the Catholic city of Amsterdam at an early age when his father became organist of St. Nicholas Church (later Oude Kerk). Sometime before 1578 the church was "reformed" by the Calvinistic Protestants, so the organ was not used in the Services. As the official municipal organist, **Sweelinck** played recitals at the Oude Kerk and directed the music for civic functions.
   2. His fame as an organist, composer, and teacher spread far beyond the Netherlands, and he attracted many pupils including **Heinrich Scheidemann, Samuel Scheidt, Melchior Schildt,** and **Jacob Praetorius.** Although he did not travel from his native land he knew Italian music and especially English virginal music of the composers **Peter Philips, John Bull,** and others who visited the Netherlands. **Sweelinck's** most important contribution is in the field of keyboard music.
   3. Keyboard music
      a. **Sweelinck's** keyboard music exists only in copies made by his pupils, colleagues, and friends. A number of doubtful works have been ascribed to him in earlier anthologies. His keyboard music may be organized into three forms: 1) fantasias, 2) toccatas in Italian style, and 3) variations on sacred and secular melodies in the English figurative style.
      b. *Fantasias* (*CE,* v. 1, pp. 1-62; *M* 9c, v. 1, fascicle 1, pp. 7-48, 57-68)

26

1) There are 14 authentic fantasias, including three echo fantasias. The contrapuntal, monothematic fantasias with fugue-like subjects, played a part in the evolution of the Baroque fugue (*AM*, v. 19, p. 28).

2) There is frequent use of imitation, and there are fantasias where the subject is used as an ostinato (*M* 9, v. 1, fascicle 1, p. 61).

  a) *Fantasia Chromatica* (*CE*, v. 1, p. 1; *M* 9b, v. 1, p. 1; 9c, v. 1, fasc. 1, p. 1; *GMB*, No. 158; *RGO*, v. 2, p. 67; *MSO*, v. 1, p. 98)

    (1) The subject of this very important composition is based on the frequently used descending chromatic fourth. The work is in three large sections which are divided into smaller groups. The theme appears with different counterpoint and is also treated in stretto.

  b) *Echo fantasias* (*CE*, v. 1, pp. 44-62; *M* 9c, v. 1, fasc. 1, pp. 69-89)

    (1) They are written in three varied sections: 1) quasi-imitative, 2) homophonic with echoes, and 3) toccata-like with increasing motion and some echoes. The three echo fantasias, characteristic of **Sweelinck**, are an adaptation of the Italian polychoral technique to the organ.

    (2) *Echo fantasia* (*CE*, v. 1, p. 51; *M* 9c, v. 1, fasc. 1, p. 76; 9b, v. 1, p. 38; *HAM*, No. 181)

c. *Toccatas* (*CE*, v. 1, pp. 63-70; *M* 9c, v. 1, fasc. 1, pp. 90-136)

  1) The 12 authentic toccatas show the influence of the Venetian **Andrea Gabrieli** by their rambling rhapsodic passages, and at the same time the influence of the English virginalists by the controlled rhythmic figurations. In several continuous sections, they may have a slow introductory section followed by the characteristic increasingly fast toccata-like section and figurations. In some, alternating with toccata-like passages, there are imitative passages in the style of **Merulo**.

  2) *Toccata in C* (*CE*, v. 1, p. 117; *M* 9c, v. 1, fasc, 1, p. 118)

    a) One chord serves as an introduction to nearly 30 different melodic figures in varied rhythms treated principally in sequence. There are no imitative sections.

  3) *Toccata in a* (*Aeolian*) (*M* 9c, v. 1, fasc. 1, p. 131; 9b, v. 1, p. 42)

    a) This short work combines the Italian and English styles.

d. Settings of Sacred Melodies (*M* 9c, v. 1, fasc. 2)

  1) There are 13 authentic settings in the form of variations on eight Lutheran chorale melodies, two Genevan Psalm tunes, and three plainsongs. The variations vary in number of parts from two to four with the majority in three parts. The melody, sometimes ornamented, appears most often in the soprano, sometimes in the tenor or bass, and rarely in the alto part.

  2) *Ich ruf zu dir* (I call to Thee) (*M* 9c, v. 1, fasc. 2, p. 33; 5b, v. 2, p. 37)

    a) There are four variations in 2, 3, 3, and 4 parts respectively with the melody in the soprano, bass, tenor, and soprano. Only rarely is the melody ornamented. The fourth variation is unusual in beginning with an imitative introduction.

e. Settings of Secular Melodies and Dances (*CE*, v. 1, pp. 99-129; *M* 9c, v. 1, fasc. 3; 9b, v. 1, pp. 19-52)

  1) Among the compositions based on secular melodies and dances, there are seven sets of variations on secular melodies and five on dance tunes. In general, the themes of the secular melodies are divided into two repeated phrases, with some variation in the repeat. The tune may appear in the upper part, with or without alteration, but rarely in a lower part.

  2) *Mein junges leben hat ein End'* (My young life is ending) (*CE*, v. 1, p. 99; *M* 9c, v. 1, fasc. 3, p. 23; 9b, v. 1, p. 52)

    a) This simple tune is made up of two repeated phrases, the first phrase of four measures and the second phrase of six measures. The written-out repeats are varied, often with brilliant passage work and rhythmic alteration.

  3) The five sets of variations on dance tunes include various dance melodies, often

in a more simple form than the settings of the other secular tunes.

    a)   The *Ballo del granduca* (*M* 9c, v. 1, fasc. 3, p. 3) is a setting of a dance tune composed by **Cavalieri** for the wedding of the Grand Duke Ferdinando of Tuscany.   The other tunes were taken from works by **John Dowland** (*M* 9c, v. 1, fasc. 3, p. 42), **Peter Philips** (*M* 9c, v. 1, fasc. 3, p. 46; *CE*, v. 1, p. 107), and a popular Dutch song *Malle Sijmen* (Silly Simon). The variations on a tune by **Cabezón** (*Pavana Hispanica*) (*M* 5c, v. 1, fasc. 3, p. 39; *CE*, v. 1, p. 128 and v. 9, p. 6) were written by **Sweelinck** and **Scheidt**.

    f.   Two other keyboard works by **Sweelinck** are a *Ricercar* (*M* 9c, v. 1, fasc. 1, p. 49: *CE*, v. 9, p. 1; *M* 9b, v. 2, p. 10) and *Praeludium* (*M* 9c, v. 1, fasc. 1, p. 137).

    4.   Vocal music

      a.   The northern part of the Netherlands was Calvinist, and church music was restricted to the unaccompanied monophonic melodies in the principal psalter of the Calvinists, the *Genevan Psalter* of 1562. **Sweelinck's** vocal music comprises chansons for voices or instruments, secular pieces with French and Italian texts, and two collections of sacred works.

      b.   *Chansons à 5,* Antwerp, 1594 (*CE*, v. 7)

        1)   These 18 chansons in five parts are generally in the style of the French chanson of the Renaissance, but harmonically more tonal.

          a)   The popular song, *Susann' un jour d'amour sollicitée* (*CE*, v. 7, p. 35), first printed in 1548, was made famous by the setting of **Orlando di Lasso**, 1560. **Sweelinck's** chanson, based on the tune, is written in motet style with each phrase treated contrapuntally.

      c.   *Rimes françoises et italiennes à 2-4,* Leiden, 1612 (*CE*, v. 8; *HM*, v. 75)

        1)   There are 12 pieces in two and three parts set to French texts, 15 to Italian texts, and one French *chanson à quatre*. This collection of secular pieces is written mostly in imitative counterpoint.

      d.   *Pseaumes de David,* 1604, 1613, 1614, 1621 (*CE*, vols. 2-5)

        1)   These settings of Genevan Psalm tunes in four to eight voices are contained in four books and represent **Sweelinck's** most important vocal works. These works by **Sweelinck**, as well as those by his French predecessors, **Claude Goudimel** (from 1551), **Claude le Jeune** (from 1564), and others, were widely known and sung by the Calvinists in their homes and at social functions. **Sweelinck** himself conducted meetings of a Collegium Musicum established to sing his music.

        2)   There are, in all, 153 settings (three Psalms have two settings each) of the 150 Psalms of David based on the metrical translations by **Beza** and **Marot**.

        3)   The devices used include imitation, word repetition, material derived from the melody, echo effects, *cantus firmus* treatment of the melody, and frequent use of a descending four-note motive.

      e.   *Cantiones sacrae à 5,* 1619 (*CE*, v. 6)

        1)   This collection of 37 motets are the only vocal works by **Sweelinck** which call for an "organ basso continuo" part, as noted in Latin on the title page. The motets are written in polyphonic style and include the well-known Christmas motet *Hodie Christus natus est* (*CE*, v. 6, p. 69).

B.   **Anthoni van Noordt** (d. *c.* 1675)

    1.   *Tabulatuur-Boeck van Psalmen en Fantasyen,* 1659 (*M* 11)

      a.   This is the first published book of Dutch keyboard music and it contains ten psalm settings and six fantasies. Based on one subject each, the fantasies are an important development from the earlier imitative forms to the fugue.

      b.   *Fantasia* (*RGO*, v. 2, p. 72)

III.   Protestant Church Music in Germany

A. The chorale
1. Originally chorales were melodies sung by the congregation in unison without accompaniment (*choraliter*), and served a liturgical function as plainsong did in the Catholic service. Organ accompaniments were added about 1604 in what was known as *cantional* style. Textual and musical sources include liturgical chants of the Catholic church, pre-Reformation German sacred songs, and German folk and fraternal songs. The substitution of a sacred text for a secular one in a composition (*contrafactum*) was a common practice. Some chorales were newly composed.
2. Polyphonic settings of chorales with the melody in the tenor (from 1524) or soprano (from 1586) were sung by the choir (*Kantorei*). Early modal settings in free rhythm, with notes of varying values, developed into tonal settings with an accented, metrical rhythm (*isometric*).
3. During the 17th century many new chorale tunes were added, principally by **Johann Cruger** (1598-1662).
   a. *Praxis pietatis melica* (Practice of piety in song), Berlin, 1647
      1) This hymnbook contains 387 hymns and was the most influential German hymnbook of the 17th century. Fifteen of the texts are by **Paul Gerhardt** (1607-1676).
B. The chorale melody and text, or in some cases only the text, formed the bases for most of the vocal music in the Protestant church during the Baroque. In the first half of the 17th century, two styles emerged using the chorale, the chorale motet and the chorale *concertato*. A third style, dramatic *concertato,* did not use the chorale.
1. Chorale motet
   a. Chorale motets were written in the conservative polyphonic style of the Renaissance with an optional continuo. Each phrase of the chorale was used as the basis for successive imitative sections in motet style, or the chorale might appear as a *cantus firmus* in various voices in alternation.
2. Chorale *concertato*
   a. The chorale was combined with the Venetian *concertato* style with an obligatory continuo. The chorale lines were introduced at various times in *cantus firmus* style, or fragments were used as motives.
      1) The free chorale *concertato* set the text only, without reference to the melody.
   b. The chorale *concertato* developed into the chorale cantata with solos, chorus, and instruments.
3. Dramatic *concertato* style
   a. A large proportion of the church music was written in this freely composed style without the use of the chorale. It made use of Latin and German texts from the Gospels and Psalms.
C. **Michael Praetorius** (Latinized form of Schultheiss) (1571-1621) (*M* 4a)
1. Praetorius composed many vocal and instrumental settings in the Venetian *concertato* style with expressive use of the chorale. He also wrote motets, Masses, Psalms, polychoral works, madrigals, and dance pieces (*M* 1, pt, 1, v. 4; pt, 2, v. 4; *CW,* v. 51).
2. *Urania* (*CE,* v. 16)
   a. This collection contains 28 settings of chorales for two, three, and four choirs of four parts each. **Praetorius** gives detailed directions for the performance of his works. He suggests that the second choir be given to instruments, or that one or more voices be played by instruments.
3. *Musae Sioniae* (The muses of Zion), 1605-1610 (*CE,* vols, 1-9)
   a. There are 1244 chorale motets for ensembles of from two parts to three choirs of four voices each in the collection. Volume 7 closes with four chorale fantasies for organ (*Pro organicis: sine textu*) (pp. 263-304).
   b. *Geborn ist uns Emanuel* (*CE,* v. 6, p. 28; *GMB,* No. 161)
      1) This is a Christmas chorale for four-voice choir alternating with solo ensembles.
4. *Musarum Sinoar[um] Motectae et Psalmi latini,* 1607 (*CE,* v. 10)

    a.   Included are 52 choral compositions in 4-16 parts with organ *accommodatae* (doubling the vocal parts).

    b.   *Beati omnes* (p. 112) is for two four-part choirs singing antiphonally and together.

    c.   *Confitemini Domino* (p. 310) makes use of four four-part choirs, some antiphonally and in groups of two choirs antiphonally.

5.   *Polyhymnia caduceatrix & panegyrica* (Songs of peace and rejoicing), 1619 (*CE*, v. 17)

    a.   In the collection there are 40 *concertato* compositions with German or Latin texts in from one to 21 parts (p. 599) for two to six choirs (p. 477) including instruments and continuo.

6.   *Polyhymnia exercitatrix*, 1620 (*CE*, v. 18)

    a.   This contains 14 compositions in from two to eight parts, including instruments. Many diminutions are written out below the simple vocal lines of the chorales.

    b.   The eight Latin compositions have continual repetition of the word "Hallelujah" superimposed upon the Latin text. Six compositions have German texts.

7.   *Puericinium*, 1621 (*CE*, v. 19).

    a.   These 14 elaborate works for various seasons of the church year are German church songs and other concert songs for two to five choirs with three to 14 parts and instruments. A four-voice boys choir, a four-voice adult choir, and a four-voice choir of violins doubled by the organ, and other instruments are included in some compositions (pp. 94, 140).

8.   *Syntagma Musicum* (Treatise on Music), 1615-1619

    a.   This treatise is one of the most important sources of information on music in the Early Baroque. Volume I is on Theory of Music, Volume II (*De Organographia*) contains pictures of instruments drawn to scale with explanations, and organ specifications, and Volume III has to do with performance of music, forms, and instruction on the performance of his works (Chapter 8, part 3).

D. **Johann Hermann Schein** (1586-1630) (*M 7*; *CW*, vols. 12, 116; *M 1*, pt. 1, v. 5)

  1.   With **Schütz** and **Praetorius, Schein** introduced the Italian monodic, *concertato*, and instrumental styles. He wrote church music with elaborate treatment of chorale melodies, secular continuo songs, and instrumental dance suites. The chorale motet is his most important contribution. From 1616 to his death he was cantor at St. Thomas Church, Leipzig, a post **J. S. Bach** held from 1723-1750.

  2.   *Cymbalum Sionium*, 1615 (*CE*, v. 4)

    a.   This collection includes 30 motets, 15 on Latin and 15 on German texts, in 16th-century style for 5 to 12 voices. An instrumental *Canzona a 5* is also included.

  3.   *Opella Nova* (New Little Works), Part I, 1618 (*CE*, v. 5); Part II, 1626 (*CE*, vols. 6-7)

    a.   Schein called these works *Geistliche Konzerte* (Sacred concertos).

    b.   Part I contains 30 pieces with German texts of from three to five voices, with continuo and bass instrument. Twenty-nine are settings of Lutheran chorales.

    c.   Part II contains 32 pieces in solo and large ensemble settings based on chorale and Biblical texts. Five are in Latin and 27 are in German. Sometimes both melody and text of the chorale is used and at other times only the text. Melodic fragmentation, varied rhythms, and ornamentation are characteristic.

    d.   *Erschienen ist der herrliche Tag* (The glorious day has dawned) (*CE*, v. 6, p. 115; *TEM*, 220)

    e.   *Gelobet seist du, Jesu Christ* (Praise be Thou, Lord Jesus Christ) (*CE*, v. 5, p. 5; *GMB*, No. 188)

  4.   *Cantional oder Gesangbuch Augsburgischer Konfession*, 1627, 1645

E. **Samuel Scheidt** (1587-1654) (*M 6*)

  1.   **Scheidt** frequently used the chorale in the form of variations in which each stanza of the chorale is set in a combination of voices and instruments in chorale *concertato* style. He is best known as a composer of organ music.

  2.   *Cantiones sacrae*, 1620 (*CE*, v. 4)

      a.   These polychoral compositions are mostly for two four-part choirs and are settings of Biblical and chorale texts in Latin and German.

   3. *Concertus sacri,* 1622 (*CE,* vols, 14, 15)

      a.   The sacred compositions of two to 12 voices include solo ensembles, echo choruses, instrumental sinfonias and also a parody Mass.

   4. *Neue geistliche Konzerte,* Parts I to IV, 1631-1640 (*CE,* vols. 8-12; *NOH,* 691-695)

      a.   These small ensembles of two to six parts and continuo are based on texts from the Psalms and Gospels. Affective passages elaborating the texts are common.

   5. *Liebliche Kraftblümlein* (Lovely little flowers), 1635 (*CE,* v. 16)

      a.   This is **Scheidt's** last concerted work and, as stated in the title, is "set for a two-part heavenly choir as a foretaste of eternal life." Based mostly on the Psalms, these two-voiced compositions are characterized by musical expression and emotional effects.

   6. *Siebzig Symphonien auf Concerten-Manier,* 1644 (*CE,* v. 13)

      a.   This contains 70 three-part instrumental works to be played "as a prelude before concertos, motets or sacred madrigals with instruments." There are 10 preludes in each of seven keys.

F. **Andreas Hammerschmidt** (1612-1675) (*DdT,* v. 40; *M* 1, pt. 1, v. 5)

   1. **Hammerschmidt,** a Bohemian organist and composer, was obliged to move to Freiburg in 1626 because of his Protestant beliefs. He became organist there in 1635 and in 1639 moved to a similar position at Zittau where he remained until his death.

   2. His many works became renowned throughout northern Germany and hold an important position in the development of Lutheran church music. The Italian *concertato* style is shown in his works which include a variety of vocal compositions for solo voice and continuo, solo ensemble pieces with instrumental accompaniment, large choral motets for as many as twelve voices including instruments, Latin motets for two voices and accompaniment, and five- and six-voice *a cappella* compositions in *madrigalmanier.*

   3. *Musicalische Andachten* (Musical devotions), 1638-1653

      a.   This collection of 157 compositions divided into five parts includes pieces from one voice and continuo up to elaborate polyphonic choral works with instrumental accompaniment, as well as *a cappella* pieces. The compositions **Hammerschmidt** has subtitled *concerten, madrigalien, symphonien,* or *motteten.*

   4. *Dialogi oder Gespräche zwischen Gott und einer gläubigen Seele* (Dialogues between God and the believing soul), 1645 (*DTÖ,* v. 16; *DdT,* v. 40)

      a.   These 22 dialogues, all but two with German texts, are written in dramatic *concertato* style for 2, 3, and 4 voices with continuo and *sinfonie.* The dialogues are worked out by a text of prayer or supplication being answered with a text of promise or comfort sung by a different voice.

      b.   *Wende dich, Herr* (Turn Thee, O Lord) (*DTÖ,* v. 16, p. 131; *HAM,* No. 213) is a dialogue between an alto and a bass voice with continuo accompaniment.

G. **Franz Tunder** (1614-1667)

   1. A pupil of **Frescobaldi, Tunder** was the father-in-law and predecessor of **Buxtehude** at the Marienkirche in Lübeck. He wrote chorale monodies and chorale variations in *concertato* style, leading to the later chorale cantata.

   2. *Wachet auf* (Awake) (*DdT,* v. 3, p. 107; *HAM,* No. 214)

      a.   The chorale cantata for solo voice consists of a short 13-measure *sinfonia* for three string instruments and continuo followed by the chorale. A two-measure interlude then introduces the closing section in triple meter which makes use of motives from the chorale.

   3. *Helft mir Gott's Güte preisen* (Help me praise God's goodness) (*DdT,* v. 3, p. 118)

      a.   This six-stanza chorale cantata makes use of solos, duets, and a four- and five-part chorus with strings and continuo.

H. **Heinrich Schütz** (1585-1672) (*M* 8abc)

1. In Italy **Schütz** used the name **Enrico Sagittarius.** He studied with **Giovanni Gabrieli** from 1609 to 1612 and later with **Monteverdi.** He was Kapellmeister to the Saxon court at Dresden from 1617 to his death. During this time he visited Italy and was court conductor at the court of King Christian IV in Copenhagen during the Thirty Years War.
2. **Schütz** developed a semi-dramatic style of church music based on various styles which included the Venetian dramatic *concertato,* 16th-century contrapuntal, and the monodic style of **Monteverdi.** He interpreted texts with unusual expressive and dramatic effect, but made little use of the chorale. His church music includes Psalms, motets, oratorios, and Passions, but no independent instrumental music.
3. *Psalmen Davids,* 1619 (*CE,* v. 16; *NASW,* vols. 23-26; *SWV,* 22-47)
    a. The Psalms are written in the Venetian polychoral style with 2, 3, and 4 choruses, soloists (*favoriti,* selected voices from the choir), and instruments. Included is a *contrafactum* in which **Schütz** set German words to **Gabrieli's** madrigal *Lieto godea.*
        1) Psalm 121: *Ich heb mein' Augen sehnlich auf* (I will lift up mine eyes) (*CE,* v. 16, p. 108; *GMB,* No. 189)
        2) Psalm 92: *Es ist fürwahr ein köstlich Ding* (It is a good thing to give thanks) (*CE,* v. 16, p. 80; *NASW,* v. 6, p. 93; *GMB,* No. 189)
4. *Cantiones Sacrae,* 1625, *SWV* 53-93 (*CE,* v. 4; *NASW,* vols. 8-9)
    a. These 40 sacred songs, based on Latin texts, are in the advanced *concertato* style with four voices and a *basso seguente,* added at the request of **Schütz's** publisher.
    b. Subjective qualities of the texts are expressed in extreme pictorial dissonance by augmented triads, simultaneous cross relations, and chromatic dissonance in melodies.
5. *Symphoniae Sacrae,* Part I, 1629; Part II, 1647; Part III, 1650 (*CE,* vols, 5, 7, 10, 11; *NASW,* vols. 13-21; *AM,* v. 45, p. 38; *NagMA,* v. 102; *SR,* 432; *BM,* 94; *NOH,* v. 5, pp. 714-720)
    a. These "sacred symphonies" show the influence of **Schütz's** second journey to Italy when he again studied with **Monteverdi** whose style he greatly admired. **Schütz** included several of his German adaptations of compositions by **Monteverdi** and **Grandi.**
    b. Part I shows the mature Italian *concertato* style applied to compositions of one to three voices with particular instruments specified for coloristic effects. Part II continues the small ensemble, few-voiced *concertato* style of Part I. Part III, published in 1650 after the Thirty Years War, makes use of dramatic *concertato* style with multiple choirs, ensembles of soloists, a variety of instruments, and continuo.
    c. *Tractatus compositionis augmentatus* (An augmented treatise on composition), *c.* 1660, written by **Schütz's** assistant, **Christoph Bernhard** (1627-1692) (*BM,* 96), discusses many of the "new" devices, such as the use of dissonance, embellishments, and affections used by **Schütz** and other composers of his time.
    d. *Saul, Saul, was verfolgst du mich?* (Saul, Saul, why persecutest thou Me?) (*CE,* v. 11. p. 99; *HAM,* No. 202, *NS,* 62)
        1) This dramatic concerto for six soloists (*favoriti*), two four-part choirs, two violins, and organ is based on St. Paul's experience narrated in Acts 9:1-31. It makes dramatic and pictorial use of the polychoral texture alternating with soloists and instruments.
    e. *Veni de Libano* (Come from Lebanon), *SWV,* 266 (*CE,* v. 11, p. 80; *NASW,* v. 13, p. 88; *MSO,* 95)
6. *Kleine geistliche Konzerte* (Little sacred concertos), 1636-1639 (*CE,* v. 6; *NASW,* vols. 10-12; *AM,* v. 45, p. 39)
    a. The concertos are based on texts of chorales and Latin hymns, and make use of one to five voices in monodies or solo ensembles with organ continuo.
        1) The smaller number of voices reflects the shortage of musicians during the Thirty Years War.

      b.   *Was hast du virwerket, o du allerholdseligster Knab, Jesu Christ?* (What have you lost, O most gracious child, Jesus Christ?) (*CE*, v. 6, p. 48; *NASW*, v. 10, p. 16; *GMB*, No. 190)

    7.   *Geistliche Chormusik,* 1648, *SWV*, 369-397 (*CE*, v. 8; *NASW*. v. 5)

      a.   This collection of sacred music was dedicated to the St. Thomas choir and the city of Leipzig.

      b.   In these 29 motets of five to seven voices, Schütz was particularly interested in discriminating between motets which could have the parts doubled with instruments (*a cappella* style) and those in which the choral and instrument parts were kept separate or alternate in *concertato* style. The continuo was not obligatory.

    8.   Oratorios

      a.   *Historia der Auferstehung Jesu Christi* (Story of the Resurrection of Christ), 1623, *SWV*, 50 (*CE*, v. 1; *NASW*, v. 3)

         1)   This large work for soloists, chorus, and instruments is a free arrangement of a work by Antonio Scandello (1517-1580), an Italian musician living in Germany.

         2)   The fact that the texts generally sung by a single person are set for more than one reflects an older style.

      b.   *Die sieben Worte Jesu Christ am Kreuz* (The seven last words of Christ on the cross), 1645, *SWV*, 478 (*CE*, v. 1, p. 147; *NASW*, v. 2, p. 3)

      c.   *Historia der Geburt Jesu Christi* (Story of the birth of Christ), 1664, *SWV*, 435 (*CE*, v. 17; *NASW*, v. 1)

         1)   Both the "Seven words" and the "Christmas story" are written in dramatic style for soloists, chorus, and instruments. They open and close with elaborate choruses accompanied by instruments, and between are recitatives and vocal ensembles which tell the story.

         2) In the "Seven words" a chorale text is used but not the chorale melody. The words of Christ in monody are accompanied with strings and continuo.

         3)   *Sinfonia* and *Und es war um die dritte Stunde* (And this was the third hour) from "Seven words" (*CE*, v. 1, p. 149; *NASW*, v. 2, p. 10; *GMB*, No. 191)

         4)   *Da Jesus an dem Kreuze stund* (As Jesus stood at the cross) (*CE*, v. 1, p. 147; *NASW*, v. 2, p. 15; *HAM*, No. 201 a, b)

   9.   Passions

      a.   Passions according to St. Matthew, *SWV*, 479; St. Luke, *SWV*, 480; and St. John, *SWV*, 481 (*CE*, v. 1; *NASW*, v. 2)

         1)   The St. Mark passion is not authentic.

         2)   No chorales, instrumental accompaniment, or continuo were used in the Passions. The words of Jesus and other soloists are set to freely-composed recitatives in plainsong style, unaccompanied. The words of the people (*turba*) and the disciples are set to four-part chorus in dramatic style.

           a)   The settings follow the Biblical text, without additions, and there is some attempt at word-painting (the crowing of the cock, descent of the angel).

         3)   Two scenes from *St. Matthew Passion*, 1666 (*CE*, v. 1, pp. 52, 67; *NASW*, v. 2, pp. 113, 135; *GMB*, No. 192).

I.   During the Early Baroque, Passions, dramatic *concertatos,* and oratorios were written in large numbers and by many other composers. Recitatives, arias, use of the orchestra, dramatic *concertato* style, free treatment of the text with poetic interpolations are all characteristic features of these larger choral works. Some use of plainsong and polyphonic styles are still present in the early 17th century.

    1.   **Melchior Vulpius** (1560-1615) (*M* 1, pt. 1, v. 3)

      a.   Vulpius makes use of the early plainsong Passion concept in which the *turba* (crowd) text is set in homophonic choruses above a plainsong tenor. There is no accompaniment for soloists or choruses.

         1)   *St. Matthew Passion* (*Denkmäler thüringischer Musik,* v. 1)

2) *Von der Geburt Jesu Christ* (On the birth of Jesus Christ), 1609 (*NagMA*, v. 44)
3) *Weissagung des Leidens und Sterbens Jesu Christi* (Prophecies of the suffering and death of Jesus Christ) (*CW*, v. 27, p. 31
   a) An oratorio for six-part chorus based on Isaiah 53.
2. **Christoph Demantius** (1567-1643) (*M*, 1, v. 4; *CW*, vols, 36, 39)
  a. *Deutscher Johannes-Passion*, 1631 (*CW*, v. 27, p. 6)
   1) Along with the plainsong Passion, the early through-composed motet Passion gradually died out during the early 17th century, this one being about the last.
3. **Thomas Selle** (1592-1663)
  a. *Johannes-Passion*, 1643 (*CW*, v. 26)
   1) This is a dramatic oratorical Passion which makes use of three solo voices, five-part orchestra, and continuo, six-part chorus, and a solo violin. The Evangelist, accompanied with two bassoons, uses recitative and the soloists, accompanied with various instruments, sing in monodic style. A chorale and verses from the Psalms and Isaiah are inserted for reflective elements in the Passion story.
4. **Johann Sebastiani** (1622-1683)
  a. *Das Leyden und Sterben unser Herrn und Heyland Jesu Christi* (The sufferings and death of our Lord and Saviour Jesus Christ), 1663 (*DdT*, v. 17, pp. 1-103)
   1) This Passion story from St. Matthew is for soloists, five-part choir, six instruments, and continuo. It includes one-voice chorales with accompaniment: *Vater unser in Himmelreich* for tenor (p. 31), *O Lamm Gottes unschuldig* (p. 49), and *O Traurigkeit* (p. 94) for soprano.
5. **Johann Rosenmüller** (*c.* 1620-1684)
  a. *Aleph. Ego vir* (A. I am the man) (*HAM*, No. 218)
   1) This dramatic Latin monody is based on the Lamentations of Jeremiah 3:1-9. **Rosenmüller** makes use of the Hebrew letters, *Aleph, Beth,* and *Ghimel,* in vocal melismas to set off the beginnings of the verses.

IV. Catholic Church Music

A. Catholic musicians, many of whom were opera composers, held important positions in south Germany and Austria. They followed the Italian style of Rome and to some extent Venice, therefore a German style of Catholic church music did not develop. The music includes elaborate Masses, Requiems, and Magnificats in the *concertato* style with large multiple choral groups and instruments, including brass and timpani.
B. **Gregor Aichinger** (1564-1628) (*CO*, v. 7; *RRMB*, v. 14)
  1. Aichinger's music shows the influence of the *stile antico* of **Palestrina** as well as the Venetian **Gabrieli** with whom he studied.
  2. *In lectulo meo. Viderunt eam* (*M* 1, pt. 1, v. 4; *DTB*, v. 18)
C. **Johann Stadlmayr** (1560-1648)
  1. *Hymnen*, 1628 (*DTÖ*, v. 5)
  a. These 34 four-part harmonizations of plainsong hymns in motet style are for various services of the Catholic church year.
D. **Johann Heinrich Schmelzer** (*c.* 1623-1680)
  1. *Missa Nuptialis* (*DTÖ*, v. 49, p. 48)
  a. This wedding Mass calls for soloists, solo ensembles, six-part chorus, and orchestra including four trombones.
E. **Johann Kaspar Kerll** (1627-1693) (*RRMB*, v. 3)
  1. *Missa cujus toni* (*DTÖ*, v. 49, p. 74)
  a. The Mass is for soloists, four-part choir, and orchestra, including three trombones. In the Kyrie an instrumental sonata for two violins, bassoon, and continuo separate the *Kyrie* from the *Christe* and another sonata separates the *Christe* from the following *Kyrie*.

    2. *Missa à tre cori* (*DTÖ*, v. 49, p. 106)

      a. This Mass is for three four-voice choirs and a large orchestra including two clarin trumpets, two cornetti, and three trombones. A descending sequence of four echoes on the word "*miserere*" in the *Agnus Dei* may be noted.

    3. *Missa pro defunctis* (*DTÖ*, v. 59, p. 73)

      a. In the *Dies irae* of this Requiem, **Kerll** uses the strings in an interesting tremolo oscillating between 16th and 8th notes.

  F. **Heinrich Franz Biber** (1644-1704)

    1. *Missa St. Henrici,* 1701 (*DTÖ*, v. 49, p. 1)

      a. This Mass requires a large orchestra of strings and brass and a five-voice choir with continuo accompaniment. Sometimes the instruments double the voice parts.

    2. *Requiem* (*DTÖ*, v. 59, p. 41)

V. Continuo Song

  A. The continuo *lied* (strophic song) flourished throughout Germany and Austria during the 17th century. Large collections of continuo songs not only included songs in monodic style to which a second voice was often improvised, but also polyphonic songs. Parodies on English, French, and Italian songs were common. Many collections made no distinction between secular and sacred, and dance songs, chorales, recitatives, or choral songs were all mixed together. Five-part ritornellos often separate the strophes.

  B. **Johann Hermann Schein** (1586-1630)

    1. *Venus Kräntzlein* (Little Venus garland), Wittenburg, 1609 (*CE*, v. 1; *NAW*, v. 6)

      a. These secular strophic songs are for five to eight voices in Italian *canzonetta* (dance-song) style and include instrumental pieces in five to eight parts.

      b. *Gleichwie ein kleines Vögelein* (Just as a little bird) (*CE*, v. 1, p. 14; *GMB*, No. 187b)

    2. *Musica boscareccia* or [Ger.] *Waldliederlein* (Little forest songs), 3 volumes, 1621, 1626, 1628 (*CE*, v. 2; *NAW*, v. 7; *AM*, v. 45, p. 41)

      a. There are 59 three-voiced songs with continuo in this collection which was published in Leipzig. They are in the style of the Italian *villanella.*

      b. *Viel schöner Blümelein* (Many beautiful little flowers) (*CE*, v. 2, p. 62; *GMB*, No. 187a)

    3. *Diletti pastorali* [Ger.] *Hirten-lust* (Shepherd's pleasure), 1624 (*CE*, v. 3; *NAW*, v. 8)

      a. These five-voice continuo madrigals are through-composed and in the style of **Monteverdi**. Included also are five five-voice pieces from the *Studentenschmauss* (student feast), 1626.

  C. **Heinrich Albert** (1604-1651), a cousin of **Heinrich Schütz**.

    1. *Arien*, 8 volumes, 1638-1650   (*DdT*, vols, 12, 13; *HM*, v. 150; *M* 1, pt. 2, v. 5)

      a. In this large collection of 190 songs there are strophic songs with continuo, recitatives, dance songs, and a few choral songs, some through-composed. These songs, sacred and secular, were commonly sung in middle class homes and at student gatherings.

      b. *Auf, mein Geist* (Rise, my soul) (*DdT*, v. 12, p. 11; *HAM*, No. 205; *AM*, v. 32, p. 100)

      c. *Der Mensch hat nichts so eigen* (Nothing becomes man better than being faithful) (*DdT*, v. 12; p. 53; *GMB*, No. 193a; *AM*, v. 14, p. 21)

      d. *Gespräch einer Jungfrauen mit einem verdorreten Rosenstock* (The maid spoke with the withering rose-tree) (*DdT*, v. 12, p. 13; *GMB*, No. 193b)

      e. *Vorjahrslied* (Last year's song) (*DdT*. v. 12, p. 91; *GMB*, No. 193c)

  D. **Andreas Hammerschmidt** (1611-1675)

    1. *Weltliche Oden* or *Liebes Gesänge* (Secular odes or Love songs), 1642 (*EDM*, vols, 43, 49)

      a. *Kusslied* (Kiss song) (*GMB*, No. 194), a strophic song with continuo.

  E. **Adam Krieger** (1634-1666)

    1. *Neue Arien,* 1676 (*DdT*, v. 19)

      a. *Adonis Tod* (*DdT*, v. 19, p. 16; *HAM*, No. 228; *AM*, v. 32, p. 101)

VI.   Keyboard Music

A.   Organ music was the principal type of keyboard music in the Early Baroque. In the Middle Baroque, idiomatic harpsichord and clavichord music began to appear. The principal keyboard forms were the chorale prelude, chorale fantasia, chorale variation, prelude and fugue, and toccata. The north German composers were strongly influenced by **Sweelinck**, the "maker of German organists."

B.   **Michael Praetorius** (1571-1621)

   1.   *Hymnodia Sionia,* 1611 (*CE,* v. 12)

     a.   Six organ settings are included in this collection of Latin hymn melodies in which the *cantus firmus* is in the bass and some imitation is used in the upper parts.

   2.   *Musae Sioniae* (*CE,* v. 7, p. 263; *M* 4bc; *NagMA,* v. 40)

     a.   This collection also includes four organ settings of German chorales, three of which are monumental fantasias in motet style, a new type of organ chorale created by **Praetorius.**

C.   **Samuel Scheidt** (1587-1654)

   1.   **Scheidt,** a pupil of **Sweelinck** and the outstanding organ composer of his time, was organist at the Moritzkirche and Kapellmeister to the Margrave of Brandenburg at Halle.

   2.   *Tabulatura Nova,* 1624 (*DdT,* v. 1; *CE,* vols, 6, 7; *LO,* vols. 6, 7)

     a.   The "new tablature" was written with a separate five-line staff for each voice instead of the Anglo-Flemish (**Sweelinck**) and Italian usage of two staves of six or more lines each.

     b.   This work is divided into three parts and includes the following types of compositions.

       1)   Chorale variation (*versus*)

         a)   *Warum betrübst du dich, mein Herz?* (Why are you so sorrowful, my heart?) (*CE,* v. 6, pt. 1, p. 48; *DdT,* v. 1, p. 33)

         b)   *Da Jesus an dem Kreuze stund* (As Jesus stood before the cross) (*CE,* v. 6, pt. 1, p. 102; *DdT,* v. 1, p. 71; *AM,* v. 11, p. 26)

       2)   Chorale fantasia

         a)   *Wir glauben all' an einen Gott*   (We all believe in one God) (*CE,* v. 6, pt. 1, p. 2; *DdT,* v. 1; *RGO,* v. 2, p. 219)

       3)   Fugue (*AM,* v. 19, p. 37)

         a)   *Fuga Contraria* (*CE,* v. 6, pt. 2, p. 1; *DdT,* v. 1, p. 89)

           (1)   The *Fuge,* worked out in contrary motion, is an expanded fantasia in contrapuntal style which presents the theme in augmentation and diminution. Phrasing is indicated which imitates that of the violin.

       4)   Secular variations

         a)   *Est-ce Mars* (*CE,* v. 6, pt. 1, p. 93; *DdT,* v. 1, p. 65)

       5)   Echo

         a)   *Echo ad manuale duplex, forte et lene* (*CE,* v. 6, pt. 2, p. 10; *DdT,* v. 1, p. 95)

       6)   Toccata

         a)   *Toccata super In te Domine speravi* (*CE,* v. 6, pt. 2, p. 10; *DdT,* v. 1)

           (1)   The theme bears no relation to the traditional plainsong.

   3.   *Tabulaturbuch hundert geistlicher Lieder und Psalmen,* 1650 (*CE,* v. 1)

     a.   Published in Görlitz and known as the *Görlitzer Tabulaturbuch,* this collection contains 114 different harmonizations of 100 chorales and is the first book of written-out organ accompaniments for Protestant congregational singing.

D.   **Heinrich Scheidemann** (1596-1663) (*M* 5abc)

   1.   **Scheidemann,** a student of **Sweelinck,** composed toccatas, preludes, organ chorales, Magnificats, intabulations, pieces in the style of the fantasie, and several dance pieces.

   2.   *Praeludium* (*HAM,* No. 195a); *Praeludium* from *Prelude and Fugue* (*HAM,* No. 195b)

   3.   Organ chorales (*CEKM,* Ser. 10, v. 2); *Magnificats* (*M* 5b)

E.   **Delphin Strunck** (1601-1694)

1. **Strunck's** limited works include arrangements of motets for organ, a setting of the Magnificat, and a lengthy toccata.
   a. *Lass mich dein sein und bleiben* (Let me be Thine) (*RGO*, v. 2, p. 207)
      1) This expressive chorale prelude is based on the widely used secular melody which has been set to various religious texts including *Herzlich tut mich verlangen* and *O Haupt voll Blut und Wunden*.
F. **Franz Tunder** (1614-1667) (*M* 10)
   1. *Prelude and Fugue* (*HAM*, No. 215); Organ chorales (*CEKM*, Ser. 10, v. 2)
G. **Jan Adam Reincken** (1623-1722) (*CEKM*, Ser. 16)
   1. Almost a centenarian, **Reincken** was born in Alsace and later studied with **Scheidemann** in Hamburg, where in 1663 **Reincken** succeeded **Scheidemann** as organist at St. Catherine's. Included in his few remaining keyboard compositions are suites, chorale settings, variations, a fugue, and a toccata.
   2. *Partite diverse sopra l'Aria: Schweiget mir vom Weibernehmen, altrimente chiamata La Meyerin* (*CEKM*, Ser. 16; *GMB*, No. 207)
      a. Each of these 18 variations consistently maintains its characteristic rhythmic and melodic patterns, and the concluding three variations show definite dance features.
H. The south German composers, mostly Catholic, were influenced by the Italians **Andrea Gabrieli, Merulo**, and **Frescobaldi**, as well as by the "colorists" such as **Elias N. Ammerbach** (1530-1597). They used elaborate ornamentation in arranging vocal music for the keyboard (intabulations).
   1. The principal forms used were the canzona, ricercar, verset, the toccata in several movements, and the suite. Catholic composers rarely used the chorale.
I. **Hans Leo Hassler** (1564-1612) (*CE*, v. 4; *DTB*, v. 7)
   1. **Hassler** was born in Nuremberg, studied with **Andrea Gabrieli** in 1584, and on his return to Germany was employed by the **Fugger** family in Augsburg, and later in Dresden. Known principally as a composer of vocal music, **Hassler's** keyboard output is nevertheless quite substantial. His 110 keyboard works include ricercars, canzonas, fugues, toccatas, intratas, chorales, Magnificats, and an organ Mass.
   2 *Ricercare* (*RGO*, v. 2, p. 115)
      a. This polythematic ricercar in the Lydian mode is one of 24 ricercars and is divided into three sections, each based on a separate theme.
J. **Christian Erbach** (1573-1635) (*CEKM*, v. 36; *DTB*, v. 7; *CO*, vols, 1, 2, 4, 8, 9, 12; *LO*, v. 6; *HM*, vols, 7, 156)
   1. In 1596 **Erbach** became organist for the **Fugger** family in Augsburg and remained there the rest of his life. His keyboard output, larger than **Hassler's**, consists of the same types of compositions.
   2. *Fuga* (*RGO*, v. 2, p. 148); *Kyrie* (*RGO*, v. 2, p. 150)
K. **Johann Ulrich Steigleder** (1593-1635) (*CEKM*, v. 13)
   1. *Tabulaturbuch darinnen das Vatter unser 40 mal variiert wird . . .*, 1627 (*RGO*, v. 2, pp. 139, 140) is a collection of 40 variations on the chorale, *Vater unser im Himmelreich*, presents the chorale in a variety of ways: as a *cantus planus* in soprano, tenor, or bass, ornamented, broken into two voices, or as a motet or fantasie. **Erbach** explains the type as a heading to each variation. The closing variation is a toccata in which imitation and motivic development foreshadow the later north German toccata.
L. **Johann Jacob Froberger** (1616-1667) (*DTÖ*, vols. 8, 13, 21; *CO*, v. 13; *LO*, v. 5)
   1. Born in Stuttgart, **Froberger** went to Vienna about 1630 and became organist at the Austrian court. In 1637 he went to Rome where he studied with **Frescobaldi** for four years. He made concert tours to Paris and London and was strongly influenced by the French style.
   2. **Froberger** was the first important composer for the harpsichord and excelled in composing toccatas, variation canzonas, ricercars, and suites. Common techniques found in his works include free doubling in particular chords, arpeggiated cadences, orna-

mentation, and casual entering and dropping out of parts.

3. His suites are made up of the allemande, courante, and saraband with a gigue as a middle movement when present. The publisher of the posthumous edition of 1693 placed the gigue at the end.

   a. *Suite in G minor, No. 9* for harpsichord (*DTÖ*, v. 13, p. 23; *GMB*, No. 205)

   b. *Suite in E minor, No. 22* for clavichord (*DTÖ*, v. 13, p. 64; *MM*, 148)

   c. *Lamento sopra la dolorosa perdita della Real Maestà di Ferdinando IV, Rè de Romani* (*DTÖ*, v. 13, p. 32; *HAM*, No. 216)

      1) This is the first movement of *Suite No. 12* in C major and is in the style of an Allemande. It ends with an ascending scale to symbolize the ascent to heaven.

   d. *Toccata* for organ (*DTÖ*, v. 8, p. 5; *HAM*, No. 217)

M. **Alessandro de Poglietti** (d. 1683) (*AM*, v. 26, p. 113; *CO*, v. 13; *DTÖ*, v. 56)

   1. **Poglietti** was an Italian harpsichord virtuoso who lived in Vienna where he was court organist from 1661 to 1663. He wrote programmatic harpsichord suites imitating bird calls, animal sounds, tolling of bells, and even the history of the Hungarian rebellion in 1671.

   2. *Aria Allemagna con alcuni Variazioni sopra l'Età della Maestà Vostra* (German aria with variations on the age of her majesty), 1677 (*DTÖ*, v. 27, p. 13; *HAM*, No. 236)

      a. This set of 20 harpsichord variations from the suite *Rossignolo* was supposed to have one variation for each year of her majesty's age, although at this time she was 22. They are based on programmatic ideas from various provinces of the Austrian empire.

   3. *Capriccio über dass Hennengschrey* (Capriccio on the cackle of a hen) (*DTÖ*, v. 27, p. 37; *TEM*, 232) is the second of three pieces in fugal style. Double notes in the subject make the theme unique.

   4. *Ricercar on the 6th tone* (*RGO*, v. 2, p. 44)

N. **Johann Kaspar Kerll** (1627-1693) (*CO*, vols. 2, 13; *DTB*, v. 3)

   1. **Kerll** spent most of his life in Vienna and Munich, and was sent to Rome to study with **Carissimi** and **Frescobaldi**. **Kerll** wrote canzonas, toccatas, and versets on the Magnificat in the Italian style.

   2. *Modulatio organica*, 1686, is a collection of 56 versets on the Magnificat, seven for each of the eight tones. Fugal imitation and toccata style are well worked out.

VII. **Ensemble Music**

A. Ensemble Suite

   1. The suite was a combination of stylized dances all in the same key and one of the popular instrumental forms of 17th-century German Baroque music.

      a. The dances were written for solo instruments and ensembles for various combinations of instruments.

   2. In the Early and Middle Baroque the most usual dances were the pavane, galliarde, allemande, and courante which were published separately and also grouped in various ways. A festive introduction, call *intrada,* prelude, or sinfonia, was often added or sometimes published separately.

   3. The variation suite was the most important development in the German ensemble suite in the 17th century. The same key and thematic material was used throughout the suite. The principal theme might be varied in each dance, or only a suggestion of the theme might be used.

   4. **Hans Leo Hassler** (1565-1612)

      a. *Lustgarten neuer teutscher Gesänge*, 1601 (*PAM*, v, 15; *HM*, v. 73)

         1) There are 11 instrumental pieces included in this song collection. They are for four to six string or wind instruments without continuo. The *entradas* are all for six instruments.

5. **Melchior Franck** (*c.* 1573-1639) (*M*, 1, pt. 1, v. 5; *CW*, vols. 24, 38, 53)
   a.   *Neuer Pavanen, Galliarden, und Intraden,* 1603 (*DdT*, v. 16, pp. 1-50)
      1)   In this collection there are 37 dances in the usual four to six parts, as well as some secular German songs.
   b.   *Neue musicalische Intraden* (*DdT*, v. 16, pp. 53-86)
6. **Valentin Hausmann** (*c.* 1565-1615) (*M 1*, pt. 2, v. 4)
   a.   *Neue fünfstimmige Paduane und Galliarde auff Instrumenten,* 1604 (*DdT*, v. 16, p. 115; *GMB*, No. 155)
   b.   *Neue artige . . . Täntze,* 1602-1604 (*DdT*, v. 16)
7. **Christoph Demantius** 1567-1643)
   a.   *Convivium deliciae,* 1608
      1)   Intrada on the text *Es ist nit zu ermessen* (It is not to judge) (*GMB*, No. 154)
         a)   An example of the technique of using a familiar melody for audience participation.
8. **Samuel Scheidt** (1587-1654) (*HM*, v. 96)
   a.   *Ludi musici,* 1621 (*CE*, vols. 2, 3)
      1)   These 32 instrumental pieces with continuo include, *paduana, galliarda, coranta, alemande, intrada,* and *canzonetto.*
9. **Johann Schultz** (1582-1653)
   a.   *Musikalischer Lustgarten,* 1622 (*EDM Landschaftsdenkmale* 6, v. 1)
10. **Paul Peuerl** (Peurl) (*c.* 1580-1630)
   a.   **Peuerl** was the creator of the German variation suite.
   b.   *Newe Padouan, Intrada, Däntz unnd Galliarda,* 1611 (*DTÖ*, v. 70; *GMB*, No. 157) is a collection of 12 variation suites for four instruments.
11. **Johann Hermann Schein** (1586-1630)
   a.   *Banchetto musicale* (Musical banquet), 1617 (*CE*, v. 1, p. 198; *NAW*, v. 9; *AM*, v. 26, p. 108), an important collection of 20 variation suites written for viols in five parts. The movements include the *padouano, gagliarda, courente, allemande,* and *tripla,* the latter a variation of the *allemande.* One *intrada* and one *padouano* are scored for four krummhorns.
      1)   *Intrada* (*CE*, v. 1, p. 198; *HAM*, No. 197), is an independent composition at the end of the collection.
   b.   *Venus Kräntzlein,* 1609 (*CE*, v. 6; *NAW*, v. 6)
      1)   Ensemble music for five instruments is included in this collection of four *intrada,* two *gagliarda,* and three *canzon.*
12. **Isaac Posch** (*fl. c.* 1620)
   a.   *Musikalische Tafelfreudt,* 1621 (*DTÖ*, v. 70, p. 79; *AM*, v. 34, p. 45)
      1)   Included in this work are nine *Paduana* and *Gagliarda a 5* in the variation suite form and 12 *intrada* and *courante a 4.*
13. **Johann Jacob Loewe** (1628-1703) (*NagMA*, No. 67)
   a.   **Loewe** was one of the earliest to make use of an introductory movement such as the sinfonia in his suites.
14. **Johann Heinrich Schmelzer** (*c.* 1623-1680) (*EDM*, v. 14)
   a.   *Ballettos,* 1669 (*DTÖ*, v. 56)
15. **Johann Christoph Pezel** (1639-1694)
   a.   **Pezel** was a municipal trumpeter in Leipzig from 1664 to 1681 and published several collections of music for wind instruments.
      1)   Musicians were employed by the city council to play for weddings, funerals, civic celebrations, and various other functions. A brass choir played chorales, sonatas, folk songs, and dance music (*turmsonaten*) from the city hall tower or a church, and led processions.
   b.   *Hora decima Musicorum Lipsiensium,* 1670 (*DdT*, v. 63)
      1)   A collection of tower music for two cornetti and three trombones or five strings

which includes harmonized chorales, military signals, sonatas, and dances.

    2)   *Turmsonate, No. 9* (*DdT*, v. 63, p. 18; *GMB*, No. 221)

16. **Johann Rosenmüller** (*c.* 1620-1684)

  a.   *Sonate da camera cioe Sinfonie,* 1670 (*DdT*, v. 18)

    1)   Each of these 11 chamber sonatas or sinfonias are for five string or other instruments and consists of an introductory sinfonia followed by an *alemanda, correnta, ballo,* and *sarabanda.* The keys of these sonatas are F, D, C, g, d, a, G, e, B, A, c. In the opening sinfonias **Rosenmüller** was influenced by the Venetian opera overture.

    2)   *Sinfonia No. 11* (*DdT*, v. 18, p. 124; *GMB*, No. 220)

B.   Ensemble Canzona-Sonata

  1.   The Baroque sonata evolved from the multi-sectional ensemble canzona of contrasting sections. These sections, when decreased in number, were known as "movements." The term "sonata" gradually replaced the term "canzona" during the Middle Baroque.

    a.   Sonatas were written for many different combinations of wind and string instruments. Solo, duo, and trio sonatas with continuo bass for harpsichord or organ were almost always for violin and continued to be used throughout the 17th and early 18th centuries.

    b.   Virtuoso possibilities of the violin were exploited by developing advanced bowing techniques, using higher positions and multiple stops. *Scordatura* tuning (mistuning) was used to facilitate the playing of chords and difficult passages.

  2.   **Johann Heinrich Schmelzer** (1623-1680) (*DTÖ*, vols. 111, 112)

    a.   *Sonatae unarum fidium,* 1664 (*DTÖ*, v. 93)

      1)   In these solo violin sonatas **Schmelzer** makes extensive use of the ostinato and variation form as well as some use of *scordatura.*

    b.   *Duodena selectarum sonatarum,* 1659 (*DTÖ*, v. 105)

      1)   Most of these 12 sonatas are for two string instruments and continuo and make use of imitation and considerable virtuosity.

  3.   **Johann Jacob Walther** (1650-*c.* 1695)

    a.   *Scherzi da Violino solo con il Basso continuo,* 1676 (*EDM*, v. 17)

      1)   *Saraband* and *gigue* from the first of twelve sonatas (*GMB*, No. 239)

    b.   *Hortulus chelicus,* 1688

      1)   This collection consists of dance pieces, arias, preludes, and sets of variations. The closing "serenata" for solo violin is a set of variations in which **Walther** imitates various instruments: the guitar with pizzicato, trumpet, lyre, and harp. Sounds of nature, the cuckoo and nightingale, are also imitated in these pieces.

  4.   **Thomas Baltzar** (*c.* 1630-1663)

    a.   A renowned violinist, **Baltzar** went to England in 1655 and was the first great violin virtuoso to appear in England. In 1661 he was appointed director of King Charles II band of 24 violins. His music features double stops and polyphonic playing.

    b.   *Allemande* for solo violin (*GMB*, No. 237), is printed in John Playford's *The Division Violin* and in Hawkins, *A General History of the Science and Practice of Music,* 682.

  5.   **Heinrich Franz Ignaz Biber** (1644-1704) (*DTÖ*, vols. 97, 106, 107; *M 2*)

    a.   **Biber**, an outstanding composer and violinist, became director of music to the Archbishop of Salzburg in 1670. He was knighted in 1690 and thereafter signed his name "von Bibern." He did much to advance the techniques of the violin.

    b.   *Sechzehn Violinsonaten, c.* 1675 (*DTÖ*, v. 25)

      1)   The "15 Sacred Mysteries of the Virgin and Christ" for violin and continuo (organ) represent abstract commentaries on the scenes portrayed in the engravings at the beginning of each sonata. These scenes are the fifteen subjects of religious meditation used in the recitation of the Rosary.

      a)   The sixteenth sonata is a passacaglia with an engraving portraying the

Guardian angel (*DTÖ*, v. 25, p. 82; *AM*, v. 11, p. 71)

2) The sonatas make considerable use of dance movements in binary form and variations over a ground bass. Rhapsodic style, motivic development, and free imitation are found in the sonatas. Multiple stops, echo effects, fast repeated notes, ornaments, and virtuoso passages are characteristic. *Scordatura* is used in all but the first sonata and the closing passacaglia.

3) *Christi Gebet auf dem Ölberg* (The prayer of Christ on the Mount of Olives), Sonata No. 6 (*DTÖ*, v. 25, p. 24; *GMB*, No. 238)

4) *Surrexit Christus hodie* from Sonata No. 11, the "Resurrection" sonata (*DTÖ*, v. 25, p. 52; *HAM*, No. 238)

a) The Resurrection hymn, *Surrexit Christus hodie*, serves as the theme for this passacaglia of eight variations.

c. Eight Violin Sonatas, 1681 (*DTÖ*, v. 11)

1) Known for their advanced violin techniques, these sonatas include high positions, double stops, arpeggios, bariolages, frequent embellishments, and unique staccato passages. They contain ostinatos, theme and variations, and dances.

SELECTED BIBLIOGRAPHY

Books

1. Apel, Willi. *The History of Keyboard Music to 1700,* tr. and rev. Hans Tischler. Bloomington, IN: Indiana University Press, 1972.
2. Bittinger, Werner. *Schütz-Werke Verzeichnis (SWV).* Kassel: Bärenreiter, 1960.
3. Blume, Friedrich. *Protestant Church Music, A History.* New York: W. W. Norton, 1974.
4. Boyden, David D. *The History of Violin Playing from its Origins to 1761 and its Relationship to the Violin and Violin Music.* London: Oxford University Press, 1965.
5. Bunjes, Paul G. *The Praetorius Organ.* St. Louis: Concordia Publishing House, 1966.
6. Curtis, Alan. *Sweelinck's Keyboard Music.* Leiden: Leiden University Press, 1969; New York: Oxford University Press, 1969.
7. Dannreuther, Edward. *Musical Ornamentation.* London: Novello & Co., 1891. Reprint, complete in one volume, Edwin F. Kalmus. (Sweelinck, Praetorius)
8. La Rue, Jan. "Bifocal Tonality: An Explanation for Ambiguous Baroque Cadences," in *Essays on Music in Honor of Archibald Thompson Davison.* Cambridge: Department of Music, Harvard University, 1957.
9. Moser, Hans Joachim. *Heinrich Schütz, a Short Account of His Life and Works,* tr. Derek McCulloch. New York: St Martin's Press, 1957.
10. Norman, Gertrude and Miriam Lubell Shrifte, eds. *Letters of Composers: An Anthology, 1603-1945.* New York: Alfred A. Knopf, 1946. (Sweelinck, Scheidt, Schütz)
11. Peeters, Flor and Maarten A. Vente. *The Organ and Its Music in the Netherlands 1500-1800.* Antwerp: Mercatorfonds, 1971.
12. Praetorius, Michael. *Syntagma Musicum,* 3. vols., 1615-1619. Facsimile reprint, Kassel: Bärenreiter, 1951.
13. Praetorius, Michael. *Syntagma Musicum, De Organographia* (Parts I and II), tr. Harold Blumenfeld. New York: Bärenreiter, 1962.
14. Thomas, Richard H. *Poetry and Song in the German Baroque: A Study of the Continuo Lied.* London: Oxford University Press, 1963.
15. Tusler, Robert L. *The Organ Music of Jan Pieterszoon Sweelinck.* Bilthoven: A. B. Creyghton, 1958.
16. Vente, Maarten A. *Die Brabanter Orgel.* Amsterdam: H. J. Paris, 1958. (Summary in English, pp. 199-220).
17. Weiss, Piero, ed. *Letters of Composers Through Six Centuries.* Philadelphia: Chilton Book Co., 1967.

Articles

1. Bruinzma, Henry A. "The Organ Controversy in the Netherlands Reformation to 1640," *JAMS* 7 (1954), p. 205.
2. Gleason, Harold. "A Seventeenth-Century Organ Instruction Book," *BACH* 3, No. 1 (Jan. 1972), p. 3.
3. Marcuse, Sibyl. "Transposing Keyboards on Extant Flemish Harpsichords," *MQ* 38 (1952), p. 414.
4. Russell, Theodore. "The Violin 'Scordatura'," *MQ* 24 (1938), p. 84.

Music

1. *Antiqua Chorbuch,* Part I, vols. 1-5, sacred music; Part II, vols. 1-5, secular music. Mainz: B. Schott's Söhne, 1951.
2. Biber, Heinrich Ignaz Franz. *Fidicinium sacro-profanum,* 12 sonatas for strings and continuo in *Diletto Musicale,* vols. 464–469.
3. *Dutch Keyboard Music of the 16th and 17th Centuries,* ed. Alan Curtis. *Monumenta Musica Neerlandica,* v. 3. Amsterdam, 1961.
4. Praetorius, Michael
   a. (CE) *Gesamtausgabe der Musikalischen Werkes,* 21 vols. Berlin: Georg Kallmeyer Verlag, 1928-1941, 1960.
   b. *Phantasy on the Chorale A Mighty Fortress is Our God,* ed. Heinrich Fleischer. St. Louis: Concordia Publishing House, 1954.
   c. *Phantasy on the Chorale We All Believe in One God,* ed. Heinrich Fleischer. St. Louis: Concordia Publishing House, 1960.
5. Scheidemann, Heinrich
   a. *Choral-Bearbeitungen.* Kassel: Bärenreiter, 1966.
   b. *Magnificat-Bearbeitungen.* Kassel: Bärenreiter, 1970.
   c. *46 Choräle für Orgel von J. P. Sweelinck und seinen deutscher Schülern,* in *Musikalische Denkmäler,* v. 3.
6. Scheidt, Samuel. (CE) *Gesamtausgabe,* 13 vols. Hamburg: Ugrino Gemeinschaft, 1923-1953.
7. Schein, Johann Hermann. (CE) *Neue Ausgabe sämtlicher Werke,* 10 vols. Kassel: Bärenreiter, 1963-
8. Schütz, Heinrich
   a. (CE) *Sämtliche Werke,* 18 vols. Leipzig: Breitkopf & Härtel, 1885-1927.
   b. *Neue Ausgabe sämtliche Werke (NASW).* Kassel: Bärenreiter, 1955- (in progress)
   c. *Stuttgarter Ausgabe sämtlicher Werke.* Stuttgart: Hänssler, 1967- (in progress)
9. Sweelinck, Jan Pieterszoon
   a. (CE) *Werken,* 12 vols., ed. Max Seiffert. Leipzig: Breitkopf & Härtel, 1895-1903.
   b. *Ausgewählte Werke für Orgel und Klavier,* 2 vols. New York: C. F. Peters, 1957.
   c. *Opera Omnia,* v. 1, fascicles 1-3, ed. Gustav Leonhardt, Alfons Annegarn, Frits Noske. Amsterdam: Vereniging voor Nederlandse Musiekgeschiedenis, 1968.
10. Tunder, Franz. *Sämtliche Orgelwerke.* Wiesbaden: Brietkopf & Härtel, 1974.
11. van Noordt, Antoni. *Psalmenbearbeitungen für Orgel,* ed. Pierre Pidoux. Kassel: Bärenreiter, 1954.

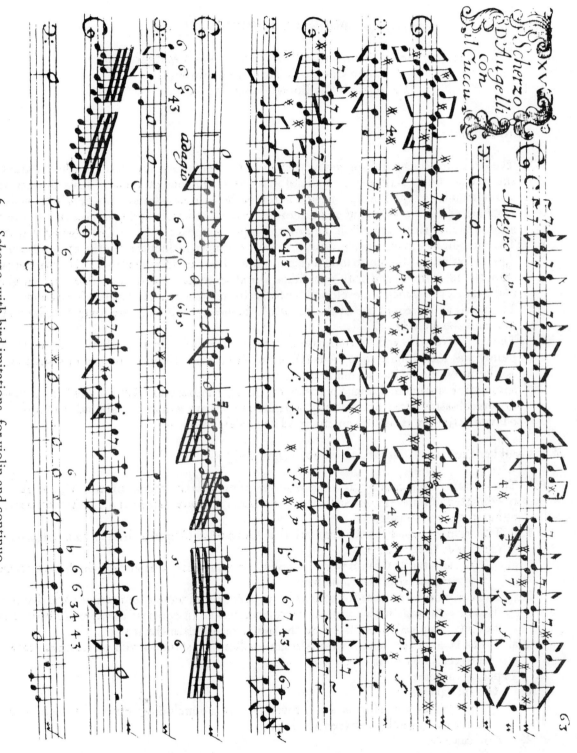

6.   *Scherzo*, with bird imitations, for violin and continuo.
From Johann Jacob Walther's *Hortulus Chelicus* (1688).

OUTLINE IV

MUSIC IN ITALY

MIDDLE BAROQUE

Introduction – Chamber Cantata – Oratorio – Opera in Venice
Comic Opera – Instrumental Music
Bibliography of Books – Articles – Music

I.   **Introduction**

A.   The *bel canto* (beautiful singing) style was one of the most important developments in the Italian Middle Baroque. It had a dominating influence on musical style throughout the remainder of the Baroque period and into the Classic period. The *bel canto* style emphasized beauty of sound and a more restrained style of singing in contrast to the exaggerated dramatic expression, and often empty virtuosity, of the Early Baroque in Italy.

B.   The melodic line, bass line, and rhythm were strongly influenced by the stylized ternary dance rhythms of the sarabande and courante. The melodies were often in short phrases, smooth and refined, and with occasional florid sections. The harmony became simple and triadic, and tonality developed with the frequent use of the authentic cadence. There was an increased use of the "motto" theme, a preliminary statement of the initial motif of the melody.

C.   The recitative was used for narrative sections; the aria for lyrical effects and most commonly was found in *da capo* (A-B-A) form. The arioso, often expressive in character, lies between the recitative and aria in style.

D.   Idiomatic instrumental music became increasingly important. Ritornellos for continuo or several instruments occasionally separated recitative and aria, and keyboard and chamber music was written by many of the lesser composers.

II. **Chamber Cantata** (*Cantata da camera*) (*BM*, 103)

A.   The cantata (from *cantare*, to sing) was one of the developments of monody. It generally consisted of a number of separate movements and was based on a continuous text, either sacred or secular.

  1.   The term was used for the first time by **Alessandro Grandi** in his *Cantade ed arie a voce sola*, 1620 (see p. 9).

   a.   The cantatas of **Grandi** were monodic, strophic-bass cantatas in which each stanza is a variation over the same bass.

  2.   The early cantatas were for solo voice or voices, and were often either narrative recitatives or lyric arias with continuo accompaniment. In contrast to the early Florentine monody, emphasis was placed on the music rather than the text.

   a.   The Neapolitan School with **Alessandro Scarlatti** standardized the cantata form into recitative—aria—recitative—aria.

B.   Types of cantatas

  1.   Refrain cantata

   a.   The first section of an aria was often used as a concluding refrain. It might also occur occasionally between sections.

  2.   Aria cantata

   a.   The aria cantata was made up of an aria, usually in short two-part form, repeated for each stanza of the text. The repeats might be varied and were always written out (A A'—B B'; A—B B'). The strophic bass continued to be used.

      b.   The first section often returned at the end in a brief da capo form (A—B—A, or A—B B'—A', or A—B—A').

   3.   Rondo cantata

      a.   The aria was repeated from time to time between the arioso and recitative sections.

   4.   Composite cantata

      a.   The composite cantata, which expanded the form, usually included recitatives, ariosos, arias, duets, and choruses combined in various ways. Some composite cantatas were in many short sections as in the early instrumental *canzon da sonar.*

C.   **Luigi Rossi** (1598-1653)

   1.   **Rossi**, a singer, organist, and composer of nearly 375 solo cantatas and some duet and trio cantatas, was largely responsible for the creation of the free composite cantata and the development of the da capo aria (*BM*, 104).

   2.   *Io lo vedo, ò luci belle* (I see it, ye fair eyes) (*HAM*, No. 203)

   3.   *Due labra di rose* (Two rose lips) (*AMI*, v. 5, p. 190)

      a.   An aria cantata for two sopranos with the same music for each stanza.

D.   **Giacomo Carissimi** (1605-1674) (*CS*, vols. 8, 16, 37, 48, 57)

   1.   Born near Rome, **Carissimi** was organist at the Cathedral of Tivoli. From about 1640 he was chapel master at the Church of Sant' Apollinare in Rome where he had many famous pupils.

   2.   One hundred forty-five of his cantatas have been preserved, and they are some of the same types of cantatas as those of **Rossi**. Some humorous subjects were introduced. Although his chief contribution was in the field of the sacred oratorio, his cantatas are generally more advanced harmonically. In common with his contemporaries, he made use of the so-called Neapolitan-sixth chord. At the cadence he frequently used the broadening effect of hemiola.

   3.   *Il Ciarlatano* (The Charlatan) (*AMI*, v. 5, p. 238)

      a.   The cantata for three sopranos is based on a humorous subject. It includes solos, a duet, trios, and many key and tempo changes.

E.   **Marc'Antonio Cesti** (1623-1669) (*M* 2b)

   1.   **Cesti** was a pupil of **Carissimi**, **Giovanni Legrenzi**, and **Alessandro Stradella** and continued the development of the free composite cantata. He wrote some 55 solo cantatas, including nine to which another voice had been added.

   2.   *Pria ch'adori* (Before you do homage) (*M* 2a, Ser. 2, v. 1, p. 1); *Lacrime mie* (My tears) (*M* 2a, Ser. 2, v. 1, p. 27; *Quante volte giurai* (How often I swore to love you) (*M* 2a, Ser. 2, v. 1, p. 49); *Disperato moriro* (In despair I die) (*M* 2a, Ser. 2, v. 1, p. 59)

III.   **Oratorio**

A.   The oratorio, named for the hall in which it was performed, had its beginnings in musical dramatizations of Bible stories as far back as the devotional songs known as *laude*. In the early 17th century, dramatic Latin dialogues were set by **Giovanni Anerio**, **Giovanni Capello**, and **Marco Marazzoli**, among others. The center of the oratorio was in Rome where **Carissimi** established the form as a short, dramatic composition on a Biblical subject. Culminating composers of the Middle Baroque oratorio were **Giovanni Legrenzi**, **Alessandro Stradella**, and **Antonio Draghi** (*c.* 1635-1700), director of music at the court in Vienna. There he wrote some 40 oratorios as well as operas, cantatas, and Masses (*DTÖ*, v. 46).

B.   Oratorio and opera had many features in common for some years, however, the lack of staging and the use of the narrator (*testo* or *historicus*) distinguished the oratorio from opera. Greater emphasis was placed on the chorus in the oratorio than in the opera. A shortened form of the oratorio was called *cantata da chiesa* (church cantata).

   1.   The Latin text, generally from the Old Testament, was set to music for solo voices in recitatives, arias, ariosos, and ensembles, and in chorus, sometimes in double and

      triple chorus. A narrator was often used to introduce the characters and relate the events. The simple instrumental accompaniment was for continuo and at times two violins were added.

  2.   The chorus played an important role, often taking part in the dramatic sections which represented action. The music was in chordal style with simple harmonies and strong rhythms.

  3.   The arias were in *bel canto* style with short phrases. Recitatives were usually assigned to the leading characters.

C. **Giovanni Francesco Anerio** (*c.* 1567-1630)
  1.   *Dialogo* (The Offering of Isaac), 1619   (*AM*, v. 37, p. 32)

D. **Giovanni Francesco Capello** (*fl.* early 17th century)
  1.   *Abraham! Abraham!,* Venice, 1615 (*GMB*, No. 180)
    a.   This oratorio dramatizes the story of Abraham's sacrifice of Isaac and the interception of the angel. It opens with a short sinfonia for four-part strings and is followed with dialogue recitatives accompanied with unfigured continuo, and has instrumental ritornellos. A three-part narrative accompanied chorus closes the oratorio.

E. **Marco Marazzoli** (*c.* 1604-1662)
  1.   *S. Tommaso* (St. Thomas), 1640   (*AM*, v. 37, p. 36)

F. **Giacomo Carissimi** (1605-1674)
  1.   There are 16 extant oratorios by **Carissimi.** (*CE*, vols. 1-8)
  2.   *Judicium Salomonis* (Judgment of Solomon) (*ICDMI*, v. 5)
    a.   *Afferte gladium et dividite infantem vivum* (Take the sword and divide the child) (*MM*, 130)
      1)   As part of a short *cantata da chiesa,* this recitative dramatizes the wisdom of Solomon when two mothers contest the ownership of a child. A motet-like chorus, praising the wisdom of Solomon, closes the work.
  3.   *Jephte,* 1645 (*ICDMI*, v. 5; *GMB*, No. 198; *MSO*, v. 1, p. 85; *CMA*, 307; *AM*, v. 37, p. 41)
    a.   *Cum vidisset Jephte*
      1)   In this recitative between Jephte (tenor) and his daughter (soprano), Jephte bewails the vow he made to the Lord.
  4.   *Jonas* (*ICDMI*, v. 5)
    a.   *Miserunt ergo sortum* (They therefore cast lots) (*HAM*, No. 207)
      1)   A double four-part chorus emphasizes the narrative. Some use of text-painting is obvious on such words as "tempest," "winds," and "flood."

G. **Alessandro Stradella** (1645-1682) (*M 2b*, v. 7)
  1.   *Susanna,* 1681 (*BMB*, v. 82)
    a.   *Da chi spero aita ò cieli?* (*GMB*, No. 230)
      1)   A strophic aria of two stanzas sung by Susanna and accompanied with two violins and continuo.
  2.   *S. Giovanni Battista* (St. John the Baptist), 1675 (*AM*, v. 37, p. 59)

IV. **Opera in Venice**

A. **Francesco Cavalli** (1602-1676)
  1.   **Cavalli** was a famous pupil of **Monteverdi** and his successor as chapel master at St. Mark's in Venice. He was the leading opera composer in the early period of Venetian opera.
  2.   **Cavalli** wrote about 40 operas which were lavishly produced in the first public opera house founded in Venice in 1637, and also in Paris. In his early works he followed the model of **Monteverdi** in the use of dramatic recitatives, *stile concitato,* and composite strophic arias. These composite arias included short arioso and recitative

sections. **Cavalli** made extensive use of melodious *bel canto* arias and, in his late works, separated the arioso (used for expressive sections) from the *secco* recitative, which was used for narrative or dialogue.

3. *Gaisone*, Venice, 1649 (*PAM*, v. 12, *Prologue and Act I*; *SHO*, 91)

  a. The story of Jason, Medea, and the Golden Fleece is the basis of this opera. **Cavalli** made use of composite arias (aria–recitative or arioso–aria) (*PAM*, v. 12, p. 73), and strophic arias, often with instrumental ritornellos. In the comic aria he introduced a new type of parlando. The stammering of the servant Demo is imitated in the music (p. 41, line 3; p. 45, line 1).

  b. The *Overture* (p. 3) is in two parts (slow–fast) which are thematically related, an unusual feature at this time.

  c. *Dell'antro magico stridenti cardini* (The magical cave-door hinges squeaked) (*GMB*, No. 201)

    1) In scene 15 of Act I, **Cavalli** established a mood by persistently repeating a four-note motif some 21 times in the initial arioso. A recitative then follows.

4. *Ormindo*, Venice, 1644

  a. *Io moro* (I die) (*GMB*, No. 200)

    1) A recitative in dialogue form is sung by Ormindo and Erisbe as she dies. The following aria, *Piangete, Amori* (I mourn, my love), makes use of a ground bass.

  b. *Se nel sen di giovinetti sol desia* (Though my soul demands admirers) (*SS*, 223)

    1) Sinfonia, arias using a ground bass, ariosos, and *secco* recitatives are included.

5. *Xerxes* (*Serse*), Venice, 1654

  a. *Ecco la lettra, Elviro* (Here is the letter, Elviro) (*HAM*, No. 206)

6. Other operas by **Cavalli** include *Didone*, 1641; *Egisto*, 1642; *Ercole amante* (Hercules in love), Paris, 1662. The latter was produced at the marriage of Louis XIV and employs a large chorus and orchestra with interludes and many ballets composed by **Lully**. The opera makes use of a larger number of instruments even in the *accompagnato* recitatives.

B. **Marc' Antonio Cesti** (1623-1669)

1. **Cesti**, born in Arezzo, was a pupil of **Carissimi**, 1640-1645, and became musical director at the court of Ferdinand II de' Medici in Florence in 1646. He was a tenor singer in the papal choir in Rome in 1659, and assistant music director at the Imperial Court of Leopold I in Vienna in 1666. **Cesti** was the chief representative of the second generation of the Venetian opera school and is said to have composed over 100 operas of which only 11 have been preserved.

  a. **Cesti's** style is more lyrical, his harmony less experimental, and his rhythms more regular than **Cavalli's**. He completed the separation between recitative and aria, and used many types of arias, including popular and comic styles.

2. *Orontea*, Venice, 1649 (*M* 2b, v. 11; *BM*, 125)

  a. **Cesti's** first opera tells the story of Orontea, Queen of Egypt. Along with *La Dori*, it was an immediate success and widely performed throughout Italy and in Innsbruck, Vienna, Paris, and Munich.

3. *La Dori*, Florence, 1661 (*PAM*, v. 12, pp. 86-177, *Prologue* from Act I and scenes from Acts II and III)

  a. *Rendete mi il mio bene* (Return to me my good) (*PAM*, v. 12, p. 129)

    1) An example of a rondo aria.

4. *Il Pomo d'Oro* (The Golden Apple), Vienna, 1667 (*DTÖ*, v. 6, *Prologue* and Act I; *DTÖ*, v. 9, Acts II to V)

  a. This famous opera is based on the story of Paris and the golden apple and was written for the marriage of Emperor Leopold I of Austria and the Infanta Margherita of Spain. It was lavishly produced with 24 elaborate stage settings and a variety of stage machines.

  b. There are five acts, 67 scenes, 48 roles all sung by men, a chorus, an orchestra of violins, viols, flutes, trumpets, harpsichord, small organ, and lutes. Additional instruments include cornetts, trombones, a bassoon, and a regal.

    c.   The *Overture* (*DTÖ*, v. 6, p. 3; *GMB*, No. 202) is in the French overture form (slow 4/4 – fast 3/4). There are instrumental introductions called sonatas for each act, ritornellos and sinfonias, and some accompanied recitatives.

    d.   Cesti makes use of various types of arias, including the da capo aria, martial airs with virtuostic passages, and some *buffo* (comic) arias. There are several ballets in each act and a grand ballet at the conclusion of the opera.

    e.   *Di Bellezza e di valore* (Every honor for beauty and valor) (*DTÖ*, v. 9, p. 173; *HAM*, No. 233)

        1)   This four-part chorus in Act 4, scene 12, opens with homophonic chords for three measures then changes to a contrapuntal imitative texture in 3/4 time. An instrumental ritornello of two violins and continuo follows.

    f.   *E dove t'aggiri Tra l'alma dolenti* (*MSO*, 81)

        1)   This aria sung by Proserpino in Act I, scene 1, is accompanied with four-part brass.

  5.   *L'Argia,* Venice, 1669

    a.   *Alma mia e che sara?* (*GMB*, No. 203)

        1)   A da capo aria which shows characteristic use of the "motto" theme. The instrumental accompaniment and ritornellos are for two violins and continuo.

  6.   Other operas by **Cesti** include *Le disgrazie d'Amore,* 1667; *La Seminarmis,* 1667; and *La magnanimità d'Alessandro,* 1662 (*PAM*, v. 12)

C.   Later Venetian opera composers

  1.   In music of this period, counterpoint began to appear more frequently. The instrumental introduction sometimes began with the "motto" theme in the bass; other basses were purely instrumental. The operatic style became more simple and popular. The continuo generally accompanied the voice and the orchestra was used in beginning and ending ritornellos.

  2.   **Antonio Sartorio** (*c.* 1620-1681)

    a.   *L'Adelaide,* Venice, 1672

        1)   *Sinfonia* for two trumpets, two violins, two violas, and continuo (*GMB*, No. 223)

        2)   *Vittricci schiere* (Victorious hosts) (*GMB*, No. 223)

          a)   A through-composed aria from Act I, scene 1, which makes dramatic use of bravura passages already suggested in the sinfonia.

  3.   **Giovanni Legrenzi** (1626-1690)

    a.   **Legrenzi** was a versatile composer of operas, oratorios, cantatas, motets, and chamber music.

    b.   *Il Giustino,* Venice, 1683

        1)   *Ti lascio l'alma impegno* (I leave my soul imprisoned with thee) (*GMB*, No. 231. This edition should probably have two sharps.)

          a)   From Act I, scene 3, this aria on a ground bass makes frequent use of instrumental interludes.

  4.   **Carlo Pallavicino** (1630-1688)

    a.   After some time in Venice, **Pallavicino** was active in Dresden where he held various positions at the court.

    b.   *Il Diocletiano,* Venice, 1675

        1)   *Sinfonia* for trumpet, two violins, and continuo (*GMB*, No. 224)

    c.   *La Gerusalemme liberata* (Jerusalem liberated), Dresden, 1687 (*DdT*, v. 55)

        1)   **Pallavicino** wrote this opera almost entirely for solo voices. It includes short da capo arias, many of which are in popular style (*In defesa*), ballets, orchestral ritornellos based on a motif from the aria, echo effects, a few accompanied recitatives, and arias on an ostinato bass (Act I, scene 1).

5. **Agostino Steffani** (1653-1728)
   a. As with **Pallavicino, Steffani** spent most of his active life in Germany and was the last important composer of Venetian opera there.
   b. *Henrico Leone,* 1689
      1) *Un balen d'incerta speme* (A flash of uncertain hope) (*HAM,* No. 244)
6. **Alessandro Stradella** (*c.* 1645-1682)
   a. *Il Corispero,* 1665
      1) *Tra cruci funeste* (Amidst fatal tortures) (*HAM,* No. 241)
7. **Luigi Rossi** (1598-1653)
   a. **Rossi** was the last Roman composer of serious opera. He was a singer as well as a composer of operas of which only two are extant.
   b. *Il palazzo incantato* (The enchanted palace), Rome, 1642
      1) *Prologue* (In *Outline II,* p. 20, *B* 17, v. 1, p. 385)
   c. *L'Orfeo,* Paris, 1647 (In *Outline II. B* 17, v. 1, p. 299)
      1) *Dormite, begli'occhi* (*GMB,* No. 199) is a solo ensemble lullaby for three sopranos.

V.   Comic Opera

A. **Stefano Landi** (*c.* 1590-1655) was the first to insert comic episodes in serious opera. These episodes are found in the following: **Landi,** *La mort d'Orfeo,* 1619; **Monteverdi,** *L'incoronazione de Poppea,* 1624; **Landi,** *Sant' Alessio,* 1634; **Cesti,** *Il Pomo d'Oro,* 1667.
B. The first independent comic operas were composed by **Virgilio Mazzocchi** and **Marco Marazzoli.**
   1. **Virgilio Mazzocchi** (1597-1646) and **Marco Marazzoli** (*c.* 1604-1662)
      a. *Chi soffre, speri* (Who suffers may hope), Rome, 1639 (In *Outline II, B* 17, v. 1, p. 312)
         1) Set to a text by **Rospigliosi,** this comic opera is a dialogue in parlando-style recitative (*recitativo secco*), a most effective medium for comedy.
   2. **Antonio Abbatini** (*c.* 1598-1670) and **Marco Marazzoli**
      a. *Dal male il bene* (Good from evil), Rome, 1654 (*AM,* v. 31, p. 37; .In *Outline II, B* 17, v. 1, p. 325)
         1) Included are parlando recitatives (p. 328); arias of various types; and ensemble finales (p. 330).
         2) *E che farete* (*GMB,* No. 204; see *Outline II, B* 17, v. 1, p. 327)
         3) *Il piu bello dell' eta tra gli spassi io spender vo* (see *Outline II, .B* 17, v. 1, p. 335)
   3. **Jacopo Melani** (1623-*c.* 1673)
      a. *La Tancia, overo il podestà di Colognole* (Tancia, or the Mayor of Colognole) (see *Outline II, B* 17, v. 1, p. 349)
         1) A comic opera which includes a parody scene from **Cavalli's** *Giasone* (*GMB,* No. 201), ensembles, recitatives, and arias of various types: 1) strophic with a ritornello or recitative between stanzas (p. 357), 2) through-composed (pp. 349, 355), and 3) chaconne bass (p. 360).

VI. Instrumental Music

A. Keyboard Music
   1. Keyboard music in the Early Baroque reached its height with **Frescobaldi.** Following **Frescobaldi** there was comparatively little Italian keyboard music written until **Domenico Scarlatti** (1685-1757) in the Late Baroque.
   2. **Michelangelo Rossi** (*c.* 1600-*c.* 1670)
      a. *Toccate e Corenti d'Intavolatura d'Organo e Cimbalo,* 1657 (*CEKM,* Ser. 15;

AMI, v. 3, p. 273; *ICDMI*, v. 26)

    1)   The 14 *Toccatas* show **Rossi** as an imitator of his teacher, **Frescobaldi**, except for the long imitative sections not common to **Frescobaldi**. **Rossi** sets his 10 *Correntes* (*CEKM*, Ser. 15, p. 41; *AMI*, v. 3, p. 331) as **Frescobaldi** does, essentially in three voices with irregular length of phrases.

  3. **Bernardo Pasquini** (1637-1710) (*CEKM*, Ser. 5, vols. 1-7; *M* 3, vols. 4, 5; *AMI*, v. 3, p. 261)

    a. **Pasquini**, a composer of many operas, oratorios, and cantatas, is known principally for his keyboard works. Among these works are toccatas (*CEKM*, Ser. 5, vols. 5, 6), variations (vols. 3, 4), dance suites and arias (v. 2), and sonatas (v. 7), 14 for one harpsichord and 14 for two harpsichords. These 28 sonatas are written to be improvised on figured basses.

  B. Chamber Music

    1. Chamber music was cultivated in northern Italy in Modena by **Stradella** and **Uccellini**, in Venice by **Legrenzi**, and in Bologna by **Vitali**. The Bologna school played an important part in the development of the solo violin and cello sonata and the trio sonata. The influence of the *bel canto* style is seen in the refined, lyrical writing and in the reaction to virtuosity.

    2. In the Early Baroque the term "sonata" (sound piece) indicated almost any type of instrumental music, usually in one movement with many contrasting sections. After about 1650, sonatas developed into a series of independent movements. These usually consisted of fugal first and last movements (often based on the same theme), and a slower homophonic middle movement in triple time, preceded and followed by short adagio sections. In many cases tempo markings were indicated.

    3. **Alessandro Stradella** (1645-1682), Modena

      a. *Sinfonia*, 1670, for violin, cello, and continuo (*GMB*, No. 229)

    4. **Marco Uccellini** (*c.* 1620-1680) (*AMI*, v. 7, pp. 265-300)

      a. **Uccellini**, along with **Giovanni M. Bononcini** (1640-1679) was another composer of the Bologna school. He was chapel master from 1654 on and he increased the virtuosity of violin playing.

      b. *Sinfonie Boscarecie*, Antwerp, 1669 (*AIM*, 51)

        1) These two pieces for violin and continuo, *La Suavissimi* and *La Gran Battaglia*, emphasize the legato effect and the use of the *stile concitato* by battle trumpets respectively. Both works are in binary form.

    5. **Giovanni Legrenzi** (1626-1690) (*HM*, vols. 31, 83, 84; *LP*, v. 4)

      a. **Legrenzi** was one of the outstanding composers of chamber music before **Corelli** and played an important part in the development of the church sonata.

      b. *Sonate a due, e tre*, Venice, 1655, for two violins and continuo

        1) *La Conara* (*AIM*, 42)

      c. *Sonate a due, tre, cinque, e sei stromenti, Op. 8*, Bologna, 1671, a reprint of the original edition, Venice, 1663.

        1) *La Rosetta* (The little rose) (*AIM*, 52)

        2) *La Fugazza* (The escape) (*AIM*, 43)

        3) *La Buscha* (The search) (*HAM*, No. 220)

    6. **Maurizio Cazzati** (1620-1677)

      a. **Cazzati** was the founder of the Bologna school in 1657 with its center at the church of S. Petronio.

      b. *Sonate a due instrumenti cioe violino e violone*, Op. 55, 1670

        1) *Sonata prima La Pellicana* (*HAM*, No. 219) is in four movements (fast, slow, fast, fast). In the frequent points of imitation **Cazzati** was one of the first to use the tonal answer.

        2) *Triosonate* (*HM*, v. 34)

    7. **Domenico Gabrielli** (Gabrieli) (1650-1690)

    a.   Gabrielli was one of the first to write for unaccompanied cello.

    b.   *Ricercar* for cello alone, *c.* 1689 (*GMB,* No. 228)

       1)   This virtuoso piece follows the plan of the multi-movement sonata and makes use of extended leaps, sequence, and double stops.

8.   **Giovanni Battista Vitali** (1644-1692)

    a.   A pupil of **Cazzati, Vitali** was director of music at the ducal court of Bologna from 1684. His sonatas had an important influence on the development of the form. He made a clear distinction between the *Sonata da camera* and the *sonata da chiesa.*

       1)   The chamber sonata consists of a series of dance movements in binary form. The church sonata is made up of four or five alternating fast and slow movements. The first and last are usually fugal and in duple meter (*HM,* vols. 38, 100; *SCMA,* v. 12).

    b.   *Correnti, e balletti da camera a due violini, col suo basso continuo,* Op. 1, Bologna, 1666.

       1)   *Balletto a tre* and *Corrente* (*AIM,* 46)

    c.   *Sonate a due violini col suo basso continuo,* Op. 2, Bologna, 1667 (*AIM,* 47)

    d.   *Sonate a due, tre, quattro, e cinque stromenti,* Op. 5, Bologna, 1669

       1)   *Sonata a due Violini e continuo, La Graziani* (*HAM,* No. 245; *AIM,* 48)

       2)   *Capriccio a 4, Capriccio detto il Molza* (*AIM,* 49)

    e.   *Artificii musicali,* Op. 13, 1689 (*AMI,* v. 7, p. 154; *SCMA,* v. 14)

       1)   Published for instruction purposes, this work makes use of unusual time signatures and contrapuntal writing, including "canons, double counterpoints, and curious inventions."

SELECTED BIBLIOGRAPHY

Books

1.   Arnold, Frank T. *The Art of Accompaniment from a Thorough Bass.* London: Oxford University Press, 1931.

2.   Dannreuther, Edward. *Musical Ornamentation.* London: Novello & Co., 1891. Reprint complete in one volume, Edwin F. Kalmus. (Carissimi)

3.   Newman, William S. *The Sonata in the Baroque Era.* Chapel Hill: University of North Carolina Press, 1959, 1966.

Articles

1.   Allen, Warren D. "Baroque Histories in Music." *MQ* 25 (1939), p. 195.

2.   Collins, Michael. "The Performance of Triplets in the 17th and 18th Centuries." *JAMS* 19 (1966), p. 281.

3.   Jander, Owen. "Concerto Grosso Instrumentation in Rome in the 1660's and 1670's." *JAMS* 21 (1968), 168.

4.   Mishkin, Henry G. "The Solo Violin Sonata of the Bologna School." *MQ* 29 (1943), p. 92.

5.   Prunières, Henry. "Opera in Venice." *MQ* 17 (1931), p. 1.

6.   Rose, Gloria. "The Cantatas of Giacomo Carissimi." *MQ* 48 (1962), p. 204.

7.   Schmidt, Carl B. "Antonio Cesti's *Il pomo d'oro:* A Reexamination of a Famous Hapsburg Court Spectacle." *JAMS* 29 (1976), p. 381.

8.   Silva, Giulio. "The Beginnings of the Art of 'Bel Canto'." *MQ* 8 (1922), p. 53.

9.   Smithers, Howard E. "The Baroque Oratorio." *Acta Mus* 48, No. 1 (1976), p. 50.

10. Tarr, Edward H. "Original Italian Baroque Compositions for Trumpet and Organ." *Diapason* 61 (Apr. 1970), p. 27.

Music

1. Carissimi, Giacomo. (CE) *Monumenti 3, Instituto Italiano per la Storia della Musica.* Publicazioni. Roma: 1941.
2. Cesti, Antonio.
    a. *Collegium Musicum,* Ser. 2, v. 1. Four Chamber Duets.
    b. *The Wellesley Edition,* v. 5. *The Italian cantata.*
3. Pasquini, Bernardo. *Musiche vocali e strumentali sacre e profane,* vols. 4, 5.

7.   Two four-part harmonizations of the chorale, *Nun komm der Heyden Heyland.* From the first edition of **Scheidt's** *Tabulaturbuch* (1650). (see *Outline III*)

OUTLINE V

MUSIC IN FRANCE

EARLY AND MIDDLE BAROQUE

Introduction – Ballet de cour – Jean-Baptiste Lully
Choral Music – Lute Music – Clavecin Music – Organ Music
Bibliography of Books – Articles – Music

I. Introduction

    A.   Italian court entertainments, particularly the ballet and a few operas, were performed in France during the Early Baroque. However, it remained for the Italian-born **Lully** to establish a national French style in the 1660's under the patronage of Louis XIV.

    B.   The court ballet (*ballet de cour*) suited the French taste and was preferred to the Italian opera, although the court did enjoy the elaborate, colorful staging of the opera. Nevertheless, they found the recitatives "monotonous," the singing too "violent" and dramatic, the operas too long, and the castrati objectionable to both men and women.

II. Ballet de cour

    A.   Court entertainments (*mascarades,* ballets, and intermezzi) were brought from Italy by Catherine de' Medici in the late 16th century and became popular at the court of Henry IV (reigned 1589-1610).

      1.   The *ballet de cour* is the French counterpart of the English masque, and only a little music of the early ballets has been preserved, except for the popular *air de cour.*

    B.   **Balthasard de Beaujoyeulx (Baldassarino de Belgiojoso)** (*fl.* 1555-c. 1587)

      1.   **Baldassarino,** ballet master to Catherine de' Medici, was a dancer and inventor of dances.

      2.   *Le Balet [sic] comique de la Royne,* 1581   (*COF,* v. 1)

        a.   This ballet was written to celebrate the marriage of Margaret of Lorraine-Vaudemont to the Duc de Joyeuse at Versailles in 1581. The libretto is an elaboration of the fable of *Circe,* and it is the earliest ballet with extant music. The term "comique" indicates a quasi-dramatic performance, such as a play.

        b.   The music consists of short rhythmic homophonic choruses in two to six parts with echo effects, monodic solos for Jupiter and Glaucus, a sung dialogue, and instrumental music.

        c.   The orchestra, divided into groups, includes a chamber organ, oboes, flutes, cornetts, sackbuts, strings, lutes, lyres, and harps. Instrumental groups were placed so that they could accompany a particular *tableau* or dance. Some took part on the stage, often moving with the singers.

    C.   **Antoine Boësset (1585-1643)** and **Pierre Guédron (1565-1621)**

      1.   *La Délivrance de Renaud,* 1617

        a.   The music for the early *ballets de cour* was often the work of several composers, except for **Lully** who composed entire scores.

        b.   The "Rescue of Renaud" includes choruses, ensembles for more than 100 performers, instrumental music, and solo airs in conservative style. Louis XIII and members of the court took part as usual.

    D.   **Gabriel Bataille** (*c.* 1575-c. 1630)

      1.   *Airs de différents autheurs,* 1608-1611 (*MMF,* Ser. 1, v. 33; *MMA,* Ser. 1, v. 16)

        a.   This three-volume collection contains 214 *air de cour* (short solo songs) with lute accompaniment, arranged and possibly some composed by **Bataille.** The music consists mostly of airs, with a few dialogues, *récits,* and Psalm settings.

III.   Jean-Baptiste Lully (1632-1687)

A.   **Lully** was born in Florence and went to France at the age of 14. He entered the service of Louis XIV six years later as a violinist in *Les Vingt-Quatre Violons du Roi,* Italian comedian, and dancer. In 1653 he was appointed composer to the king, wrote his first court ballet, and from 1655 led his own group of *Petits-Violons du Roi,* numbering from 17 to 21 players. **Lully** became "superintendent" of the king's music in 1661 and finally secured an artistic and financial monopoly over opera in France.

1.   The "Twenty-four violins of the king" were made up of 6 violins, 12 violas playing three separate parts, and 6 cellos. This orchestra became famous for the doubling of the parts instead of using the usual solo ensembles, and lasted until about 1715.

B.   Ballet

1.   **Lully's** first court ballet (*ballet de cour*), with **Cambefort,** was the *Ballet de la Nuit,* 1653. By the time of his last ballet, *Le Temple de la paix,* 1685, he is said to have written or collaborated in 28 ballets.

2.   His ballets included instrumental dance music in the French style, and vocal music in the Italian *bel canto* style. New types of dances were introduced; many were originally peasant dances from various regions of France. These dances include the gavotte (4/4), passepied (3/8 or 6/8), bourrée (2/2), rigaudon (4/4), loure (6/4), and most importantly the minuet (3/4). Other dances were the hornpipe, polonaise, and canarie.

3.   *Ballet de la Raillerie,* 1659

a.   The libretto includes a humorous dialogue between the "simple" Italian and "subtle" French music.

4.   *Comédie-ballet*

a.   **Lully** collaborated with **Molière,** the playwright, actor, and creator of French high comedy, in the unification of the stage play and ballet, 1664.

b.   *Le Bourgeois Gentilhomme* (The would-be gentleman), 1670 (*CE,* Ser. 2, v. 3, p. 41)

1)   On a text by **Molière,** this *comédie-ballet* includes solo and chorus ensembles, some comic scenes, recitatives in Italian dramatic style, and strophic-variation arias. Orchestral music includes the "French overture," ritornellos, and dances.

5.   **Lully** established the musical form of the "French overture," based on the earlier so-called "Venetian overture," which consisted of a slow movement in duple meter followed by a fast movement in triple meter.

a.   The French overture, which became a standard type, was first used by **Lully** as the introduction to his ballet, *Alcidiane,* 1658.

b.   The French overture consists of two sections. The first section is a slow, stately movement in homophonic style with dotted rhythms. The second section is an allegro in a mildly imitative style. The allegro often concludes with a short adagio.

C.   Opera

1.   Italian opera, largely through the efforts of **Mazarin,** was performed in Paris from 1645 to 1662. **Cavalli's** *Egisto* was produced in 1646 and **Luigi Rossi's** *Orfeo,* ordered by Mazarin and Barberini, in 1647. *Orfeo* met with popular success, but was criticized by the literary circle as too costly, too realistic, and the singing as too violent.

2.   For the festivities surrounding the marriage of Louis XIV, **Cavalli's** *Serse,* 1660, was produced. The choruses were replaced with ballets, composed and danced by **Lully,** which were more successful than the opera. To celebrate the marriage, **Cavalli's** *Ercole amante,* 1662, was produced.

3.   The Italian style, however, did not interest the French, and the musicians at the court attempted to establish a national opera. Their first efforts were in the form of pastorales, written by **Robert Cambert** and others. These important forerunners of French opera achieved immediate success. Official existence of French opera dates from the founding by **Cambert** and **Perrin** in 1669 of the *Académie Royale de Musique et de*

Danse (now the *Académie Nationale de Musique*, or *Grand Opéra*).
4.   **Lully** composed his first opera, *Cadmus et Hermione*, in 1673 and produced 15 operas before his death in 1687. The librettos for 11 of these operas were written by **Jean-Philippe Quinault** who, like **Lully** in his operas, combined Italian and French elements.
5.   *Cadmus et Hermione* (*CE*, Ser. 3, v. 1) (*BM*, 160)
   a.   The typical **Lully** opera, usually in five acts, was often based on a libretto about courtly love and knightly conduct. A mythological or allegorical prologue in praise of royalty was included with a French overture played both before and after the prologue. The ballets continued to be elaborate and colorful. The orchestra consisted of the "24 violins" with the addition of flutes, oboes, bassoons, trumpets, and timpani for special effects.
   b.   The recitatives, usually syllabic, have frequent changes of meter to accommodate the word accentuation of the French language, one of the important contributions of **Lully.**
      1)   *Persée*, 1682
         a)   *O mort! venez finir* (O death! come put an end to my unhappy fate) (*COF*, v, 22; *GMB*, No. 232)
      2)   *Armide*, 1686
         a)   *En fin il est en ma puissance* (At last it is in my power) (*COF*, v. 17; *GMB*, No. 234)
   c.   The airs are short, sometimes ornamented, and often in minuet or other dance rhythms.
      1)   *Alceste*, 1674
         a)   *Le ciel protège les héros* (Heaven protects the heroes) (*CE*, Ser. 3, v. 2, p. 101; *COF*, v. 16; *HAM*, No. 225)
   d.   Throughout the operas spectacular and elaborate choruses and ballets (*divertissements*) are introduced.
      1)   *Roland*, 1685
         a)   *Chaconne* (*GMB*, No. 233)

IV.   **Choral Music**

A.   The cantata, oratorio, and church music in general developed slowly in France due to the greater interest in opera and ballet.
B.   **Jean-Baptiste Lully** (1632-1687)
   1.   *Miserere mei Deus* (Psalm 50), 1664 (*CE*, Ser. 4, v. 1)
   2.   *De profundis* (Psalm 129), 1683 (*CE*, Ser. 4, v. 3, p. 1)
   a.   For two choirs and orchestra, this motet, along with the *Dies irae* (*CE*, Ser. 4, v. 2, p. 211), was sung at the funeral service of Marie-Thérèse of Austria, July 30, 1683.
C.   **Marc-Antoine Charpentier** (1643-1704)
   1.   **Charpentier**, a pupil of **Carissimi**, established the oratorio in France and was an outstanding composer of cantatas, motets, Masses, Psalms, and oratorios.
   2.   *Le reniement de St. Pierre* (The denial of St. Peter), c. 1690
   a.   This Latin oratorio deals with the experience of Peter from the time of the Last Supper to Peter's sorrowful denials of Jesus.
   b.   Included are five-part homophonic choruses, recitatives, arioso passages, and a group of soloists to heighten the emotional content.
   c.   *Et introductus est Petrus in Domum* (And Peter was brought into the palace) (*AM*, v. 37, p. 79; *TEM*, No. 242)
   d.   *Dialogue entre Madeleine et Jesus* (*HAM*, No. 226)
      1)   This dialogue from **Charpentier's** Latin oratorio *Dialogus inter Magdalenam et Jesum* is inaccurately ascribed to *Le reniement de St. Pierre* in *HAM*.

V.   Lute Music

A.   Lute music reached a high point during the Middle Baroque. The lute was widely used as a solo instrument, to accompany songs, and for preludes and interludes during court ballets.

    1.   Lute music in the Early Baroque consisted mainly of stylized dances which were compiled in books according to their types. Later the separate dances were arranged in groups according to keys, forming suites.

B.   **Jean-Baptiste Besard** (born *c*. 1567) (*BMB*, vols. 28, 30)

    1.   *Thesaurus harmonicus*, 1603   (*BMB*, v. 28)

        a.   This large collection includes dances, preludes, songs with lute accompaniment, and transcriptions. **Besard** also published in 1617 a collection including transcriptions of vocal works for several lutes.

C.   **Denis Gaultier** (*c*. 1603-1672)

    1.   Famous as a lutenist and composer, **Gaultier** was particularly successful in the use of ornaments and the *style brisé* (broken style). This free-voiced style suggested moving parts and provided both melody and harmony, while playing only one note at a time.

    2.   **Gaultier's** lute collection consists mostly of stylized dances arranged in groups of several types all in the same key. The principal types were the *allemande, courante,* and *sarabande* to which might be added a number of optional dances, pieces with fanciful titles, and the *tombeau,* a miniature memorial piece created by **Gaultier.**

    3.   *La Rhétorique des dieux* (The rhetoric of the gods), *c*. 1655

        a.   A set of 69 pieces grouped in the order of the 12 modes.

        b.   *Mode sous-ionien* (a composition in the relative minor) (*Pavane, HAM*, No. 211)

        c.   *Tombeau des Mademoiselle Gaultier* (*TEM*, 227)

        d.   *Tombeau le Monsieur de Lenclos* (*GMB*, No. 215a)

        e.   *La Consolation aux amis du Sr. Lenclos* (*GMB*, No. 215b)

D.   **Esajas Reusner** (1636-1679) (*EDM*, v. 12)

    1.   **Reusner** studied with French lutenists and was the first German composer to introduce the dance suite with a prelude.

    2.   *Deliciae Testudinis*, 1667

        a.   *Prelude* (*HAM*, No. 233)

        b.   *Suite in F* (Courante, Sarabande, Gigue) (*GMB*, No. 216)

        c.   *Suite in G minor* (*Allemanda, Courant, Sarabande, Aria, Gigue, Aria*) (*MOB*, 67)

VI.   Clavecin Music

A.   Clavecin (harpsichord) and organ music flourished during the reign of the "Sun King," Louis XIV (1643-1715), and many composers were active at the court.

    1.   The composers were strongly influenced by the lute music, including the various types of dances, "broken style," imaginative titles, ornamentation, variations, and grouping of dances according to keys.

B.   **Jacques Champion de Chambonnières** (*c*. 1602-1672)

    1.   **Chambonnières** was the first outstanding French clavecin composer, clavecinist at the court of Louis XIV, and a famous teacher. He also influenced south German keyboard composers through **Froberger.**

    2.   *Les Pièces de Clavessin*, Books 1 and 2, 1670 (*MMF*, Ser. 1, v. 3)

        a.   The two books contain 60 dances arranged in groups according to keys, and include single dances as well as groups of the same types. The basic dances—allemande, courante, and sarabande—are followed by various optional dances including the chaconne. The player could make up a "suite" by selecting a number of dances in the same key.

        1)   The chaconne is in rondeau form which alternates a refrain with contrasting

couplets, a type found only in the French Baroque.
  b. *Allemande, "la Rare"* (Book I, p. 1)
  c. *Sarabande, "Jeunes Zéphirs"* (Book II, p. 59; *GMB*, No. 218)
  d. *Chaconne* (*HAM,* No. 212)
C. **Louis Couperin** (*c.* 1626-1661)
  1. **Louis** was the uncle of **François le Grand**, a pupil of **Chambonnières**, and organist at Saint-Gervais from 1653 until his death.
  2. *Oeuvres Complètes* (*LP,* v. 18)
    a. **Couperin** composed over 100 dance pieces and 14 unusual and original *Préludes*.
      1) The dances are arranged in groups by keys and then by type. In each group there are one or more dances of the same type. The first group in C major, consists of 15 pieces with all the allemandes, courantes, sarabandes, and other dances together.
      2) The *Préludes* are grouped together at the beginning. They may be in one, two, or three sections. The first section is written in whole notes without a time signature. The player is free to improvise the meter, rhythm, and melodic lines within the framework of the notes. The second section, when included, is written out in conventional notation, and a third section returns to the style of the first.
    b. *Menuet de Poitou* (*LP,* v. 18, p. 140; *HAM,* No. 229)
      1) An early example of the minuet with three-measure phrases and a "double." The minuet became a popular dance at the court and often replaced the older dances in the suite. Minuets were also written for a trio of two oboes and a bassoon, and in the 18th century the term "trio" was used for the middle section of the minuet.
D. **Nicolas-Antoine Lebègue** (1630-1702)
  1. Born in Laon, **Lebègue** became organist at the Chapell Royale and Saint-Merry in Paris. He and **Marchand** are also known as composers for organ as well as clavecin.
  2. *Pièces de Clavecin,* 1677
    a. These *Pièces* include a *Prélude* and a number of dances in each of several key groups. The *Préludes* are somewhat similar to those of **Louis Couperin**, but are more clearly notated and the second section is omitted.
  3. *Second livre de Clavecin,* 1687
    a. This book includes several groups of dances, although the *Préludes* are omitted and the groups are called *Suites.* The chaconnes are divided in type between the French rondeau and the ostinato.
E. **Jean-Henri d'Anglebert** (1628-1691)
  1. Born in Paris, **d'Anglebert** was a student of **Chambonnières**, whom he succeeded as clavecinist at the court of Louis XIV in 1644. **D'Anglebert** represents the culmination of clavecin music in the French Baroque which was followed by the *style galant* of the rococo.
  2. *Pièces de Clavecin,* 1689 (*MMF,* Ser. 1, v. 4)
    a. The pieces are arranged in four "modes" (G, g, d, D). *Préludes* are followed by dances and other pieces, transcriptions of compositions by **Jean-Baptiste Lully**, concluding with five fugues on the same subject, and a *Quatuor sur le Kirie de la Messe* which could be played on four keyboards or three keyboards and pedals. The *Préludes* follow, in general, the type of free rhythm and patterns of **Lebègue** and **Louis Couperin.**
    b. An extensive table of ornaments (*agréments*), known to **J. S. Bach**, and principles of accompaniment are added in an appendix.
    c. *Prélude, Allemande, Sarabande* (*HAM,* No. 232)
    d. *Tombeau de Mr de Chombonnières* (*MMF,* Ser. 1, v. 4, p. 109)
    e. *Variations sur les folies d'Espagne* (*MMF,* Ser. 1, v. 4, p. 88)

   f.   *Fugue* (*RGO*, v. 2, p. 77);   *Quatuor sur le Kirie* (*RGO*, v. 2, p. 78)
F. The clavecin music of **François Couperin** and **Jean-Philippe Rameau** will be included in *Outline IX*.

VII.   Organ Music

A. The French organ evolved into its classic form during the early 17th century and remained fairly uniform until the late 18th century. The organs were often rather large instruments and included a variety of principal, flute, mutation, mixture, and reed stops of various pitches. The pedal division, however, was small, rarely including a 16' stop, and was used principally for playing a *cantus firmus* with a brilliant 8' Trompette.

B. The music, mostly intended for liturgical use, consisted of attractive and often highly ornamented pieces which became increasingly secular, even dance-like in style. The pieces were often grouped in suites or used as versets in an organ Mass; both collections were usually entitled *Livre d'orgue.*

1.   The organ Mass usually consists of the versets of the Ordinary (Kyrie, Gloria, Sanctus, Agnus Dei) played in alternation on the organ with plainsong sung by the choir (*alternatim* practice).

2.   The titles of the pieces often indicated the stops to be used, singly and in combination, or the form of the piece. These titles include the *Basse de Trompette, Récit de Cromhorne, Récit de Tierce en taille* (solo in the tenor with a Tierce 1 3/5' stop in the combination), *Cornet, Voix humaine, Grand jeu, Plein jeu, Prélude, Fugue, Dialogue, Duo,* and *Trio.*

C. **Jean Titelouze** (1563-1633)
1.   **Titelouze** was born at Saint-Omer of English ancestry. In 1588 he was appointed organist at Rouen Cathedral and remained there until his death. He often served as an organ consultant.
2.   *Les Hymnes pour toucher sur l'orgue avec les fugues et recherches sur leur plain-chant,* 1623 (*AMO,* v. 1)
3.   *Magnificat au cantique de la Vierge pour toucher sur l'orgue suivant les huit tons de l'Eglise,* 1626 (*AMO,* v. 1)

D. **François Roberday** (1624-1680)
1.   **Roberday** was born in Paris and became organist at the Minorite church in Paris.
2.   *Fugues et Caprices,* 1660 (*AMO,* v. 3)
   a.   Included in these works are pieces by **Frescobaldi, Ebner[t]**, and **Froberger**. Other composers supplied subjects for some of the other pieces. The pieces were written in score and could be performed by instruments.

E. **Guillaume-Gabriel Nivers** (1632-1714)
1.   **Nivers** was organist at Saint-Sulpice, Paris, the *Chapelle Royale,* and *La Maison Royale de Saint-Louis et Saint-Cyr.* **Nivers** founded the great school of organ composers who flourished in France during the Baroque. His three collections of liturgical music contain over 225 compositions. These include many of the characteristics of form, style, and registration found in French organ music until well into the 18th century.
2.   *[Premier] Livre d'orgue contenant cent pièces de tous les tons de l'Eglise,* 1665 (*M* 10abc)
   a.   Contains 100 pieces grouped according to the eight church modes (*tons*) and four transposed modes.
3.   *2. [Second] Livre d'orgue contenant la Messe at les Hymnes de l'Eglise,* 1667.
   a.   Contains an organ Mass, three sequences, hymns, and an *Offerte* (Offertory). The organ Mass follows the usual *alternatim* structure. The chants of Mass IV (*Cunctipotens genitor*) are used in the first movements of the Ordinary. The other movements are mostly free composed.
4.   *3. [Troisième] Livre d'orgue des huit tons de l'Eglise,* 1675

a.   Contains 104 pieces arranged in eight groups according to the church modes. Includes *Fugues, Duos, Dialogues, Echos, Récits,* and other types.

F.   **Nicolas-Antoine Lebègue** (1630-1702)

1.   **Lebègue** was organist at the church of Saint-Merry, Paris, and at the *Chapelle Royale.* His works are generally more secular in style than those of **Nivers.** They are noted for their attractive melodies, echo effects, colorful registrations, and especially for the expressive *Récits* for solo and accompaniment.

2.   *Les pièces d'orgue,* 1676 (*AMO,* v. 9)

a.   Contains a "suite" of contrasting pieces in each of the eight church modes.

b.   *Offertoire* (*AMO,* v. 9; *RGO,* v. 2, p. 81)

c.   *Noël: Or nous ditte Marie* (*AMO,* v. 9; *RGO,* v. 2, p. 83)

3.   *Second livre d'orgue,* 1678/79 (*AMO,* v. 9, p. 97)

a.   Contains an organ Mass and *Magnificat* with versets to be performed *alternatim.*

4.   *Troisième livre d'orgue,* 1685 (*AMO,* v. 9, p. 165)

a.   Contains a collection of *Offertoires, Symphonies, Noëls, Elévations* and *Les Cloches.*

b.   *Noël: Une vierge pucelle* (*AMO,* v. 9, p. 214; *HAM,* No. 231)

G.   **Nicolas Gigault** (*c.* 1624-1707)

1.   Organist at the Paris churches of Saint-Honoré, Saint-Martin, Saint-Nicolas-de-Champs, and Saint-Esprit.

2.   *Livre de musique dedié à la Très Ste. Vierge,* 1683

a.   An all-purpose collection which **Gigault** states might be used for the organ, clavecin, lute, viols, violins, flutes, and other instruments. The book includes variations on *nöels* and a few liturgical and other pieces.

3.   *Livre de musique pour l'orgue,* 1685 (*AMO,* v. 4)

a.   Contains 185 pieces which include three organ Masses with many versets, six groups of pieces based on church modes, a *Te Deum,* and a few miscellaneous pieces.

H.   **André Raison** (1641-1719)

1.   **Raison** was organist at the Abbey of Sainte-Geneviève, and the Jacobins of the rue Saint-Jacques. His style is secular and often dance-like, although **Raison** explains that these movements should be played more slowly "because of the sanctity of the church."

2.   *Premier livre d'orgue,* 1688 (*AMO,* v. 2)

a.   Contains five organ Masses with versets in the church modes but without using the Gregorian chant. The ostinato theme of the *Christe* in the second Mass was used by **Bach** as the first half of the subject of his *Passacaglia* (*S.* 582). The concluding work is an *Offerte de 5me ton* (*Le Vive le Roy des Parisiens*), written as a salute to the king.

1)   *Kyrie* (*AMO,* v. 2; *RGO,* v. 2, pp. 79, 80)

3.   *Second livre d'orgue sur les acclamations de la Paix tant desirée,* 1714

a.   This book contains a miscellaneous collection of pieces beginning with a prelude and fugue based on the peace antiphon *Da pacem Domine.* Other movements include another prelude and fugue, an *Ouverture, Allemande grave,* and seven *Noëls.*

I.   **Jacques Boyvin** (*c.* 1649-1706)

1.   **Boyvin** was organist at the cathedral of Rouen.

2.   *Premier Livre d'orgue,* 1689 (*AMO,* v. 6); *Livre d'orgue,* 1700 (*AMO,* v. 6)

a.   Both books include groups of pieces arranged according to the eight church modes. Also included are notes on performance, especially registration and ornamentation.

J.   **Gilles Jullien** (*c.* 1653-1703)

1.   **Jullien** was organist at the cathedral of Chartres.

2.   *Premier livre d'orgue,* 1690

a.   Contains groups of pieces arranged, as in **Boyvin's** books, according to the eight church modes.

K.   **Nicolas de Grigny** (1672-1703)

1.   **Grigny** was organist at the Abbey of Saint-Denis, Paris, and the cathedral of Reims.

He represents the culmination of the 17th-century organ Mass. His music is innovative, serious, highly ornamented, and rarely influenced by secular elements.

2. *Premier livre d'orgue contenant une Messe et les Hymnes des principalles Festes de l'année*, 1699; 2nd edition, 1711 (*AMO*, v. 5)

   a. This book, which **Bach** copied in part for his own use, includes an organ Mass for the principal feasts of the church year. The first verset in each movement is based on the chants of Mass IV. An *Offertoire, Élévation*, and *Communion* are also included. Of special interest are the five-part *Fugues, Dialogues*, and the verset, *Récit de tierce en taille*, for the verse in the *Gloria*, "O Lord God, Heavenly King." The final piece for full organ with pedal points on A and E completes the book.

L. The following French composers of organ music will be included in *Outline IX*: François Couperin, Jean-François Dandrieu, Louis Marchand, Gaspard Corrette, Michel Corrette, Guilain Freinsberg, Pierre du Mage, Louis-Nicolas Clérambault, and Louis-Claude d'Aquin.

SELECTED BIBLIOGRAPHY

Books

1. Anthony, James R. *French Baroque Music from Beaujoyeulx to Rameau*. London: B. T. Batsford, 1973.
2. Demuth, Norman. *French Opera: Its Development to the Revolution*. Chester Springs, PA: Dufour Editions, 1964.
3. Isherwood, Robert M. *Music in the Service of the King: France in the Seventeenth Century*. Ithaca, NY: Cornell University Press, 1973.
4. Laurencie, Lionel de la. *Lully*. Paris, 1911. Reprint: New York: Da Capo Press, 1978.
5. Mersenne, Marin. *Harmonie Universelle,* tr. Roger E. Chapman. The Hague: Martinus Nijhoff, 1957.
6. Prunières, Henry. *Le Ballet de Cour en France avant Benserade et Lully*. Paris: Henri Laurens, 1914. Reprint: New York: Johnson Reprint Corporation, 1970.
7. Titcomb, Caldwell. "Carrousel Music at the Court of Louis XIV," in *Essays on Music in Honor of Archibald Thompson Davison*. Cambridge: Department of Music, Harvard University, 1957.
8. Tunley, David. *The Eighteenth-Century French Cantata*. London: Dennis Dobson, 1974.

Articles

1. Anthony, James R. "Printed Editions of André Campra's 'L'Europe galante'." *MQ* 56 (1970), p. 54.
2. Cohen, Albert. "The 'Fantaisie' for Instrumental Ensemble in Seventeenth Century France—Its Origin and Significance." *MQ* 48 (1962), p. 234.
3. Demuth, Norman. "A Musical Backwater." *MQ* 40 (1954), p. 533.
4. Fuller, David. "French Harpsichord Playing in the 17th Century—after Le Gallois." *Early Music* 4, No. 1 (1976), p. 22.
5. Grout, Donald J. "Seventeenth Century Parodies of French Opera." *MQ* 27 (1941), pp. 211, 514.
6. Hannas, Ruth. "Cerone, Philosopher and Teacher." *MQ* 21 (1935), p. 408.
7. Hilton, Wendy. "A dance for kings: the 17th-century French Courante. *Its character, step-patterns, metric and proportional foundations.*" *Early Music* 5 (1977), p. 160.
8. Hitchcock, H. Wiley. "The Instrumental Music of Marc-Antoine Charpentier." *MQ* 47 (1961), p. 58.
9. ——————"Latin Oratorios of Marc-Antoine Charpentier." *MQ* 41 (1955), p. 41.

10. Hsu, John. "The use of the bow in French solo viol playing in the 17th and 18th centuries." *Early Music* 6 (1978), p. 526.
11. Locke, Arthur A. "Descartes and Seventeenth-Century Music." *MQ* 21 (1935), p. 423.
12. Sandman, Susan Goertzel. "The wind band at Louis XIV's court." *Early Music* 5 (1977), p. 27.

Music

1. d'Anglebert, Jean-Henri. *Pièces de clavecin*, in *Monuments de la musique ancienne*, Ser. 1, v. 8.
2. Bataille, Gabriel. *Airs ce cour pour voix et luth*, in *Monuments de la musique ancienne*, Ser. 1, v. 16.
3. Gaultier, Denis. *Le rhétorique des dieux et autres pièces de luth*, in *Monuments de la musique ancienne*, Ser. 1, vols. 6, 7.
4. Grigny, Nicolas de. *Premier Livre d'Orgue*. Paris: Schola Cantorum.
5. Lebègue, Nicolas. *Noëls varies*. Paris: Schola Cantorum, 1952.
6. Lully, Jean-Baptiste. (CE) *Ouevres complètes*. Paris: Le Revue musicale, 1930-
7. Raison, André
    a. *Premier Livre d'Orgue*, 3 Fascicles. Paris: Schola Cantorum, 1963.
    b. *Second Livre d'Orgue*, 2 Fascicles. Paris: Schola Cantorum, 1963.
8. Roberday, François. *Fugues et Caprices*. Paris: Heugel, 1972.
9. Titelouze, Jean. *Oeuvres complètes d'Orgue*. Mainz: Schott, 1898.
10. Nivers, Guillaume-Gabriel
    a. *Le Premier Livre d'Orgue*, 2 fascicles, ed. Norbert Dufourcq. Paris: Editions Borneman, 1963.
    b. *2. Livre d'Orgue*, ed. Norbert Dufourcq. Paris: Schola Cantorum, 1956.
    c. *Troisième Livre d'Orgue*, ed. Norbert Dufourcq. Paris: Heugel, 1958.

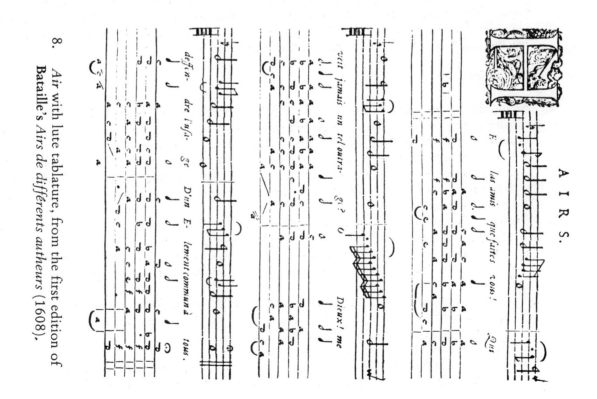

8. *Air* with lute tablature, from the first edition of Bataille's *Airs de différents autheurs* (1608).

OUTLINE VI

MUSIC IN SPAIN AND PORTUGAL

EARLY AND MIDDLE BAROQUE

Introduction — Organ Music
Church Music — Opera
Bibliography of Books — Articles — Music

I. Introduction

A. In the 17th century the music of Spanish composers was known in various countries of Europe. The influence of the Spanish guitar was felt in France by the publication of **Luis de Brizeño's** *Método para Aprender a Tañer la Guitarra a lo Español,* Paris, 1626. In Italy the publication of **Nicolas Doisi de Velasco's** *Nuevo Método de Cifra para Tañer Guitarra,* Naples, 1630, also advanced the popularity of the guitar. The organ continued to be an important instrument and many compositions were written for it.

B. The principal entertainment of the Spanish court was the *zarzuela,* a dramatic production of singing, dancing, and spoken dialogue which originated about 1650 and continued throughout the Baroque. Italian opera troupes began to appear in Spain by 1700 and ultimately took over the musical responsibilities of the court. The presence of the famous Italian singer **Farinelli** (1737-1759) and harpsichordist **Domenico Scarlatti** (1729-1757) in Spain was a major triumph for Italian music. In Spanish church music, the influence of the multi-choral, polyphonic, and monodic styles of the Early Italian Baroque are apparent.

C. Various Baroque techniques were applied to the forms used by Spanish composers. The *tiento* [Portuguese, *tento*] is a fantasie made up of imitation in the style of the ricercar, toccata-like passages, motivic development, and thematic variation. In the 17th century the *villancico* was a religious work similar to the church cantata or anthem. By 1723 it was banned from the church because of its secularization.

II. Organ Music

A. **Sebastián Aguilera de Heredia** (*c.* 1565-1627) (*CEKM,* v. 14, pp. 50-121; *M* 6)
   1. There are 17 organ works by **Aguilera** which include two settings each of *Pange lingua* and *Salve regina,* and 13 *tientos,* some called *obras* (works).
   2. Some characteristics of **Aguilera's** music are strict and free imitation, sequence, modulating figures, echo effects, mixture of styles as suggested by the term *ensalada,* and freedom of voice leading when a note and its chromatic variant appear simultaneously (*punto intenso contra remisso*).

B. **Francisco Correa de Araujo** (*c.* 1575-1663) (*M* 5)
   1. *Libro de tientos . . . Facultad Organica* (Art of organ playing), Alcalá, 1626
      a. This method of organ playing not only includes compositions, but also instruction in theory. Special performance techniques mentioned include fingering, ornamentation, and *notes inégales.*
      b. Comprising the music section of the *Facultad* there are 69 compositions arranged in order of difficulty including 62 *tientos,* variations, and some liturgical pieces.

C. **Manuel Rodriguez Coelho** (*c.* 1555-1635) (*M* 4)
   1. *Flores de musica,* Lisbon, 1620
      a. This large collection of 133 pieces by the Portuguese composer includes *tentos,* liturgical pieces based on chants, and versets in the eight church modes.

      b.   The 23 versets for the *Magnificat* are written in five parts; four to be played by the organ and the upper part to be sung.

          1)   *Verso do primeiro tom* (*HAM,* No. 200)

  D. **Juan Cabanilles** (1644-1712)

      1.   **Cabanilles**, the outstanding Spanish composer of the Middle Baroque, at the age of 21 became organist at the Valencia cathedral. His fame spread throughout France as well as Spain. He composed several hundred organ works including *tientos,* toccatas, sets of variations, versets, and hymns.

        a.   *Paseos* (*M* 3, v. 8, p. 120; *HAM,* No. 239)

          1)   This chaconne of 53 measures is based on a four-measure harmonic sequence of I, I, IV, V, chords.

III.   Church Music

  A.   The conservative style of **Tomás Luis de Victoria** (*c.* 1549-1611) was followed by the Spanish church composers until the Late Baroque.

  B.   **Juan Pujol** (*c.* 1573-1626)   (*M* 7)

      1.   **Pujol** was the most outstanding composer of religious music during the Early Baroque in Spain. In his music there are 89 *villancicos* for the Holy Sacraments and Christmas, and 120 other compositions including Masses, Psalms, motets, responsories, and Passions. Generally in four to eight parts, some are with continuo.

        a.   **Pujol's** *Officium Hebdomadae Sanctae* has been sung in the cathedral of Barcelona until the present time.

        b.   *Requiem aeternam* (*GMB,* No. 179) is a four-part introit in motet style for the Requiem Mass with plainsong *cantus firmus* (*LU,* 1807) in the upper voice.

  C.   **Joan Cererols** (1618-1676)

      1.   **Cererols** entered the monastery at Montserrat in 1636 where he studied organ and violin. He composed much sacred music including Masses, Psalms, *villancicos,* and Vespers.

        a.   *Señor mio Jesu Cristo* (*HAM,* No. 227)

          1)   This *villancico,* the counterpart of the cantata, opens and closes with an accompanied four-part chorus called *estribillo* (refrain). Between the choruses there are solos with accompaniment called *coplas.*

IV. Opera

  A.   Spanish opera came under the influence of Italian composers, but very little Spanish operatic music exists before the Late Baroque. The first Italian opera company appeared in Madrid in 1703.

  B.   The *zarzuela* (a term taken from King Philip IV's palace, *Real Sitio da la Zarzuela*) was the popular entertainment in the Spanish court. It was composed of dialogues, arias, recitatives in Italian style, choruses, and native *villancicos* and *seguidillas* (moderately fast triple-meter dances). The French *ballet de cour* and the English masque are comparable to it. The orchestra was made up of strings, winds, and percussion, including timpani and castanets.

      1.   **Juan Hidalgo** (*c.* 1600-1685)

        a.   **Hidalgo**, harpist at the Royal Chapel from 1631, composed operas, comedies, and sacred and secular songs.

        b.   *Zarzuela: Celos Aun del Aire Matan* (Jealousy, even when it comes from the air, can kill), 1660

          1)   On a text by **Pedro Calderón**, this is the oldest Spanish opera.

      2.   **Sebastian Duron** (d. *c.* 1716)

        a.   *Veneno es de Amor la Envidia* (Envy is the poison of love), 1697

1)   This typical *zarzuela,* on a mythological theme, includes arias and recitatives as well as native *seguidillas* and *villancicos.*

SELECTED BIBLIOGRAPHY

Books

1.   Apel, Willi. *The History of Keyboard Music to 1700,* tr. and rev. Hans Tischler. Bloomington, Indiana: Indiana University Press, 1972.
2.   Chase, Gilbert. *The Music of Spain.* New York: W. W. Norton, 1941. 2nd ed. rev., New York: Dover Publications, 1959.

Articles

1.   Apel, Willi. "Spanish Organ Music of the Early Seventeenth Century," *JAMS* 15 (1962), p. 174.
2.   Bradshaw, Murray C. "Juan Cabanilles: The Toccatas and Tientos," *MQ* 59 (1973), p. 285.
3.   Chase, Gilbert. "Origins of the Lyric Theatre in Spain," *MQ* 25 (1939), p. 292.
4.   Livermore, Ann. "The Spanish dramatists and their use of music," *ML* 25 (1944), p. 140.
5.   López-Calo, José. "Vespers in Baroque Spain," *MT* 112 (1971), p. 439.

Music

1.   *Anthologia de Organistas Espanoles del Siglo XVII,* 4. vols, ed. Higinio Angles. Barcelona: Biblioteca Central, 1965-1968   (de Heredia, Correa de Arauxo, Cabanilles, etc.)
2.   *Biblioteca de Catalunya,* 20 vols. Barcelona: Institut d'estudio Catalans, 1921-
3.   Cabanilles, Johannis. *Biblioteca de Catalunya,* vols. 4, 8, 13, 17.
4.   Coelho, Manuel Rodriguez. *Portugaliae Musica,* vols. 1 A, 3A.
5.   Correa de Arauxo, Francisco.
    a.   *Biblioteca de Catalunya,* v. 20.
    b.   *Monumentos de la Musica Española,* vols. 6, 12.
6.   Heredia, Sebastián Aguilera de, *Biblioteca de Catalunya,* v. 20.
7.   Pujol, Joannis (Juan). *Biblioteca de Catalunya,* vols. 3, 7.
8.   *Spanish Organ Masters after Antonio de Cabezón,* ed. Willi Apel. *CEKM,* v. 14 (Hernando de Cabezon, Aguilera de Heredia)

OUTLINE VII

MUSIC IN ENGLAND

EARLY AND MIDDLE BAROQUE

Introduction – The Masque – Instrumental Music
Anglican Church Music – Henry Purcell
Bibliography of Books – Articles – Music

I. Introduction

A. The transition from Renaissance to Baroque style took place during the reign of James I (1603-1625), the first Stuart king.

1. In the reign of Charles I (1625-1649) Early Baroque characteristics are evident, particularly in the masque. These included recitatives, songs of various types, dances, choruses, and instrumental pieces. The Middle Baroque saw the use of the French overture and the adaptation of the Italian *bel canto* style to the English air and recitative during the Commonwealth (*Interregnum*, 1649-1660).

2. The use of violins and *basso continuo* became a part of the Restoration style which began during the reign of Charles II (1660-1685) and culminated in the works of **Henry Purcell** (*c.* 1659-1695).

a. **Samuel Pepys** (1633-1703), a public official and amateur musician, mentions many of the musicians of his time and comments on music that he heard and books that he read.

II. Masque

A. The court masque was introduced into England in the late 16th century and had many features in common with the French *ballet de cour,* the Italian *intermezzo,* and the Spanish *zarzuela.*

B. Early masques were designed for court entertainment and were seldom repeated. Outstanding writers of masques were poet laureate **Ben Jonson** (1572-1637) and the poet **John Milton** (1608-1674), a supporter of the Commonwealth. The unpretentious music, much of which has been lost, was usually composed or adapted by several composers. In 1605 with the production of *The Masque of Blackness,* Inigo Jones, an English architect, began a long association of 20 years with **Ben Jonson** staging masques. This masque was performed by the Queen, eleven of her ladies, and professional instrumentalists.

C. Masques were based on allegorical plots and used elaborate stage machines and lavish scenery and costumes. They included three principal ballets: 1) Entry, 2) Main Dance, and 3) Going-off), spoken and sung prologues, songs with figured bass, short homophonic choruses, dialogues and instrumental music. The principal acting and singing parts were taken by professionals.

1. Masquers, the nobility, danced with the spectators during the "revels" which took place after the "Going-off." General ballroom dancing followed.

2. Antimasques, intermediate scenes of a comic burlesque or ridiculous nature, were first introduced into the masque in 1609 by **Jonson** in his *The Masque of Queens.*

D. **Thomas Campion** and **Alfonso Ferrabosco** (*c.* 1575-1628) were early composers of masques. **Nicholas Laniere** (1588-1666), **Henry Lawes** and **William Lawes** (1602-1645) introduced the new Italian recitative style adapted to English words. This met with little success because the English preferred spoken dialogue. **Locke, Blow,** and **Purcell** were the principal composers of music for masques and stage productions of the

Restoration (1660).
- E. **Thomas Campion** (1567-1619)
  1. *Masque in Honor of the Marriage of Lord Hayes,* 1607
     a. Three instrumental consorts were used when this was first given at Whitehall: 1) 6 "hoboys," 2) 2 lutes, 1 bandora, 1 sackbutt, 1 harpsichord, and 2 violins, and 3) 9 violins, 3 lutes, 6 cornetts, and 6 voices.
- F. **Henry Lawes** (1595-1662)
  1. *Masque of Comus,* 1634, on a text by **John Milton**
     a. *Sweet echo* (*HAM,* No. 204)
- G. **Matthew Locke** (*c.* 1630-1677)
  1. **Locke** uses some of the experimental harmonies of the Early Italian Baroque combined with English diatonic harmony. Recitative-like passages, popular airs, short choruses, and instrumental pieces are found in his works.
  2. *Cupid and Death* (*MB,* v. 2) (1653)
     a. The music was written by **Locke** and **Christopher Gibbons** on a text by **James Shirley**, and it was produced privately during the Commonwealth.
     b. In the five entries the music is written mostly in two parts, violin and bass, with the occasional use of two violins. The vocal parts are accompanied with bass. There is use of four-part choruses.
- H. During the Commonwealth (1649-1660), opposition to the stage prevented public performances of masques. The masque, still performed in the court and in schools, gradually declined. The presentation of **Davenant's** *Salmacida spolia* (Salmacida plundered) in 1639 ended the performance of court masques until the Restoration in 1660.
  1. The first English opera, *The Siege of Rhodes,* 1656, by **Sir William Davenant** (1606-1668), was performed as a five-act "representation" to avoid the displeasure of the Puritans. The music by **Henry Lawes, Captain Cooke, Matthew Locke,** and others has not survived.
- I. During the Restoration Italian opera was introduced at the court, and Italian musicians settled in England and encouraged the performance of Italian music. Among them were the composer **Giovanni Batista Draghi** in 1667 and the violinist **Nicola Matteis** in 1672.
  1. The French opera composer **Robert Cambert** arrived in 1674. When Charles II returned from exile in France, he organized a string orchestra of 24 violins in imitation of that of Louis XIV and appointed the Frenchman **Louis Grabu** to be Master of the King's Music in 1666.
     a. **Pelham Humfrey** (1647-1674) in 1664 was sent by Charles II to France and Italy to perfect himself in composition. Upon the death of **Captain Henry Cooke** in 1672, he was appointed Master of the Chapel Royal.
- J. **John Blow** (*c.* 1648-1708)
  1. **Blow**, a teacher of **Henry Purcell**, was organist at Westminster Abbey and organist-composer in the Chapel Royal.
  2. *Venus and Adonis, c.* 1682
     a. This short pastoral opera in three acts is the earliest extant English opera which has music throughout. It includes a French overture, prologue ballet, recitatives, arias in the Italian *bel canto* style, dialogues, and choruses. The instrumental music includes a "ground" and a sarabande.
     b. *Mourn for thy servant* (*HAM,* No. 243)
        1) There are frequent harmonic surprises in this women's chorus, but the rhythm is regular and sombre.

III. Instrumental Music

- A. Keyboard music
  1. The term "virginal" included other plucked keyboard string instruments, such as

spinet, clavicymbal, and harpsichord.

2. The remarkable development in keyboard music which began during the reign of Queen Elizabeth (1558-1603) and continued into the Early Baroque was dominated by **William Byrd** (1543-1623) (*MB*, vols. 27, 28); **John Bull** (1562-1625) (*MB*, vols. 14, 19); **Orlando Gibbons** (1583-1625) (*MB*, v. 20); and **Thomas Tomkins** (1572-1656) (*MB*, v. 5).

   a. Many of the early 17th-century collections of these composers include compositions for both the virginal and the organ. The works for the virginal are dance movements, variations, fantasies, grounds, and preludes. Those for the organ are liturgical pieces, fantasies, and voluntaries. By the middle of the 17th century the most common forms of keyboard music were suites of dances for the virginal and voluntaries for the organ.

     1) The first printed collections of virginal music were *Parthenia* in 1611 with 21 compositions by **Byrd, Bull,** and **Orlando Gibbons**, and *Parthenia In-violata, c.* 1614, containing 20 compositions with a viol added to double the bass parts.

     2) The voluntary (verse) during the Restoration often consisted of two imitative sections and a free postlude to conclude. The Late Baroque voluntary frequently consisted of a slow imitative introduction followed by a lively *concertato* movement.

3. The Early Baroque church organ was usually a two-manual instrument, called a "double" organ. During the Commonwealth many church organs were destroyed, but during the Restoration which began in 1660, many were replaced or rebuilt.

4. **Thomas Tomkins** (*c.* 1585-1656)

   a. *Paris Holograph,* 1646-1654 (*MB*, v. 5)

     1) A manuscript collection of 79 compositions by **Byrd, Bull,** and **Tomkins** of which 59 were written by **Tomkins** in the last decade of his life. Included are dance movements, variations, and fancies which show the instrumental interplay of melodic patterns and contrapuntal lines. About half of these works are liturgical pieces for organ.

5. **Christopher Gibbons** (1615-1676)

   a. Son of **Orlando, Christopher** became organist at Westminster Abbey in 1660. His music includes five voluntaries, three for "double" organ, a *Corrente* and *Saraband* (*CEKM*, v. 18).

6. **Matthew Locke** (1630-1677)

   a. *Melothesia: or Certain General Rules for Playing upon a Continued Bass,* 1673 (*M* 8bc; *MMF*, Ser. 2, v. 30)

     1) The *Melothesia* includes definitions of ornaments, four suites for harpsichord, and seven voluntaries "for the organ," including one for double organ. Some other composers represented in the collection are **Christian Preston, John Banister,** and **John Roberts**.

7. **John Blow** (1649-1708)

   a. *A Choice Collection of Lessons for Harpsichord,* 1698-1704

     1) Includes dances, one suite, preludes, and grounds.

   b. Organ music comprises about 30 extant works, often called "voluntaries," with slow and fast fugal sections. Five are double voluntaries.

8. **Henry Purcell** (*c.* 1659-1695) (see Section VI, p. 71)

9. **Jeremiah Clarke** (1674-1707), Five Suites from *Choice Lessons* (*M* 6, v. 5)

10. **William Croft** (1678-1727), 12 Suites (*M* 6, vols. 3, 4)

B. Consort music

1. Viol making, playing, and composition reached its height in England during the Middle Baroque. Viols were made in three principal sizes: 1) treble, 2) tenor (*viola da braccio*), and 3) bass (*viola da gamba*). The largest viol was the double-bass (*violone*). A chest of six viols contained two each of the treble, tenor, and bass viols.

a. The violin began to supplant the viols in concerted and solo music after the Commonwealth. Viols, however, continued to be used, particularly by amateurs, during the entire English Baroque.

2. The term "consort" was used for instrumental chamber ensembles and also for the music. A "whole" consort was a group of instruments of the same family; a "broken" consort was a mixed group of instruments.

3. The principal form of consort music was the "fancy" (ensemble fantasia). It was in ricercar style at first, but developed in the early 17th century into movements in several sections in contrasting tempos and varied textures. **Locke** and others followed the fantasia by dance movements and the whole work was known as a "suite."

4. **Giovanni Coperario** (**John Cooper**) (1570-1627) (*MB*, v. 9)

   a. **Cooper's** consort music includes fantasias in consorts of two to six parts, and suites for string instruments with continuo for organ.

5. **William Lawes** (1602-1645)

   a. A brother of **Henry** and a student of **Cooper, Lawes** received appointment to the court under Charles I in 1635. He met an untimely death in the service of the king during the Civil War. Individualistic style, wide skips, irregular rhythms, and experimental harmonies are evident in **Lawes'** music.

   b. **Lawes'** consort music includes five- and six-part suites, harp consorts, the "Royal Consorts," and "Sonatas" (*Fantasia, Alman,* and *Galliard*) for one and two violins, bass viol, and organ (*MB*, v. 21).

   c. *"Harpe" Consorts* (*MB*, v. 21, pp. 64-89)

   1) Containing some of the first known written-out harp parts, these eleven consorts comprise 30 individual dance movements with written-out divisions. The first 25 dances are organized into suites (*alman–corant–corant–saraband*). The remaining dances include three *Pavens* (*MB*, v. 21, pp. 69-89) which show the most outstanding writing of the entire collection.

   d. *The Royal Consort* (*MB*, v. 21, p. 127)

   1) A large and popular collection of instrumental music containing 66 movements. They were scored originally for four viols, and later arranged by **Lawes** for two violins, two bass viols, and unfigured bass for two theorbos.

   e. *Sonata* No. 8 in D Major for violin, bass viol, and organ (*MB*, v. 21, p. 100)

6. **John Jenkins** (1592-1678)

   a. A prolific composer of instrumental music, **Jenkins** is known to have composed more than 800 compositions. These include the prevailing forms of the day–fantasias, suites, and other dance movements. He began to compose for viols in the old polyphonic style, but later wrote for violin under the influence of the Italian trio sonata and concertato style.

   b. Eight Suites (g, a, d, F, B-flat, F, e, D) (*MB*, v. 26, pp. 78-132)

7. **Matthew Locke** (*c.* 1630-1677) (*MB*, vols. 31, 32)

   a. **Locke** was another prolific composer of consort music and many of his airs and dances were composed for the king's band of violins. Included in his consort music are eight suites for two parts, 10 suites for three parts (*The Little Consort,* 1656), five suites (*The Flat Consort 'For my Cousin Kemble'*), 10 suites for broken consort, and two six-part canons, 1654.

   b. *Consort of ffoure* [*sic*] *Parts, c.* 1672 (*MB*, v. 32, pp. 57-97)

   1) Contains six suites: *Fantazia, Courante, Ayre, Saraband*

   2) *Fantazia* (*HAM*, No. 230; *MB*, v. 32, p. 91)

8. **Christopher Simpson** (*c.* 1610-1669)

   a. *The Division-Violist*, London, 1659

   1) This book includes a method of gamba playing, elements of harmony and counterpoint, a table of ornaments, ways of playing "divisions," and sample divisions. Encouragement is given to emotional expression, tempo changes, dynamics, and

contrast.

    2)   The second edition published in 1667 was called *The Division-Viol* and also contained a Latin translation.

  b.   Divisions on a ground were improvised by a gamba player who "broke" the ground into florid figures or added a new "descant" counterpoint to the ground resulting in a series of variations. The ground might be either a short or a long melody, and it could also be played on the organ or harpsichord with the thorough-bass chords realized.

  9.   Other composers of consort music (*MB*, v. 9) include **Christopher Gibbons** (1615-1676); **Thomas Lupo** (early 17th century) with 80 viol fantasias for three to six parts; **Thomas Simpson** (early 17th century), *Taffelconsort*, 1621, for four viols and continuo; and **Tobias Hume** (d. 1645), *Captaine Humes Poeticall Musicke,* 1607, includes 18 instrumental pieces.

IV.   Popular Music

  A.   **John Playford** (1623-1686) was an important music publisher from 1648 to 1684. His *The English Dancing Master,* 1651, contained popular music, country dances, and songs. **John Playford** was succeeded in the publishing business by his son, **Henry** (1657-1709).

  B.   Catches and rounds are characterized by ingenious construction and clever manipulation of secular texts, sometimes of a bawdy nature, which dealt with drinking, popular events, and characters of the time. Canons generally had religious texts. Many collections continued into the 18th century.

    1.   **Thomas Ravenscroft** (*fl.* 1607-1621)

      a.   *Pammelia, Musicke Miscellanie. Or, Mixed Varietie of Pleasant Roundelayes, and delightfull Catches,* 1609 (*M 3*, pp. 11, 35, 45, 85)

        1)   The collection of rounds and canons from three to ten parts is one of the first to be printed.

      b.   *Deuteromelia: Or The second part of Musicke melodie,* 1609 (*M 3*, pp. 64, 68)

      c.   *Melismata. Musicall Phansies,* 1611 (*M 3*, p. 47)

    2.   **John Hilton** (1599-1657)

      a.   *Catch that Catch can, or A Choice Collection of Catches, Rounds & Canons for 3 or 4 Voyces,* 1652 (*M 3*, pp. 18, 41, 73)

        1)   This book contains 133 catches published by **John Playford** and is an enlargement of a portion of *A Musicall Banquet,* 1649, which contained only 20.

    3.   **Henry Lawes** (1596-1662)

      a.   **Henry Lawes** wrote more than 350 songs.

      b.   *Select Musicall Ayres, and Dialogues, for one and two Voyces, to sing to the Theorbo, Lute, or Basse Violl,* 1652

    4.   **Henry Purcell** (*c.* 1659-1695)

      a. Some 50 catches by **Purcell** were printed in various collections. (*M 3*, pp. 6, 17, 24, 25, 40, 42, 52, 56, 58, 75, 76, 83, 87)

        1)   *I gave her cakes,* London, 1673 (*CE*, v. 22, p. 6; *GMB*, No. 248; *M 3*, p. 42)

V.   Anglican Church Music

  A.   The principal types of music sung in the Church of England are Anglican chants, anthems, and Services.

  B.   Anglican chant is the singing of prose Psalms and canticles in speech rhythm. In the late 16th and early 17th centuries, Gregorian Psalm tones were harmonized in the tenor by **Tallis, Byrd,** and **Gibbons,** and were published in 1641. In the 18th century, the melody was placed in the treble part with simple harmonies to which was sung each line (verse) of the Psalm ("single chant"). Two lines of the Psalms were sung to chants which were

double in length ("double chants").
C.   Anthem and Services
  1.   The English anthem corresponds to the Latin motet. The first anthems were written in the middle of the 16th century by **Christopher Tye** (*c.* 1500-*c.* 1573) and **Thomas Tallis** (*c.* 1505-1583). They were, however, more harmonic and syllabic, had shorter phrases, a more regular rhythm, and an English text.
    a.   The "full" anthem was for chorus throughout and was often unaccompanied and contrapuntal in style.
    b.   The "verse" anthem was for one or more solo voices alternating with short sections for chorus. It was accompanied throughout with organ or viols. The verse anthem was introduced by **William Byrd** and became widely used during the 17th century. About 1630 a new Italian solo arioso style was introduced and instruments with continuo were added to accompany the solo sections.
  2.   The "Service" consists of musical settings of the unvarying parts of Morning and Evening Prayers and Holy Communion. The "Short Service" was in chordal style in contrast to the "Great Service" which was in a more elaborate contrapuntal style.
D.   The Restoration composers were influenced by French as well as Italian styles. They featured trio writing for alto, tenor, and bass, dotted rhythms, short "echo" repetitions at ends of sections, instrumental symphonies and ritornellos, and a "Hallelujah" chorus at the end of the work.
E.   **Matthew Locke** (1622-1677)
  1.   Ten anthems (*MB*, v. 38)
    a.   These verse anthems make use of solo sections, accompanied with instruments, and choruses. Scored in a variety of combinations they generally fluctuate from two to five or eight parts with introductory instrumental symphonies and ritornellos.
    b.   *Be Thou exalted, Lord* (*MB*, v. 38, p. 52)
     1)   A large scale anthem written for three four-part choruses and five-part strings.
  2.   Six motets (*MB*, v. 38)
    a.   In general, these Latin motets are written for one to three voices and accompanied with three-part strings (2 violins and bass).
    b.   *Audi Domine* (*MB*, v. 38, p. 7) is written in five parts.
F.   **Pelham Humfrey** (1647-1674)
  1.   *Complete Church Music* (*MB*, vols. 34, 35), contains 18 verse anthems and one Service in E minor.
G.   **John Blow** (1648-1708)
  1.   **Blow** used jagged and irregular vocal lines, expressive ornaments and inflections, rich and sometimes startling harmonic progressions.
  2.   *I said in the cutting off of my days* (*MB*, v. 7, p. 78)
    a.   A three-part verse anthem (2 tenors and alto) with four-part strings.
  3.   *God spake sometime in vision* (*MB*, v. 7, p. 1)
    a.   This anthem was written for the coronation of James II (1685) and makes use of an eight-part chorus. The work is unusual in that the vocal parts are written with a lower tessitura accompanied with high string parts. It opens with a French overture.
  4.   *Service in G*
    a.   *Jubilate Deo* (*Psalm 100*) (*TEM*, 253)
     1)   Written for two choirs (*cantoris* and *decani*) and a solo quartet. The middle section is a two-part double canon and the final section is the *Gloria Patri* in a four-part strict canon.
H.   The *Gostling Manuscript* (*c.* 1706)
  1.   This double-ended manuscript, copied by **John Gostling** (*c.* 1650-1733), contains 64 anthems by various composers of the Restoration period (**Matthew Locke, William Turner, Jeremiah Clark, Pelham Humfrey,** and others) including 16 by **Purcell** and 22 by **Blow.** This manuscript "is probably the most important authority for the

correct text of Purcell's anthems."

I. Following **Purcell** were **William Croft** (1678-1727) (*HAM*, No. 268), **Maurice Greene** (1695-1755) (*HAM*, No. 279), and finally **Handel** who culminated the Baroque anthem in England.

VI. **Henry Purcell** (*c.* **1659-1695**)

A. **Purcell** was one of the great composers in the history of English music and represents the culmination and perfection of Middle Baroque styles in England. He was a singer in the Chapel Royal where he studied with **Cooke**, **Humfrey** (a pupil of **Lully**), and **Blow**. He succeeded **Matthew Locke** as "Composer in Ordinary for the Violins" (1677) and **John Blow** as Organist and Choirmaster of Westminster Abbey, 1679. He became one of the organists of the Chapel Royal in 1682, "Keeper of the King's Wind Instruments" in 1683, and composer to the court.

  1. **Purcell** was influenced by Italian and French music, but he developed a style peculiarly his own. He was a highly imaginative composer and a master in his use of free and original forms, bold harmonies, sharp dissonances, massive contrapuntal effects, musical characterization, attractive melodies, the expressive style, and English declamation.

  2. His compositions include church music, odes and welcome songs, chamber music, incidental music for some 40 theatrical productions, and a few keyboard works.

B. Church music

  1. **Purcell** wrote about 70 anthems (mostly verse), three Services, and some 50 duets, hymns, Psalms, canons, chants, religious songs, and part-songs.

  2. Full anthems

    a. **Purcell** composed most of his anthems from the time he went to Westminster Abbey in 1679 until about 1688. His comparatively few full anthems (about a dozen) were mostly in the older motet style with close imitations, sharp dissonances, including simultaneous cross relations, and expressive treatment of affective words. They show a gradual development toward functional harmony.

    b. *In the midst of life* (*Z.* 17A) (*CE*, v. 13, p. 1); 2nd version (*Z.* 17B) (*CE*, v. 28, p. 215)

    c. *Lord, how long wilt Thou be angry* (*Z.* 25) (*CE*, v. 29, p. 19)

  3. Verse anthems (*CE*, vols. 13, 14, 17, 28, 29, 32)

    a. **Purcell's** verse anthems usually include a French overture and instrumental ritornellos between the solo sections. The verse sections are often highly dramatic and expressive, with considerable use of word-painting, wide skips, and dotted rhythms. The chorus sections are contrasted in style with the verse sections and varied from polyphonic to massive chordal writing. Anthems often conclude with "Alleluias" which are sometimes in *concertato* style.

    b. *My heart is inditing* (*Z.* 30) (*CE*, v. 17, p. 69; *GMB*, No. 246), Coronation anthem for James II, 1685.

  4. Services (*Z. 230-232*) (*CE*, v. 23; *CW*, v. 17)

    a. **Purcell's** three *Services* comprise settings of the canticles for Morning and Evening Prayers, and the Holy Communion.

    b. *Te Deum* and *Jubilate* from the *Service in D* (*Z.* 232) (*CE*, v. 23, p. 90)

      1) This elaborate work for five-part chorus, six solo voices, strings, trumpets, and organ was printed by the composer's widow in 1697 with the commentary "Made for St. Cecilia's Day, 1694."

  5. Sacred songs

    a. **Henry Playford** in his *Harmonia Sacra; or Divine Hymns and Dialogues,* Part I, 1688; Part II, 1693, published this collection of sacred songs and hymns. This includes 12 in Part I and 5 in Part II by **Purcell**. These songs were intended for private devotional use and were mostly composed in a sombre, recitative style, somewhat resembling a solo cantata.

    1) *Now that the sun hath veiled his light,* 1688 *(Z. 193) (CE,* v. 30, p. 70)

    2) Other composers included in **Playford's** collection are **Blow, Locke, William Turner, John Weldon,** and **Pelham Humfrey.**

C.   Odes and welcome songs *(Z. 320-344)*

  1.   **Purcell** composed about 25 Odes and Welcome Songs for various occasions. They are lengthy compositions for chorus, soloists, and strings, with the occasional addition of oboes, trumpets, and recorders. The texts, generally unsuitable except for the occasion for which they were written, are full of extravagant flattery and praise.

  2.   *Fly, bold rebellion (Z. 324) (CE,* v. 15, p. 116), a welcome song for Charles II, September 9, 1683.

  3.   *"The Yorkshire Feast Song" (Of old when heroes thought it base) (Z. 333) (CE,* v. 1, p. 1)

  4.   Six Odes for Queen Mary's Birthday, April 30, 1689-1694 *(Z. 332, 320, 338) (CE,* v. 2, pp. 1, 36, 72) *(Z. 331, 321) (CE,* v. 24, pp. 1, 36)

    a.   *Come, Ye Sons of Art,* 1694 *(Z. 323) (CE,* v. 24, p. 87; *CMA,* 347)

      1) This birthday ode is for four solo voices, four-part chorus, two oboes, two trumpets, timpani, strings, and continuo. The overture in D major is the same as used for *The Indian Queen,* Act 2, transposed to C major.

  5.   Secular songs *(CE,* v. 25)

    a.   **Purcell** wrote some 90 extant independent secular solo songs in addition to those found in his large works. Furthermore, there are 13 solo songs with a unison or two-part chorus. In these, as in his other vocal music, he achieved a perfect union of text and music. There are 46 two-part (soprano and bass) songs with *basso continuo (CE,* v. 22).

    b.   *Orpheus Britannicus,* 1698, Book I; 1702, Book II *(M* 12f; *MMF,* Ser. 1, v. 1)

      1) A collection of single songs with selections from stage plays and odes published after **Purcell's** death by his widow.

      2) *How Pleasant is the Flow'ry Plain and Grove (Z. 543) (CE,* v. 22, p. 74; *HM,* v. 164)

D.   Dramatic music

  1.   **Purcell** composed only a few incidental pieces for stage plays before writing his masterpiece, *Dido and Aeneas (c.* 1689). His instinct for dramatic style is seen in many early works for chorus and solo voices. The through-composed style of Italian and French opera did not suit English taste, and in its place incidental music was inserted in plays to strengthen and illustrate the drama.

  2.   *Dido and Aeneas, c.* 1689 *(Z. 626) (CE,* v. 3)

    a.   The only real opera that **Purcell** wrote, *Dido and Aeneas,* had as its predecessor only one surviving English opera, *Venus and Adonis, c.* 1682, by **John Blow.**

    b.   *Dido and Aeneas* was written for a girls' school in Chelsea near London. The libretto, by the poet laureate, **Nahum Tate,** is based on Virgil's *Aeneid.* It tells the story of Dido of Carthage and Prince Aeneas. Dido and her court accompany her guest Aeneas to a hunt in a nearby grove, when a sudden storm brewed by the witches, frightens the courtiers back to Carthage. A sorceress, an enemy of Dido, appears to Aeneas in the guise of Mercury and tells him that he must set sail for Italy. Torn between love and duty, the prince bids farewell to Dido. As his ships sails out to sea, the forsaken queen sings her lament and dies in the arms of her maidens.

    c.   The opera is scored for a four-part string orchestra and harpsichord, and includes a four-part mixed chorus and 10 solo voices (7 sopranos, one tenor, one bass, and one baritone).

    d.   The forms include two-part, three-part, small rondo, da capo, motet style, recitative, aria, arioso, canon, ground bass, and a French overture.

    e.   The opera also includes dances and instrumental pieces. The choruses, both polyphonic and homophonic, either take part in or comment on the action. There is considerable use of text-painting.

    f.   Characteristic is **Purcell's** use of dotted rhythms, unusual dissonances (suspensions, augmented triads, cross relations), dramatic expressiveness, musical characterization, and his superb English declamation.

    g.   *Lament* (*CE*, v. 3; *HAM,* No. 255; *NS,* 81; *MSO,* v. 1, p. 102)

        1)   Dido's famous farewell song is written over a chromatic ground, similar to the ones used by **Cavalli** in *Didone,* **Lully** in *Alceste,* and **Bach** in the *Crucifixus* from the *Mass in B Minor.* The free melodic line, independent of the bass, the varied and poignant harmonies, and the apparent simplicity of the *Lament* contribute to its remarkable dramatic effect.

   3.   Incidental music

    a.   **Purcell** wrote music for masques and plays as early as 1680, *King Richard the Second* (*Z.* 581) (*CE*, v. 20, p.43) and *Theodosius* (*Z.* 606) (*CE*, v. 21, p. 115). During his last years he wrote some of his finest music for stage productions. This music is often on a large scale with lengthy recitatives, arias, choruses, and extended forms. Spoken dialogue was inserted between the musical numbers. Influences of the Late Italian Baroque are seen in the da capo arias, use of concertato style, and a more established tonality.

    b.   *The Prophetess, or the History of Diocletian,* 1690 (*Z.* 627) (*CE*, v. 9)

    c.   *King Arthur, or the British Worthy,* 1691 (*Z.* 628) (*CE*, v. 26)

        1)   *I call you all to Woden's hall* (*GMB*, No. 247)

    d.   *The Fairy Queen,* 1692 (*Z.* 629) (*CE*, v. 12; *HM*, vols. 50, 58), an adaptation of **Shakespeare's** Midsummer Night's Dream.

    e.   *The Indian Queen,* 1695 (*Z.* 630) (*CE*, v. 19, p. 1)

    f.   *The Tempest, or the Enchanted Isle,* 1695 (*Z.* 631) (*CE*, v. 19, p. 111)

    g.   Instrumental suites from various plays include *entr'actes* known as "act-tunes."

E.   Instrumental music

   1.   Keyboard music (*CE*, v. 6)

    a.   In comparison to his total output, **Purcell's** keyboard works are relatively few. They include two collections of harpsichord pieces and six organ voluntaries (*M* 12e; *LO*, v. 10). Some keyboard works ascribed to **Purcell** are doubtful.

    b.   *A Choice Collection of Lessons for the Harpsichord or Spinnet Composed by ye late Mr. Henry Purcell* (*CE*, v. 6; *M* 12b; *MMF,* Ser. 1, v. 26)

        1)   This instruction book, published posthumously by **Purcell's** widow in 1696, contains eight suites (G, g, G, a, C, D, d, F) and five single pieces with examples of fingering and ornaments. The three- or four-movement suites are in French style and include dances called *Almand, Corant, Saraband* or *Minuet,* with two *Hornpipes* and one *Jigg.*

        2)   *Suite No. 1 in G* (*Z.* 660) (*CE*, v. 6, p. 1; *SS,* 65)

        3)   Instruction for the performance of the ornaments appeared only in the second edition, 1697 (lost), and the third edition, 1699.

    c.   *Musick's Hand-maide,* 1663

        1)   It contains 81 compositions by various composers, including **Benjamin Sandley, William Lawes, Benjamin Roger, Matthew Locke,** and **Albertus Bryan.** Music by **Purcell,** as well as **John Blow,** did not appear until *The Second Part of Musick's Hand-maid,* 1678 (*M* 12h).

        2)   *Musick's Hand-maid* is a collection of short harpsichord instruction pieces and is one of the richest compilations of mid-17th century keyboard music in England. It was published jointly by **John** and **Henry Playford.** In 1689 **Henry Playford** brought out another edition of *The Second Part* "carefully Revised and Corrected by the said Mr. Henry Purcell."

      3) *A New Ground* (from *The Second Part*) (Z. T682) (CE, v. 6, p. 30)

         a) A transcription of the ground "Here the Deities approve" (CE, v. 10, p. 8), from the Ode for St. Cecilia's Day, 1683, *Welcome to all the pleasures* (Z. 339) (CE, v. 10, p. 1).

   d. *Voluntary on the 100th Psalm,* for organ (Z. 721) (CE, v. 6, p. 59)

  2. Chamber music

   a. *Fantazias* for viols, 1680 (CE, v. 31; M 12d)

      1) **Purcell's** string music without continuo consists of 15 *Fantazias* in three, four, and five parts (Z. 731-745) (CE, v. 31, p. 1), two *In Nomines* in six and seven parts (Z. 746, 747) (CE, v. 31, p. 37), a *Chacony* in four parts (Z. 730) (CE, v. 31, p. 61), and five *Pavans* in three and four parts (Z. 748-752) (CE, v. 31, p. 42).

      2) These works, the last of the English fantasias for viols, were written when **Purcell** was only 21 years of age and reveal an extraordinary mastery of contrapuntal and harmonic techniques. The fantasias are of sectional construction, with sudden contrasts of tempo and bold dissonance treatment.

      3) *Fantazia a 4* in G minor (Z. 735) (CE, v. 31, p. 7; HAM, No. 256; M 12d, p. 4)

      4) *Fantazia upon one note a 5* in F major (Z. 745) (CE, v. 31, p. 34)

   b. **Purcell** composed two sets of sonatas, the first published in 1683 and the second published posthumously in 1697 by his widow. **Purcell** wrote in "a letter To the Reader" in the first set of sonatas that he had "Faithfully endeavour'd a just imitation of the most fam'd Italian Masters; principally, to bring the seriousness and gravity of that sort of Musick into vogue, and reputation among our Countrymen, whose humor, 'tis time now, should begin to loath the levity, and balladry of our neighbors."

      a) The "Italian Masters" to whom **Purcell** referred were probably **Maurizio Cazzati** and **Giovanni Battista Vitali,** who published sonatas in 1677, and the "levity" referred to the dance rhythms frequently used in French instrumental music.

   c. *[Twelve] Sonnata's of III Parts: two viollins and basse: to the Organ or Harpsecord,* 1683 (Z. 790-801) (CE, v. 5; M, 12g)

   d. *Ten Sonata's in Four Parts* (Z. 802-811) (CE, v. 7)

      1) The first set of sonatas has an unusual sequence of keys: the first eight *ascending* in thirds (g, B-flat, d, F, a, C, e, G), and the last four *descending* in thirds (c, A, f, D). The organization of the keys of the Sonatas in four parts in general is ascending by fourths (b, E-flat, a, d, g, g, C).

      2) In both sets of trio sonatas, there are places where the bass and continuo are not the same. The second set, 1697, was designated, but not by **Purcell,** "in four parts" for this reason.

      3) Most of the sonatas have five movements, the others have either four or six, except No. 6 (Z. 807) of the second set, which is a chaconne with 44 variations.

      4) The sonatas are of the church sonata type, and the movements are usually contrapuntal. Seventeen of the sonatas include a movement marked "canzona."

         a) The movements alternate slow—fast in about half of the sonatas, and the others have no set order.

SELECTED BIBLIOGRAPHY

Books

1. Bergeron, David Moore. *English Civic Pageantry, 1558-1642.* London: Edward Arnold, 1971.

2. Bridge, Sir Frederick. *Shakespearean Music in the Plays and Early Operas.* New York: Haskell House, 1965 (Reprint of 1923 edition)

3. ————*Samuel Pepys, Lover of Musique.* London: Smith, Elder, & Co., 1903.

4.   Bumpus, John S. *A History of English Cathedral Music, 1549-1889*. London: T. Werner Laurie, 1908. (Reprint, London: Gregg International Publishers, 1972) 2. vols.

5.   Burney, Charles. *A General History of Music*. London: 1776-1789. (Reprint, 2 vols., ed. Frank Mercer. New York: Harcourt, Brace & Co., 1935).

6.   Clarke, Henry Leland. "Moll Davies, First Lady of English Opera," in *Essays on Music in Honor of Archibald Thompson Davison*. Cambridge: Department of Music, Harvard University, 1957.

7.   Daniel, Ralph T. and Peter G. Le Huray. *The Sources of English Church Music, 1549-1660*. 2 vols. London: Stainer & Bell, 1972.

8.   Dearnley, Christopher. *English Church Music 1650-1750 in Royal Chapel, Cathedral and Parish Church*. London: Barrie & Jenkins, 1970; New York: Oxford University Press, 1970.

9.   Dent, Edward J. *The Foundations of English Opera*. Cambridge: The University Press, 1928. (Reprint, New York: Da Capo Press, 1965)

10. Fiske, Roger. *English Theatre Music in the Eighteenth Century*. London: Oxford University Press, 1973.

11. Harley, John. *Music in Purcell's London*. London: Dennis Dobson, 1968.

12. Harris, Bernard. *A Book of Masques*. London: Cambridge University Press, 1966.

13. Hawkins, Sir John. *A General History of the Science and Practice of Music*. London, 1776. New York: J. L. Peters, 1875. (Reprint, New York: Dover Publishers, 1963)

14. Holst, Imogen, ed. *Henry Purcell 1659-1695. Essays on His Music*. London: Oxford University Press, 1959.

15. Kastendieck, Miles Merwin. *England's Musical Poet, Thomas Campion*. New York: Oxford University Press, 1938. (Reprint, New York: Russell & Russell, 1963)

16. Lampe, John Frederick. *A Plain and Compendious Method of Teaching Thorough Bass*. London: 1737. (Facsimile, New York: Broude Brothers, 1969)

17. Lefkowitz, Murray. *William Lawes*. London: Routledge and Kegan Paul, 1960.

18. Le Huray, Peter. *Music and the Reformation in England 1549-1660*. New York: Oxford University Press, 1967.

19. Long, Kenneth R. *The Music of the English Church*. London: Hodder and Stoughton, 1971.

20. Mace, Thomas. *Musik's Monument*. London: 1676. (Facsimile, New York: Broude, 1966)

21. Meyer, Ernst Hermann. *English Chamber Music* (Middle Ages to Purcell). London: Lawrence & Wishart, 1946. (Examples of music)

22. Moore, Robert Etheridge. *Henry Purcell and the Restoration Theatre*. London: Heinemann, 1961.

23. Nalbach, Daniel. *The King's Theatre 1704-1867: London's First Italian Opera House*. London: The Society for Theatre Research, 1972.

24. Pasquali, Nicolo. *Thorough-Bass Made Easy*. Edinburgh: 1757. (Facsimile, London: Oxford University Press, 1974.

25. Playford, John. *The English Dancing Master*. London: 1651. (Facsimile, ed., M. Dean-Smith. London: 1957. New York: Dance Horizons, 197-)

26. Pulver, Jeffrey. *A Biographical Dictionary of Old English Music*. London: Kegan Paul, Trench, Trubner & Co., 1927. (Reprint, New York: Burt Franklin, 1969)

27. Routh, Francis. *Early English Organ Music from the Middle Ages to 1837*. New York: Harper & Row, 1973.

28. Shaw, Watkins. *Eight Concerts of Henry Purcell's Music*. London: Arts Council of Great Britain, 1951.

29. Simpson, Christopher. *The Division Viol*. London: 1667. (Facsimile, London: Curwen, 1955.

30. Sumner, William Leslie. *The Organ*, 4th edition. London: Macdonald, 1973.

31. Weiss, David G. *Samuel Pepys, Curioso*. Pittsburgh: University of Pittsburgh Press, 1957.

32. Westrup, Jack Allan. *English Cathedral Music*, 5th edition. London: Methuen & Co., 1969.
33. Wienandt, Elwyn A. and Robert H. Young. *The Anthem in England and America.* New York: The Free Press, 1970.
34. Woodfill, Walter L. *Musicians in English Society; from Elizabeth to Charles I.* New York: Da Capo Press, 1969.
35. Zimmerman, Franklin B. *Henry Purcell 1659-1695: An Analytical Catalogue of His Music.* New York: St Martin's Press, 1963.
36. Zimmerman, Franklin B. *Henry Purcell, 1659-1695. His Life and Times.* New York: St Martin's Press, 1967.

Articles

1. Ashbee, Andrew. "John Jenkins 1592-1678: the viol consort music in four, five and six parts," *Early Music* 6 (1978), p. 492.
2. Brett, Philip. "The English Consort Song, 1570-1625, *PMA* 88 (1961), p. 73.
3. Bryant, G. "The Restoration Verse Anthem and Its Performance," *MusicAGO* 5 (Jan. 1971), p. 26.
4. Dent, Edward J. "Italian Opera in London," *PMA* 72 (1945), p. 19.
5. Gombosi, Otto. "Some Musical Aspects of the English Court Masque," *JAMS* 1 (1948), p. 3.
6. Harley, John. "Music and Musicians in Restoration London," *MQ* 40 (1954), p. 509.
7. Holman, Peter. "Continuo realizations in a Playford songbook," *Early Music* 6 (1978), p. 268.
8. ———— "Suites by Jenkins rediscovered: with Suite No. 7 in B flat for three Violins and continuo," *Early Music* 6 (1978), p. 25.
9. Hughes, Charles W. "Porter, Pupil of Monteverdi," *MQ* 20 (1934), p. 278.
10. ————"Richard Deering's Fancies for Viols," *MQ* 27 (1941), p. 38.
11. Hutchings, Arthur. "The English Concerto with or for Organ," *MQ* 47 (1961), p. 195.
12. Johnson, Jane Troy. "How to 'Humour' John Jenkins' Three-part Dances," *JAMS* 20 (1967), p. 197.
13. Lawrence, W. J. "Foreign Singers and Musicians in the Court of Charles II," *MQ* 9 (1923), p. 217.
14. Le Huray, Peter G. "Towards a Definitive Study of Pre-Restoration Anglican Service Music," *MD* 14 (1960).
15. ————"The English Anthem, 1580-1640," *PMA* 86 (1959).
16. Love, Harold. "The fiddlers on the Restoration stage," *Early Music* 6 (1978), p. 391.
17. Mellers, Wilfrid. "John Bull and English Keyboard Music," *MQ* 40 (1954), pp. 364, 548.
18. Morehen, John. "The English consort and verse anthems," *Early Music* 6 (1978), p. 381.
19. Pike, Lionel. "The First English 'Basso Continuo' Publication," *ML* 54 (1973), p. 326.
20. Pinto, David. "William Lawes' music for viol consort," *Early Music* 6 (1978), p. 12.
21. Pulver, Jeffrey. "Music in England during the Commonwealth," *Acta Mus* 6 (1934), p. 169.
22. Reese, Gustave. "The Origin of the English *In Nomine*," *JAMS* 2 (1949), p. 7.
23. Shaw, Harold Watkins. "Blow's Use of the Ground Bass," *MQ* 24 (1938), p. 31.
24. Squire, W. B. "The Music of Shadwell's 'Tempest'," *MQ* 7 (1921), p. 565.
25. van Tassel, Eric. "English church music *c.* 1660-1700," *Early Music* 6 (1978), p. 572.
26. Wailes, Marylin. "Four Short Fantasies by Henry Purcell," *Score* 20 (1957), p. 59.
27. Westrup, Jack Allan. "Foreign Musicians in Stuart England," *MQ* 27 (1941), p. 70.
28. ————"Purcell and Handel," *ML* 40 (1959), p. 103.
29. Zimmerman, Franklin B. "Anthems of Purcell and Contemporaries in a Newly discovered 'Gostling Manuscript'," *Acta Mus* 41 (1969), p. 55.
30. ————"Musical Borrowings in the English Baroque," *MQ* 52 (1966), p. 483.

Music

1. Blow, John
   a.   *Selected Organ Music,* ed. A. V. Butcher. Hinrichsen Edition, n. d.
   b.   *Six Suites,* ed. Howard Ferguson. London: Stainer & Bell, 1965. (21 compositions from *A Choice Collection of Lessons,* 1698; *A Choice Collection of Ayres,* 1700; and *The Second Book of the Harpsichord Master,* 1700).
   c.   *Two Voluntaries,* from the Nanki Manuscript, ed. Hugh McLean. London: Novello, 1971.
   d.   *Complete Organ Works,* ed. Watkins Shaw. London: Schott, 1958.
   e.   *Amphion Anglicus,* London, 1700. (*MMF,* Ser. 1, v. 2)
2. Campion, Thomas. *The English School of Lutenist Song Writers,* ed. Edmond H. Fellowes. London: Stainer & Bell, 1920-1932; 1959-   (Ser. 1 vols. 4, 13; Ser. 2, vols. 1, 2, 10, 11).
3. *Catch that Catch Can,* ed. Mary Catherine Taylor, Margarita Windham, and Claude Simpson. Boston: E. C. Schirmer, 1945.
4. Coperario, Giovanni (John Cooper) *M* 2, Ser. 1, v. 17.
5. *English Pastime Music, 1630-1660: An Anthology of Keyboard Pieces,* ed. Martha Mass. *Collegium Musicum,* Ser. 2, v. 4 (a collection of 119 short pieces).
6. Keyboard Music: *Contemporaries of Purcell,* 7 vols. London: J. & W. Chester, 1921. (Blow, Croft, Clark, and others)
7. Jenkins, John. *Consort Music in five parts,* ed. Richard Nicholson. London: 1971.
8. Locke, Matthew
   a.   *Keyboard Suites,* ed. Thurston Dart. London: Stainer & Bell, 1959.
   b.   *Melothesia, Keyboard Suites,* ed. Anthony Kooiker. University Park, PA., 1968.
   c.   *Organ Voluntaries,* ed. Thurston Dart. London: Stainer & Bell, 1957.
   d.   *The Present Practice of Music Vindicated. MMF,* Ser. 2, v. 16.
   e.   *Stainer & Bell Keyboard Series,* vols. 6, 7   (suites and organ pieces)
   f.   *Tallis to Wesley,* v. 6 (organ music)
9. Playford, Henry. *The theater of music, or, a choice collection of the newest and best songs,* in 4 books. London: 1685-1687. (*MMF,* Ser. 1, v. 36)
10. Playford, John
   a.   *Musicks Hand-maide Presenting New and Pleasant Lessons for the Virginals or Harpsycon,* London: 1663. Modern edition by Thurston Dart, London: Stainer & Bell, 1969.
   b.   *Select Ayres and Dialogues,* 1669. Facsimile, New Jersey: The Gregg Press, 1966.
11. Porter, Walter. *Madrigales and Ayres of two, three, foure, and five voyces, with the continued bass,* London: 1632.
12. Purcell, Henry
   a.   (*CE*) *Complete Works,* The Purcell Society, London: Novello, 1876-
   b.   *Complete Harpsichord Works,* 2 vols. ed. Howard Ferguson. London: Stainer & Bell, 1964.
   c.   *Eight Concerts of Henry Purcell's Music,* ed. Watkins Shaw. London: Arts Council of Great Britain, 1951.
   d.   *Fantazias and In Nomines,* ed. Thurston Dart. London: Novello, 1969.
   e.   *Purcell: Organ Works,* 2nd rev. ed. Hugh McLean. London: Novello, 1967.
   f.   *Orpheus Britannicus,* 3rd edition with large additions in 1721. Facsimile, Ridgewood, N J: Gregg Press, 1965.
   g.   *Sonnata's of III Parts: Two Viollins and Basse: To the Organ or Harpsecord,* 1683. Facsimile, Cambridge: Magdalene College, 1975.
   h.   *The Second Part of Musick's Hand-maid,* 1689. Modern ed. Thurston Dart. London: Stainer & Bell, 1958, rev. ed., 1968, 1969.

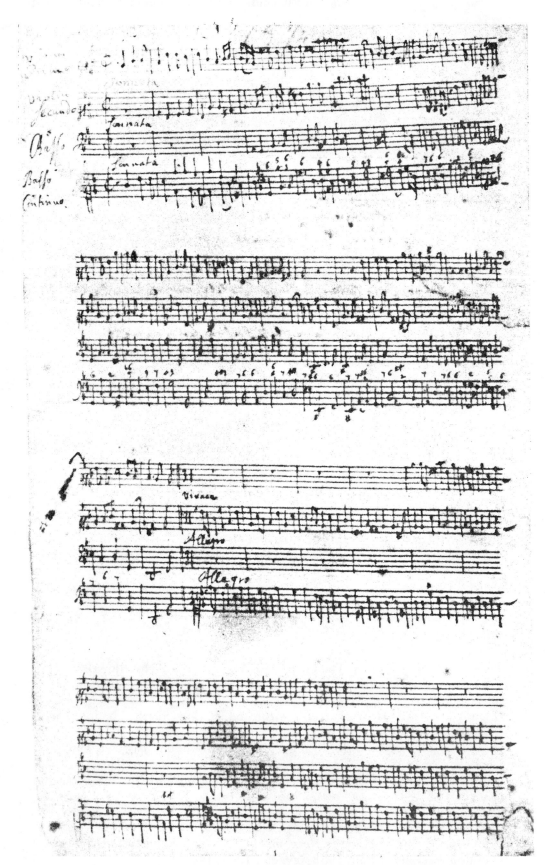

9.   The first page of **Purcell's** autograph MS of his
Sonnatas in III Parts (1683).

OUTLINE VIII

MUSIC IN ITALY

LATE BAROQUE

Introduction — The Concerto — Chamber Music
Keyboard Music — Opera Seria — Opera Buffa — Cantata and Oratorio
Bibliography of Books — Articles — Music

I. **Introduction**

    A. Tonality with functional harmony was completely established in the Late Baroque in Italy. Strong key feeling was achieved through frequent cadences, sequences of fifths (including one diminished fifth) returning to the tonic, and descending 6/3 chords used also as a means of modulation. Seventh chords appeared on all degrees of the scale and diminished seventh chords became "diatonic" rather than "altered" chords.

    B. Tonality brought in a new type of counterpoint called harmonic or tonal counterpoint. This was based on the underlying harmonic scheme. Harmonic counterpoint, initiated by **Corelli**, culminated in the music of **J. S. Bach**.

    C. Instrumental music in the Late Baroque in Italy took the lead over vocal music, and new and extended forms, particularly the concerto, developed. The concerto style made use of strong, regular rhythms, unison passages, rapid harmonic rhythm, themes emphasizing tonality, rapid scale passages, and tone repetitions. The melody was supported by a chordal-style accompaniment, which was controlled by the continuo with its rhythmical and rapidly moving bass line.

II. **The Concerto**

    A. The Baroque "concerto" (1670-1750) may be divided into three types: 1) orchestral concerto or concerto-sinfonia; 2) *concerto grosso*; and 3) solo concerto.

        1. The orchestral concerto, cultivated by members of the Bologna school, used the concerto style with continuo. Contrast was not developed by alternating *tutti* and solo sections but rather with techniques, *tutti* versus brilliant style.

        2. The *concerto grosso* was the principal type of Baroque instrumental concerto. The most outstanding *concerto grosso* composers were **Corelli**, **Torelli**, and **Vivaldi**.

          a. The *concerto grosso* used two contrasting groups of instruments: 1) solo group (*concertino*), at first consisting of two violins and continuo (cello and harpsichord); 2) full orchestral groups of strings (*ripieni, tutti,* or *concerto grosso*) and continuo.

            1) "*Senza ripieni*" indicated that a smaller group of principal players was to accompany the *concertino* and that the full orchestra (*ripieni*) was not to play.

        3. The solo concerto, the latest type, required only one player on the solo part instead of the *concertino* group.

          a. The solo concerto created an incentive to advance the technical idiom of the violin, developed a contrast in thematic material between the soloist and the orchestra, and encouraged the craftsmen to build violins of greater power and distinctive tone to compete with the orchestra.

    B. **Arcangelo Corelli** (1653-1713)

        1. **Corelli**, outstanding composer, teacher, and violinist, represents the culmination of the Bologna school. After 1681, he settled in Rome and completed his life in the service of Cardinal Pietro Ottoboni. **Corelli** laid the foundation for modern violin technique and surprisingly limited himself to composing only for bowed instruments.

Numbered among his pupils are **Geminiani, Locatelli, Giovanni Battista Somis** (1686-1763), and his brother **Lorenzo Somis** (1688-1775).

2.   *Concerti grossi*, Op. 6 (composed *c.* 1680, published in Rome, 1712, published in Amsterdam, 1714 (*CE*, vols. 4, 5; *AM*, v. 23, p. 55)

   a.   Corelli wrote 12 *concerti grossi*. The first eight are in the form of the church concerto (*concerto da chiesa*) and were intended to be played in church. The last four are chamber concertos (*concerto da camera*) with a prelude followed by suite movements. The *concertino* in the concertos is the trio sonata group of two violins, cello, and harpsichord.

   1)   The cello is occasionally dropped out of the *concertino* group (*Concerto* No. 1,) last allegro (*CE*, v. 4, p. 21); *Concerto* No. 4, adagio (*CE*, v. 4, p. 65).

   b.   The concertos have five or more short movements, as in the earlier canzonas. Some of the short adagios serve merely as connecting movements. Several short movements are sometimes combined to produce a two-part form (*Concerto* No. 8, first and last movements) (*CE*, v. 5, pp. 150, 159).

   c.   The same thematic material is often used in the short *tutti* (*concerto grosso*) and *concertino* (solo) sections, producing an echo effect: *Concerto* No. 3 (*CE*, v. 4, p. 56); *Concerto* No. 5 (*CE*, v. 4, p. 88); *Concerto* No. 9, *Gavotte* (*CE*, v. 5, p. 179). The *concertino* and *concerto grosso* groups may also alternate in quick succession in playing a continuous phrase.

   d.   Little distinction was made between the solo and *tutti* parts as regards their difficulty, and doubling of the *tutti* parts by the solo parts was optional. The first violin assumes more importance in the last concerto, *Concerto* No. 12 (*CE*, v. 5, p. 218).

   e.   **Corelli** used sequences, suspensions, unison passages, modulations to related keys, and diatonic and arpeggiated motives. Contrapuntal writing is used, particularly in the allegros of *Concerto* No. 1 (*CE*, v. 4, p. 16); *Concerto* No. 2 (*CE*, v. 4, p. 36); *Concerto* No. 3 (*CE*, v. 4, pp. 48, 52); *Concerto* No. 5 (*CE*, v. 4, p. 96), and in the preludes of concertos No. 10 (*CE*, v. 5, p. 185); No. 11 (*CE*, v. 5, p. 204); No. 12 (*CE*, v. 5, p. 219).

   f.   *Concerto grosso*, Op. 6, No. 8 (*CE*, v. 5, p. 150)

   1)   This famous concerto was "*Fatto per la notte di natale*" (composed for the night of the nativity) and includes the popular *Pastorale* as an *ad libitum* final movement (*CE*, v. 5, p. 164; *SS*, 693; *AM*, v. 23, p. 66).

C.   **Alessandro Scarlatti**   (1659-1725)

   1.   **Scarlatti** was born in Palermo and spent his productive years in Naples and Rome. Principally a composer of opera and oratorio, **Scarlatti** composed little chamber music. Included are suites and sonatas for flutes and strings, and 12 *concerti grossi* (*sinfonia*).

   2.   *Sinfonia Prima, di concerto Grosso con due Flauti*, Naples, 1715

   a.   The form of these 12 concertos is in five movements: allegro–adagio–fugue–adagio–dance. The instrumentation includes strings, one or two flutes, one flute and one oboe, and one trumpet and one flute.

   b.   *Sonate a quattro*, *c.* 1720, four sonatas for string quartet. Parts of these are included in the six concertos for strings.

   1)   *Concerto* No. 3 (*HAM*, No. 260)

D.   **Giuseppe Torelli** (1658-1709)

   1.   **Torelli**, an outstanding violinist, composer, and a representative of the Late Baroque Bologna school, settled in Germany following a concert tour in 1695. After a year in Vienna he returned to Bologna in 1701.

   2.   **Torelli** originated the typical Late Baroque three-movement concerto form (fast–slow–fast) in his orchestral concertos and *concerti grossi*. Most of the slow movements in themselves are arranged in a slow–fast–slow form.

   3.   *6 Sinfonie a 3 e 6 Concerti a quattro*, Op. 5, 1692

   a.   The six sinfonias are three-voice works written in the elaborate harmonic counterpoint of the Late Baroque. The six concertos are orchestral concertos (see above), written in concerto style without contrasting *tutti*-solo sections. The emphasis is on the strongly rhythmic melody and bass. The continuo and other instruments, moving in fast harmonic rhythm, provide the chordal background.

4. *Concerti musicali a 4,* Op. 6, 1698 (*M* 11a)
   a. Some of these twelve orchestral concertos have short solo interludes which, as **Torelli** stated in the Preface, were "to be played by one violin alone."
5. *6 Concerti grossi,* Op. 8, 1709 (published posthumously by **Torelli**'s brother, Felice.)
   a. This is a collection of six *concerti grossi* with a solo violin for the *concertino*. The solo and *tutti* sections are contrasted and of equal importance. In single movements, similar *tutti* sections (ritornellos) sometimes alternate with the solo sections in rondo style in various keys. Only the first and last *tutti* are in the same key.
   b. Characteristic features include themes based on triads, *tutti* which begin with three powerful chords (I–I–I or I–V–I), vital rhythms, and lengthy up beats. *Tutti* are sometimes treated in contrapuntal style.
   c. *Concerto grosso,* Op. 8, No. 7 (*GMB*, No. 257)
      1) In the closing movement, **Torelli** suggests for the solo violin, *solo tutto sopra il manico,* that is to shift the hand position to avoid open strings and thus avoid dissimilar tone quality. A suggestion in the adagio movement is to improvise ornaments (*con affetto*).
   d. *Concerto grosso,* Op. 8, No. 8 (*HAM*, No. 246)
E. **Antonio Vivaldi** (1678-1741)
   1. **Vivaldi** was born in Venice and studied with his father and **Legrenzi**. He received Holy Orders sometime after 1699 and became a priest on March 23, 1703. He was known as the "red priest" because of his red hair. In Venice he taught violin and conducted the orchestra of the music school of the Hospital of the Pietà for girls, 1703-1741. He traveled in Italy and other countries and was in Mantua for some time. He returned to Venice in 1735, and spent his last days in Vienna.
   2. **Vivaldi** was a highly individual and prolific composer. His works include about 445 complete concertos, 100 chamber works, 48 operas, 59 secular cantatas, and 60 sacred compositions including oratorios, motets, Psalms, and Mass movements. He developed the solo concerto for violin or flute and a new type of *concerto grosso* with two, three, or four independent wind and/or string instruments in place of the usual *concertino* for two violins, cello, and continuo.
   3. **Vivaldi** established the three movement form (fast–slow–fast), sometimes with a slow introduction. Single movements became longer, solo passages were extended, and the number of rondo-like alternations of the *tutti* and solo increased.
      a. He used descriptive titles for some of his collections of concertos. The thematic material of the solo part was often derived from the *tutti* and elaborated and expanded. The ritornello and solo sections were sometimes based on independent thematic material, but were in the same key and rhythm.
   4. Dynamic gradations from pianissimo to double forte may be found in his scores. Different simultaneous dynamic levels are often used to bring out a specific part (*P.* 241) (*La Primavera,* movement 2, *F.* v. 1, No. 22, p. 13; *Concerto* in E minor (*P.* 126) (*F.* v. 1, No. 74, p. 1).
   5. A great variety of tempo indications define expression and articulations, slurs and bowing techniques are frequently shown in the manuscript scores: *Concerto* in E-flat, (*P.* 439) (*F.* v. 1, No. 92); *Il Sospetto* (The suspicion) (*P.* 419) (*F.* v. 1, No. 2). An extended pedal point of 27 measures may be found in the third movement of *L'Inverno* (*P.* 442) (*F.* v. 1, No. 25, p. 19). *Scordatura* in the principal violin and the first and second violins of the orchestra is called for throughout in *Concerto* in A (*P.* 229) (*Tomo* 100; *F.* v. 1, No. 39).
   6. *L'Estro armonico* (Harmonious whim), Op. 3, Amsterdam 1712 (*CE, Tomo* 406-417)

a. This work is comprised of 12 concertos for one, two, or four violins and one cello *"concertante"* in six of the concertos. The *tutti* ensemble is made up of two violins, one or two violas, cello, and cembalo continuo.

b. Concertos No. 2 (*P.* 326) (*Tomo* 407); No. 4 (*P.* 97) (*Tomo* 409); and No. 7 (*P.* 249) (*Tomo* 412) open with a slow movement, and No. 11 (*P.* 250) (*Tomo* 416) uniquely opens with a short allegro movement for *concertante* instruments followed by four movements: adagio, allegro, largo, allegro.

c. **Bach** transcribed six of these concertos for other instrumental combinations: harpsichord concertos: No. 3 (*P.* 408) (*Tomo* 92) became **Bach** *S.* 978; No. 9 (*P.* 414) (*Tomo* 437) became **Bach** *S.* 972; No. 12 (*P.* 417) (*Tomo* 461) became **Bach** *S.* 976; Concerto for four harpsichords, No. 10 (*P.* 415) (*Tomo* 80) became **Bach** *S.* 1065; Concerto No. 8 (*P.* 413) (*Tomo* 427) became **Bach** Organ Concerto *S.* 593; and Concerto No. 11 (*P.* 416) (*Tomo* 133) became **Bach** Organ Concerto *S.* 596.

d. *Concerto grosso,* Op. 3, No. 8, first movement (*HAM,* No. 270)

e. *Concerto grosso,* Op. 3, No. 11 (*NS,* 84)

7. *La Stravaganza* (The Extraordinary) Op. 4, Amsterdam, 1712 (*Tomo* 418-429)

a. There are 12 concertos in Opus 4 for solo violin with four-part strings and cembalo or organ continuo. In only one case (No. 7) is there an opening slow movement.

8. *Il Cimento dell'Armonia e dell'Invenzione* (The strife between harmony and invention) Op. 8, 1728 (*Tomo* 2, 65, 76-85)

a. These 12 concertos are for two violins, viola, cello, organ or cembalo continuo and *violino principale.* Seven of them are programmatic concertos:
    No. 5, *La Tempesta di Mare* (The tempest of the sea) (*P.* 415) (*Tomo* 80)
    No. 6, *Il piacere* (The pleasure) (*P.* 7) (*Tomo* 81)
    No. 10, *La Caccia* (The *hunt) (P.* 338) (*Tomo* 83)
    Le Stagione (The seasons)
        No. 1, *La Primavera* (Spring) (*P.* 241) (*Tomo* 76; *TEM,* 286)
        No. 2, *L'Estate* (Summer) (*P.* 336) (*Tomo* 77)
        No. 3, *L'Autunne* (Autumn) (*P.* 257) (*Tomo* 78; *SS,* 340)
        No. 4, *L'Inverno* (Winter) (*P.* 442) (*Tomo* 79)

1) Each of the four Seasons is described by a sonnet, and the music depicts in the solo sections the buzzing of insects, bird calls, a flowing brook, slipping on ice, terrible wind, and many other characteristics of the seasons.

F. **Francesco Geminiani** (1687-1762)

1. **Geminiani** carried on the conservative style of his teachers **Corelli** and **Alessandro Scarlatti** in Rome. After working in Lucca (1707-1710) and Naples, he settled in London in 1714 and became a famous teacher and virtuoso. He later lived in Dublin (1733-1740), Paris (1755), London and again in Dublin (1759) until his death.

2. Although one of the lesser concerto composers, he advanced the art of violin playing. In his *concerti grossi* **Geminiani** added a viola to the traditional trio-sonata *concertino,* forming a string quartet. He was interested in contrapuntal writing, and even subtitled his *Concerto Grosso,* Op. 7, No. 1, *"l'Arte della fuga."*

3. Even though the concertos are imitations of those by **Corelli**, their popularity is evidenced by the numerous revisions and adaptations made of his works by himself and others.

4. The 25 *Concerti grossi* are generally in three or four movements.

a. *Six Concertos in 7 Parts,* Op. 2, London, 1732; Paris, 1755

b. *Six Concertos in 7 Parts,* Op. 3, London, 1733

c. *Six Concertos,* Op. 6, London, 1741

d. *Seven Concertos in 8 Parts,* Op. 7, London, 1746 (with added viola parts)

5. *The Art of Playing upon the Violin ,* 1751, is the first important treatise on violin playing in the English language. **Geminiani's** principles are still used today.

G. **Pietro Locatelli** (1695-1764)
1. A pupil of **Corelli** in Rome, **Locatelli** derived his progressive style from **Vivaldi**. He traveled as a violin virtuoso and settled in Amsterdam, where he established regular public concerts.
2. **Locatelli** used the contrapuntal style of **Corelli**, as did **Geminiani** also, but his harmonic technique is more advanced. A brilliant violinist, he wrote virtuoso cadenzas (*capricci*) for his solo concertos and expanded the trio *concertino* in his *concerti grossi* to a string quartet, and even used a string quintet.
3. His concertos include 12 *Concerti grossi*, Op. 1, 1721; 6 *Introduttioni teatrali* (*M* 4, v. 4); 6 Concertos, Op. 4, 1735; and 6 *Concerti a quattro*, Op. 7, 1741.
H. **Evaristo Felice dall' Abaco** (1675-1742)
1. An Italian violinist and composer, **dall' Abaco** went to Munich in 1704 in the employ of the Elector and in 1715 was appointed *Konzertmeister* of the court. His works include trio sonatas and concertos.
   a. [12] *Concerti a quattro da chiesa*, Op. 2 (*DTB*, v. 1)
      1) *Concerto da chiesa*, Op. 2, No. 5 (*AM*, v. 45, p. 82)
   b. *Concerti a più instrumenti*, Op. 5 and 6
      1) *Concerto*, Op. 6, No. 11 (*GMB*, No. 277)
I. Other Italian composers of concertos were **Tommaso Albinoni** (1671-1750) (*M* 1); **Benedetto Marcello** (1686-1739); **Giuseppe Valentini** (*c.* 1681-*c.* 1740); **Francesco Veracini** (1690-1768) (*HM*, v. 169); and **Giuseppe Tartini** (1692-1770) (*SCMA*, v. 9).

III. **Chamber Music**

A. *Sonata da chiesa*
1. The church sonata developed about 1680 into a four-movement form (slow—fast—slow—fast) with the addition of a slow movement at the beginning of the basic three-movement form established by **Giovanni Vitali** in 1667.
   a. The last two movements were often of a dance-like character even though the *sonata da chiesa*, as its name implies, was intended to be performed in church. Some of the Italian composers of the Late Baroque used three (**Locatelli, Tartini**), or more than four (**Veracini**) movements.
B. *Sonata da camera*
1. The chamber sonata, a suite with a prelude (*sinfonia*) followed by dance movements, was known as early as 1629, although the name *sonata da camera* was not used until about 1670. The chamber sonata was not intended for church or operatic use, but for use in the home or small concert rooms.
2. The church sonata and the chamber sonata gradually lost many of their distinguishing characteristics in the Late Baroque. These new sonatas were often called "trio sonatas" even though the old names persisted.
C. **Arcangelo Corelli** (1653-1713)
1. **Corelli** played a most important part in the development of Baroque chamber music. His style is characterized by a mastery of form, moving bass lines, expressive melodies, harmonic complexity, contrapuntal writing, proportion, and restraint.
2. **Corelli** extends the range of the violin to fifth position (*Concerto grosso I, CE*, v. 4, p. 16); exploits various bowing techniques, such as *bariolage* (*Sonata III, CE*, v. 5, p. 29) and *tremolo* (*Concerto grosso V, CE*, v. 4, p. 88); and uses other techniques such as parallel thirds in sixteenth notes (*Sonata III, CE*, v. 5, p. 28); two-part imitation (*Sonata IV, CE*, v. 5, p. 38); "arpeggio" (*Sonata I, CE*, v. 5, p. 18); and perpetual motion (*Sonata VI, CE*, v. 5, p. 62).
3. *Suonate da chiesa a tre*, Op. 1, Rome, 1683 (*CE*, v. 1); Op. 3, Modena, 1689 (*CE*, v. 2) (*NagMA*, v. 147; *AM*, v. 45, p. 60)
   a. **Corelli** established the four-movement form in his 24 church sonatas for two violins,

cello, and organ continuo. The first movements (most often *grave* and generally in duple time) may be contrapuntal, with imitations between the two violins (Op. 3, No. 4; *CE*, v. 2, p. 142), or homophonic. The bass sometimes answers the two violins antiphonally (Op. 3, No. 8; *CE*, v. 2, p. 164).

b. The second movements (*allegro*), in duple meter, are frequently in fugal style with a short counter-subject, and the subject and counter-subject are used in various ways throughout the movement.

c. The third movements (*adagio* or *largo*), in triple time, are generally homophonic and in the style of the *saraband*.

d. The fourth movements (*allegro*), in duple or compound meter, are usually in a stylized dance form and are generally homophonic with some use of imitation.

e. *Sonata da chiesa*, Op. 3, No. 7 (*NS*, 77)

4. *Suonate da camera a tre*, Op. 2, Rome, 1685 (*CE*, v. 1); Op. 4, Bologna, 1694 (*CE*, v. 2)

a. The 24 chamber sonatas for two violins, cello, and harpsichord continuo usually consist of a prelude followed by two or three dance movements in homophonic style. The dances include the allemande, courante, saraband, gavotte, and gigue, but appear in no fixed order.

1) The preludes are usually slow and in duple meter and are in a mixed homophonic and imitative style. Eight of the slow movements in Op. 4 conclude with a Phrygian cadence which leads to the following movement.

b. *Suonate da camera a tre*, Op. 2, No. 2 (*CE*, v. 1, p. 78; *GMB*, No. 240)

1) Each movement (*Allemanda, Corrente, Giga*) is in repeated bipartite form. There is some use of echo.

c. *Sonata da camera*, Op. 4, No. 3 (*AM*, v. 45, p. 63)

5. *Suonate a violino*, Op. 5, Rome, 1700 (*CE*, v. 3)

a. This set of 12 sonatas for solo violin, cello, and harpsichord continuo (*a due*) includes six church and six chamber sonatas. Op. 5, No. 12 is the famous set of 23 variations on the *Follia* theme (*CE*, v. 3, p. 96).

b. The sonatas *a due* (slow—fast—slow—fast) resemble the trio sonatas in form and content. In the fourth edition of the six church sonatas, **Corelli** has added elaborate ornamentation in the adagios, an invaluable addition for the stylistic performance of these sonatas.

c. *Suonate a violino*, Op. 5, No. 3 (*CE*, v. 3, p. 26; *HAM*, No. 252)

d. *Suonate a violino*, Op. 5, No. 8 (*CE*, v. 3, p. 76; *HAM*, No. 253)

D. **Antonio Vivaldi** (1678-1741)

1. **Vivaldi** wrote 76 sonatas for various solo and combinations of instruments, all with figured bass. Although recognized as one of the most important Venetian sonata composers, **Vivaldi**'s sonatas represent only a small portion of his total output.

2. Op. 1 (*Tomo* 382-393)

a. This opus contains 12 sonatas for two violins, cello, and cembalo. The dance movements include allemandes, correntes, gigues, and gavottes. Canonic imitation, sequence, syncopation, and arpeggios are some of the common techniques. No. 12 is a set of 20 variations on *La Follia*, possibly inspired by **Corelli**.

3. Opus 2, Venice, 1709 (*Tomo* 394-405)

a. There are 12 *sonate da camera* for solo violin and continuo in Opus 2. All the sonatas, except No. 2, begin with a slow prelude in binary form, and each of the sonatas is in a different key. (*HM*, v. 102).

4. Opus 5, Amsterdam, 1716-1717 (*Tomo* 430-435)

a. This collection includes six *sonate da camera*, four for solo violin and continuo (*NagMA*, v. 162), and the remaining for two violins and continuo (*NagMA*, v. 171). They usually include a prelude, as in the church sonata, followed by two or three dance movements.

5. Six cello sonatas, Paris, 1740 (*Tomo* 473-478)

a.   The cello sonatas are in the church sonata form with the fast movements in the typical Baroque binary style: I–V, V (short development)–I (reprise).

6.   *Il Pastor Fido [6] Sonates, pour la Musette, Viele, Flûte, Hautbois, Violon avec la Basse Continüe Del Sigr Vivaldi. Opera XIIIe,* Paris, *c.* 1737

a.   The *Sonata da camera,* Op. 13, No. 4 (*Tomo,* 470, p. 8) calls for an organ continuo in the *Pastorale,* and an independent *obbligatto* part which rather consistently plays in thirds and sixths with the solo part.

b.   In the second movement of No. 6 (*Tomo,* 472, p. 4) the fugue subject is played by the solo violin and the continuo in various voices.

E.   **Francesco Maria Veracini** (1690-1768)

1.   **Veracini** was lauded as one of the great violin virtuosi of the Late Baroque and is also known as a composer of operas. He gave great impetus to violin playing in Dresden, London during **Handel's** time, France, and Italy.

2.   With **Veracini** the separation between the church and chamber sonata became less distinct. The sonatas show the influence of the opera and concerto in the use of the French overtures, da capo forms, and ritornellos.

3.   [12] *Sonate a Violino Solo, e Basso,* Opus 1, Amsterdam, *c.* 1720; Dresden, 1721; London, 1733

a.   Sonata No. 8 (*ICDMI,* v. 34)

4.   *Sonate Accademiche a Violin Solo e Basso,* Op. 2, London and Florence, 1744

a.   In the Preface of these 12 sonatas, **Veracini** shows specific signs for crescendo and diminuendo. The direction, *come sta* (do not add ornaments), is suggested in Nos. 1, 5, and 12 (*HM,* v. 169).

F.   **Giuseppe Torelli** (1658-1709)

1.   *Sonate a tre stromenti,* Op. 1, 1686

a.   *Sonate für Violino Solo, Violoncello obligatto u. Cembalo* (*AIM,* 64)

1)   The first movement is in the style of a fanfare similar to those in the trumpet works.

2.   *Sinfonie a 2.3.4. Istromenti,* Op. 3, 1687 (*HM,* v. 69)

a.   Included in these *sinfonie* are two solo sonatas, six trio sonatas, and four multi-voice sonatas, also called *sinfonie.*

3.   In addition to the sonatas for string instruments, **Torelli** wrote 11 sonatas for trumpet (some are called *sinfonie*), nine for two trumpets, and several for trumpet and oboe or other instrument (*BMB,* vols. 87, 88, 89; *M* 11c).

G.   **Giuseppe Tartini** (1692-1770)

1.   **Tartini** was the last sonata composer of the Italian Baroque. In 1728 he founded a school for violinists, the *Scuola delle Nazioni* (School of the Nations). He made many contributions to violin technique, particularly in bowing. Among several treatises which he wrote is *Trattato di musica* (Treatise of music) (*MMF,* Ser. 2, v. 8), Padua, 1754, in which he described the principle of differential tones which he discovered.

2.   Sonatas

a. Some 200 solo and trio sonatas have been catalogued. Published during his lifetime were Opus 1, Amsterdam, 1732, which contains 12 sonatas, and Opus 2, Amsterdam, 1743, which contains 11 sonatas.

b.   The solo sonatas generally are made up of three movements (largo–allegro–presto), while the trio sonatas have been reduced to two movements, anticipating the pre-Classical *style galant.*

1)   There is a shift to homophonic texture and the fast movements, rather than being fugal, appear in a binary form. Extension of range, double and triple stops, greater variety of figurations and more sensitive expression, as noted in movement titles, is common.

c.   Sonata, Op. 3, No. 12 (*Presto assai*) (*HAM,* No. 275)

d.   Sonata, Op. 1 "Pastorale" (*Grave, Allegro*) (*GMB,* No. 295)

H.   Other Italian composers of the Late Baroque who wrote chamber music for various combinations of instruments include **Giovanni Battista Bassani** (1657-1716) (*ICDMI*, v. 2; *AMI*, v. 7; *HM*, vols. 16, 64); **Evaristo Felice dall' Abaco** (1675-1742) (*DTB*, vols. 1, 16; *HAM*, No. 269; *AM*, v. 45, p. 85); **Tommaso Vitali**, son of **Giovanni Battista Vitali**, (*c.* 1665-1747) (*HM*, vols. 38, 100; *SCMA*, v. 12; *HAM*, No. 263; *GMB*, No. 241); **Tommaso Albinoni** (1671-1750) (*NagMA*, vols. 9, 34, 74; *AM*, v. 45, p. 73); **Benedetto Marcello** (1686-1739) (*HM*, vols. 141, 151, 152); **Francesco Geminiani** (1687-1762) (*HM*, vols. 173, 174, 178; *SCMA*, v. 1); and **Pietro Locatelli** (1695-1764) (*ICMI*, v. 14; *HM*, v. 35).

IV.   Keyboard Music

A.   Keyboard music in the Italian Late Baroque is represented by the late works of **Bernardo Pasquini** (1637-1710) (*CEKM*, Ser. 5); **Domenico Zipoli** (1688-1726) (*LO*, vols. 4, 12; *AMI*, v. 3; *M* 13); and, above all, **Domenico Scarlatti**.

B.   **Domenico Scarlatti** (1685-1757)

1.   **Domenico**, son of **Alessandro**, was born in Naples and first studied with his father. He was engaged as harpsichordist in the household of the Portuguese ambassador to the Holy See in Rome. In 1708 in Venice he became a close friend of **Handel**. About 1720 he went to Lisbon and became music master to the young Portuguese princess, Maria Barbara. He remained in her service the rest of his life and accompanied her to Madrid in 1729, when she married the heir to the Spanish throne.

2.   **Scarlatti's** principal works are for keyboard, but he also composed operas, cantatas, oratorios, serenades, and church music.

3.   Almost all his 555 keyboard sonatas were written for Maria Barbara. The term "sonata" was used for most of his pieces in binary form; other designations were *aria, capriccio, fuga, gavota, gigha, minuet,* and *pastorale.* Thirty sonatas were published by **Scarlatti** in 1738 in London as *Essercizi per Gravicembalo* (Studies for the Harpsichord) (K. 1-30) (*M* 9a, v. 1; *M* 9b).

a.   There are two collected editions of the sonatas. One is edited by Ralph Kirkpatrick (*M* 9a), who points out that most of the sonatas were composed in pairs and has arranged them in chronological order, based on manuscripts, stylistic changes, and the range of the harpsichord. The other edition by Alessandro Longo (*M* 9c) has the sonatas arranged in suites without regard to chronological sequence. The Longo edition suffers from inaccuracies and editorial additions.

4.   **Scarlatti's** style developed from the Italian keyboard style of **Zipoli** and others in the *Essercizi,* many of which anticipate the technical features of the series of virtuoso sonatas of 1742 to 1749. Then a group of easier sonatas was followed by the great works of his most mature period, 1752-1757. **Scarlatti** was also influenced by the violin sonata, *L.* 93 (v. 2, p. 117); *K.* 149 (v. 7).

5.   **Scarlatti's** keyboard techniques include:

1.   wide leaps, *K.* 299 (v. 11); *L.* 210 (v. 5, p. 34)

2.   rapid broken octave passages, *K.* 22 (v. 2); *L.* 432 (v. 9, p. 137)

3.   scales in contrary motion, *K.* 367 (v. 13); *L.* 172 (v. 4, p. 77)

4.   contrary arpeggios, *K.* 411 (v. 14); *L.* 69 (v. 2, p. 56)

5.   crossing hands, *K.* 120 (v. 4); *L.* 215 (v. 5, p. 53)

6.   glissando, *K.* 379 (v. 13); *L.* 73 (v. 2, p. 66)

7.   repeated notes, *K.* 96 (v. 3); *L.* 465 (v. 10, p. 68)

8.   trilling internal pedal point, *K.* 119 (v. 4); *L.* 415 (v. 9, p. 64)

9.   parallel thirds and sixths, *K.* 524 (v. 18); *L.* 283 (v. 4, p. 129)

10.   *acciaccatura,* producing startling effects, *K.* 175 (v. 6); *L.* 429 (v. 9. p. 124; *HAM*, No. 274)

11.   trills, scales juxtaposed against full chords, crossing hands, parallel thirds and sixths, *K.* 11 (v. 1); *L.* 352 (v. 8, p. 6); (*NS*, 278; *MM*, 180)

12. repeated notes, diminished seventh arpeggios, trills, parallel thirds, and octaves, *K.* 519 (v. 18); *L.* 475 (v. 10, p. 111) (*GMB*, No. 282, 1)

13. following a French sixth there is a flourish which may imply the beginning of a cadenza, *K.* 544 (v. 18); *L.* 497 (v. 10, p. 190) (*GMB*, No. 282, 2)

6. The form of the two-part sonatas may be classified in two types:
   a. Type I: The second half begins with the same thematic material as the first half. There may be a modulatory section at the beginning of the second half.
   b. Type II: The second half does not begin with the material of the first half. There will usually be a suggestion of a development or a modulatory section at the beginning of the second half. The second half will usually end with a restatement of the material from the end of the first half.

7. The basic tonal scheme is as follows:
   a. The first half (repeated) — Tonic—modulatory—dominant
   b. The second half (repeated) — Dominant—modulatory—tonic

8. **Scarlatti's** harmonic material is made up almost entirely of triads with some use of 7th, 9th, and altered chords. About half of his modulations are made by common chords. Change of mode (major—minor) and chromatic modulations (particularly in the minor mode) account for most of the modulations.

V.   Opera Seria

A. The librettist **Apostolo Zeno** (1668-1750) and his successor, **Pietro Metastasio** (1698-1782) purged the typical 17th century opera of unessential comic and fantastic episodes, machines and other unnecessary elements, and created a more homogeneous structure. Two distinct types of opera developed: 1) *opera seria*; and 2) *opera buffa.*

B. *Opera seria* began its development in Naples and became known as Neapolitan opera. The typical opera consisted of three acts. The libretto was based mainly on legend or classical history. Each scene was divided into two parts: part I (recitative) was used for dramatic action, while part II (aria) was used for reflection on the feelings of the hero.

1. There were two types of recitative: 1) *recitativo secco,* "dry recitative," accompanied only with continuo; and 2) *recitativo accompagnato* or *stromentato,* accompanied with strings or full orchestra.

2. Arias, in da capo form, were of various types: *aria cantabile, aria parlante, aria di bravura.* They were considered the most important part of the opera.

3. Choruses were rarely used and the orchestra played a relatively unimportant part, except in overtures, ritornellos, and occasional accompaniments for arias.

4. Serious opera developed a fairly rigid form with different types of arias assigned to various singers in regular order and number. Neapolitan opera stressed the bel canto style of singing and developed a highly ornamental vocal line and virtuoso technique. Castrati had been used in opera since **Monteverdi's** *Orfeo* and they were used almost exclusively for male and female roles from 1650-1750.

5. Composers often borrowed their own and other composers' arias. Scores were not printed and operas were seldom performed the same way again. A haphazard collection of arias called a *pasticcio* might undergo considerable change from one performance to another, and from one city to another. Neapolitan opera became the standard operatic form throughout Europe, culminating in the operas of **Handel.**

6. **Francesco Provenzale** (*c.* 1630-1704)
   a. **Provenzale** was the first important Neapolitan composer of opera. His eight operas contain both serious and comic scenes.
   b. *Lo schiavo di sua moglie* (His wife's slave), Naples, 1671
      1) A humorous opera in the dignified style of the *opera seria.*
      2) *Lasciatema morir* (Let me die) (*HAM*, No. 222), an ostinato aria.

7. **Alessandro Scarlatti** (1659-1725)

      a.   **Alessandro** was a prolific opera composer. By his own count he wrote 115 operas, probably including adaptations. However, the librettos of only 80 are known and only 35 operas are extant. **Scarlatti** produced his operas in Rome, Florence, Venice, and Naples.

      b.   His early operas show the influence of Roman and Venetian opera in the use of continuo arias, extended two-part form (ABB), and ostinato basses. He made use of the da capo aria, which later became the standard type. The use of short motives in both vocal and orchestral parts is notable.

      c.   **Alessandro Scarlatti's** operas after 1703 (*BM*, 175) anticipate the stylized form of the later Neapolitan composers. He used orchestral accompaniments with horns (1718) and oboes and trumpets (1721), expanded the harmonic materials by the use of the so-called Neapolitan 6th and diminished 7th chords, and at times extended the aria with florid passages.

      d.   The Neapolitan overture, often called a "sinfonia," is in three short sections (fast—slow—fast).

          1) *Sinfonia* from *La Griselda,* Rome, 1721 (*HAM*, No. 259)
          2) *Sinfonia* from *La Caduta de Decem Viri*, 1697 (*TEM*, 261)
          3) *Sinfonia* from *Marco Attilio Regolo* (*MSO*, 90; *M* 8b, v. 2)

      e.   In his late operas, **Scarlatti** frequently concluded an act with an ensemble consisting of a duet, trio, or quartet.

      f.   *La Rosaura,* Rome, 1690 (*PAM*, v. 14, acts 1 and 2 only)

      g.   *La Griselda,* Rome, 1721 (*M* 8a, b, v. 3; *GMB*, No. 259)

    8.   The following composers also expanded the fame of the Neapolitan *opera seria* during the early 18th century. They perfected the Italian overture, enlarged the da capo form, and made extravagant use of ornamentation, cadenzas, and coloraturas. **Nicola Porpora** (1686-1766) wrote about 50 *opera seria.* **Leonardo Vinci** (1690-1730) composed 36 operas for Naples and Rome. **Leonardo Leo** (1694-1744) composed some 30 operas for various cities other than Naples.

    9.   Later Baroque Venetian opera developed along the line of Neapolitan opera. The orchestra became more important, the da capo aria was extended, the bravura arias with elaborate cadenzas and arias with unison orchestral accompaniments were featured. There were many composers stemming from the Venetian School. **Francesco Gasparini** (1668-1727) wrote more than 60 stage works. **Giovanni Battista Bononcini** (1670-1747) helped to spread Italian opera to Berlin, Vienna, Paris, and London where he became a rival of **Handel**. Thirty of his operas have been preserved (*Astartus*, 1720; *BMB*, v. 20, and *Astianatte*, 1727; *HAM*, No. 262). **Antonio Lotti** (1667-1740), (*Alessandro severo, GMB*, No. 270); **Antonio Vivaldi** (1678-1741) (*La fide ninfa, M* 12b).

VI. Opera Buffa

  A.   In the late 17th century, comic episodes, which had been taken out of serious opera, were performed as *intermezzi* between acts. In the early 18th century, Italian comic opera developed as an independent form.

  B.   A typical *opera buffa* consisted of two acts. It was written in popular style with recitatives and melodious arias, and frequently included ensemble finales. The humor was lively, and often caricatured serious opera. Much use was made of rapid parlando for comic effects.

  C.   **Giovanni Battista Pergolesi** (1710-1736)

    1.   *La serva padrona* (The Maid mistress), Naples, 1733 (*CE*, v. 11; *ICDMI*, v. 23)

      a.   This two-act comic opera, called an "intermezzo," is the most famous early Italian *opera buffa.* There are only three characters (one a mute) and no chorus or ballet. The opera was widely known throughout Europe and exerted considerable influence on other composers.

b. The orchestra is composed of a quartet of strings, and both acts conclude with a duet. The overture may be a spurious work.

c. Characteristically the acts of *La serva padrona* originally alternated with the three acts of **Pergolesi's** *opera seria, Il prigionier superbo* (The conceited prisoner), Naples, 1733. (*CE*, v. 20).

2. *Livietta e Tracollo*, Naples, 1734 (*CE*, v. 11, pt. 3)

a. *Misero* (*TEM*, 314), a recitative and aria.

3. *Il maestro di musica* (The music master), Naples, 1731 (*CE*, v. 25)

4. *Lo Frate 'nnamerato* (The brother in love), Naples, 1732 (*CE*, v. 2)

VII. **Cantata and Oratorio**

A. The early composite chamber cantata was standardized by the Neapolitan composers into a four-movement form: recitative—aria—recitative—aria. The arias are in da capo form and of contrasting character. The recitatives show considerable harmonic freedom. Chamber cantatas contain some of the finest vocal music of the Late Baroque.

B. **Alessandro Scarlatti** (1659-1725)

1. **Scarlatti** wrote 600 solo cantatas with continuo, 30 chamber cantatas for two voices, and 60 solo cantatas with continuo and instrumental accompaniment. About 30, however, are of doubtful authorship.

2. *Lascia, deh lascia al fine di tormentarmi più*, 1709 (*GMB*, No. 260)

a. In this four-movement solo cantata, **Scarlatti** makes frequent use of diminished 7th chords and text characterization, such as on the word *"tormentor"* and *"cor mi sface"* (heart is broken).

C. **Agostino Steffani** (1654-1728)

1. **Steffani's** sacred music includes settings for six-part choir, double four-part chorus, as well as motets of one to three voices. The German influence of contrapuntal techniques include canon.

2. *Occhi, perche piangete?* (Eyes, why weep?) (*GMB*, No. 242)

a. Well developed imitative counterpoint is used in this secular chamber duet.

D. **Francesco Durante** (1684-1755)

1. Although **Durante** lived in the city of Neapolitan opera, he composed chamber cantatas and church music. The influence of the opera is seen in his daring vocal lines and harmonic sequences of chromatics, diminished 7ths, and suspension.

2. *Fiero acerbo* (Bold, harsh destiny of my soul) (*HAM*, No. 273)

E. **Benedetto Marcello** (1686-1739)

1. *Stravaganze d'Amore* (The extravagances of love) is a chamber cantata which deals in music and text with the intensities of love: caprice, exuberance, power, fury, patience, and grace.

a. *Amor tu sei* (Love, thou art that cruel one) (*TEM*, 304)

1) The first part of this aria is in quintuple meter, a device almost nonexistent in the Baroque.

2. *Il teatro alla moda* (The theatre à-la-mode), Venice, 1720 (*SR*, 518)

a. This famous satire is a sarcastic exposition of the follies of Italian opera, poets, singers, composers, stage hands, orchestra members, and others connected with opera.

F. Oratorios in operatic style were written to be performed during Lent when opera houses were closed. Although well-known progressive composers wrote oratorios, their church music was usually in the older contrapuntal style.

G. **Alessandro Scarlatti** (1659-1725)

1. Rome was the chief center of the oratorio and the Passion oratorio, which became a major subject for composers of church music.

2. *Passio D. N. Jesu Christi secundum Joannem*, Rome, 1708 (*M* 8c)

3.   *Agar et Ismaele esiliati* (Hagar and Ishmael exiled), 1683 (*AM*, v. 37, p. 74)

H.   **Antonio Lotti** (1667-1740)
1.   *Masses* (*DdT*, v. 60)
   a.   Included are eight four-part *a cappella* settings of the Mass for daily use and a *Requiem* (*DdT*, v. 60, p. 115).

I.   **Antonio Caldara** (1670-1736)
1.   Chamber cantatas (*DTÖ*, v. 75, pp. 1-61) and sacred solo motets (*DTÖ*, vols. 101, 102)
2.   *Stabat Mater*, Vienna, 1725 (*DTÖ*, v. 26, p. 34; *GMB*, No. 273)
   a.   A four-part mixed chorus with soloists and an orchestra for strings and trombones.
3.   Eight motets, Rome, 1714 (*DTÖ*, v. 26, pp. 1-33; *CS*, v. 27)
4.   *Crucifixus* (*DTÖ*, v. 26, p. 144), for four four-part choruses and continuo.

J.   **Giovanni Pergolesi** (1710-1736)
1.   *Stabat Mater*, Rome, 1735 (*CE*, v. 26; *M* 7b), for soprano, alto, and orchestra.
   a.   *Eja Mater* (*CE*, v. 26, p. 18; *GMB*, No. 275). Aria for alto and orchestra.

SELECTED BIBLIOGRAPHY

Books

1.   Dent, Edward J. *Alessandro Scarlatti: His Life and Works*. London: Edward Arnold, 1905. (Reprint of the new edition, 1960; London: Edward Arnold Publishers, 1962).
2.   Gasparini, Francisco. *L'Armonico Pratico al Cimbalo*, tr. Frank S. Stillings. *The Practical Harmonist at the Harpsichord*. New Haven: Yale University Press, 1968.
3.   Geminiani, Francesco. *The Art of Playing on the Violin*, 1751. Facsimile ed. David D. Boyden. Oxford, 1952.
4.   Kirkpatrick, Ralph. *Domenico Scarlatti*. Princeton: Princeton University Press, 1953.
5.   ———————" Domenico Scarlatti's Choral Music," in *Essays on Music in Honor of Archibald Thompson Davison*. Cambridge: Department of Music, Harvard University, 1957.
6.   Klenz, William. *Giovanni Maria Bononcini of Modena*. Durham, NC: Duke University Press, 1962. (contains sonatas by Bononcini and Cazzati).
7.   Kolneder, Walter. *Antonio Vivaldi, His Life and Work*, tr. Bill Hopkins. Berkeley: University of California Press, 1970.
8.   Paymer, Marvin E. *Giovanni Battista Pergolesi 1710-1736: A Thematic Catalogue of the Opera Omnia*. New York: Pendragon Press, 1977.
9.   Pincherle, Marc. *Corelli, His Life, His Work*, tr. Hubert E. M. Russell. New York: W. W. Norton, 1956, 1968.
10.   ———————*Vivaldi, Genius of the Baroque*, tr. Christopher Hatch. New York: W. W. Norton, 1957, 1962.
11.   Robinson, Michael F. *Naples and Neapolitan Opera*. London: Oxford University Press, 1972.
12.   Selfridge—Field, Eleanor. *Venetian Instrumental Music from Gabrieli to Vivaldi*. New York: Praeger Publishers, 1975.

Articles

1.   Arnold, Denis. "Vivaldi's church music: an introduction," *Early Music* 1 (1973), p. 66.
2.   Barbour, J. Murray. "Violin Intonation in the 18th Century," *JAMS* 5 (1952), p. 224.
3.   Boyden, David D. "Ariosti's Lessons for Viola d'Amore," *MQ* 32 (1946), p. 545.
4.   ———————"Prelleur, Geminiani, and Just Intonation," *JAMS* 4 (1951), p. 202.
5.   ———————"The Missing Italian Manuscript of Tartini's *Traité des Agrémens*," *MQ* 46

(1960), p. 315.

6. Boyden, David D. "The Violin and its Technique in the 18th Century," *MQ* 36 (1950), p. 9.
7. Brainard, Paul. "Tartini and the Sonata for Unaccompanied Violin," *JAMS* 14 (1961), p. 383.
8. Jacobi, Erwin R. "G, [*sic*] F. Nicolai's Manuscript of Tartini's *Regole per ben suonar il Violino*," tr. Willis Wager, *MQ* 47 (1961), p. 207.
9. Kirkendale, Ursula. "The War of the Spanish Succession Reflected in Works of Antonio Caldara," *Acta Mus* 36 (1964), p. 221.
10. Kirkpatrick, Ralph. "Domenico Scarlatti's Early Keyboard Works," *MQ* 37 (1951), p. 145.
11. Marcello, Benedetto. "Il Teatro alla Moda," tr. Reinhard G. Pauly, *MQ* 34 (1948), p. 371; 35 (1949), p. 85.
12. Newman, William S. "The Sonatas of Albinoni and Vivaldi," *JAMS* 5 (1952), p. 99.
13. Pauly, Reinhard G. "Benedetto Marcello's Satire on Early 18th-Century Opera," *MQ* 34 (1948), p. 222.
14. Pincherle, Marc. "Vivaldi and the Ospitali of Venice," *MQ* 24 (1938), p. 300.
15. Poultney, David. "Alessandro Scarlatti and the Transformation of Oratorio," *MQ* 59 (1973), p. 584.
16. Ransome, Antony. "Toward an authentic vocal style and technique in late baroque performance," *Early Music* 6 (1978), p. 417.
17. Selfridge-Field, Eleanor. "Vivaldi's esoteric instruments," *Early Music* 6 (1978), p. 332.
18. Schnoebelen, Anne. "Performance Practice at San Petronio in the Baroque," *Acta Mus* 41 (1969), p. 37.

Music

1. Albinoni, Tomaso. *Musiche vocali e strumentali sacre e profane*, v. 24.
2. Ariosti, Attilio.
    a. *Il Coriolano, BMB*, v. 19
    b. *Musiche vocali e strumentali sacre e profane*, vols. 26, 27, 28.
3. Corelli, Arcangelo. (CE) *Les Oeuvres de Arcangelo Corelli*, ed. J. Joachim and F. Chrysander. London: Augener, 1888-1891.
4. Locatelli, Pietro. *Monumenta Musica Neerlandica*, v. 4.
5. Marcello, Benedetto
    a. *Arianna. BMB*, v. 25; *Biblioteca di Rarita Musicali*, v. 4.
    b. *Cantate. ICMI* v. 2.
    c. *Gioza*, an oratorio. *ICMI*, v. 8.
    d. Sonatas, in *Musiche vocali e strumentali sacre e profane*, v. 29.
6. Pasquini, Bernardo.
    a. *Musiche vocali e strumentali sacre e profane*, v. 4 (*Introduzione e pastorale per organo*).
    b. *Musiche vocali e strumentali sacre e profane*, v. 5 (*Toccata con lo scherzo del cuccu per organo*).
7. Pergolesi, Giovanni Battista
    a. (CE) *Opera Omnia*, ed. F. Caffarelli. Roma: Gli amici della musica da camera, 1939-1942.
    b. *Stabat mater, Musiche vocali e strumentali sacre e profane*, vols. 7, 8.
8. Scarlatti, Alessandro
    a. *La Griselda*, ed. O. Trechsler. Kassel: Bärenreiter, 1960.
    b. Operas of Alessandro Scarlatti. *Harvard Publications in Music.* Cambridge: Harvard University Press, 1979
        v. 1 *Eraclea*
        v. 2 *Marco Attilio Regolo*

        v. 3   *Griselda*
        v. 4   *The Faithful Princess*
        v. 5   *Massimo Puppieno*

    c. *Passio D. N. Jesu Christi Secundum Johannen. Collegium Musicum*, Ser. 1, v. 1.

    d. *Primo e secondo libro di Toccate. ICMI*, v. 13; *Musiche vocali e strumentali sacre e profane*, v. 2.

9. Scarlatti, Domenico

    a. *Complete Keyboard Works in facsimile from the manuscript and printed sources* ed. Ralph Kirkpatrick, 18 vols. New York: Johnson Reprint Corporation, 1972.

    b. *Essercizi per Gravicembalo.* Farnborough, Hants., England: Gregg Press, 1967 (Facsimile, 1739 edition, London).

    c. *(CE) Opere complete per clavicembalo,* ed. Alessandro Longo, 10 vols. and one supplement. Milan: G. Ricordi, 1947-1951.

10. Tartini, Giuseppe. *Sinfonie in A. HM,* v. 53.

11. Torelli, Giuseppe

    a. *Concerto musicale,* Op. 11, No. 1. *Musiche vocali e strumentali sacre e profane,* v. 23.

    b. *Diletto Musicale,* Nos. 310, 496, 499 (Sinfonia for trumpets and strings).

    c. *Italian 17th & 18th century sinfonias & sonatas for trumpets and strings.* London: Musica Rara, *c.* 1976.

12. Vivaldi, Antonio

    a. *(CE) Opere strumentali,* ed. Gian Francesco Malipiero. Milan: G. Ricordi, 1948-

    b. *La fide ninfa. Instituta et Monumenta,* Ser. 1, v. 3.

    c. *Juditha triumphans: sacrum militare oratorium. Musice vocali e strumentali sacre e profane,* v. 10.

    d. *Motetti a canto solo con stromenti, LP,* v. 7.

13. Zipoli, Domenico. *Orgel- und Cembalowerke,* ed. Luigi Tagliavini. Heidelberg: Willy Müller, 1957.

10. Portrait of **Francesco M. Veracini**
by Francesco F. Richter (1744)

(6)

SONATA II

11.   The *Grave* and the beginning of the *Vivace* movement of
Sonata da chiesa a tre, Op. 1, No. 2, by Corelli.
From the edition published by I. Walsh, London (*c.* 1735)

OUTLINE IX

MUSIC IN FRANCE

LATE BAROQUE

Introduction – Chamber Music – Clavecin Music – Organ Music
Opera – Cantata and Motet
Bibliography of Books – Articles – Music

I. Introduction

A. After the time of **Lully** (d. 1687) the serious, formal Baroque style with its strict rules, conventions and forms, gradually blended into a lighter, more varied, entertaining, highly ornamented, and elegant style. This style reached its height in France during the regency and reign of Louis XV (1715-1774) and was reflected in the pastoral and ballet operas, chamber music, and especially clavecin music. The Italian concerto forms, however, did not suit the French taste, and they were attempted only by a few composers.

II. Chamber Music

A. French composers began to write trio and solo sonatas during the late 17th and early 18th centuries, and these works show the characteristic tendency toward program music. The first group of composers included **Marin Marais** (1656-1728), who wrote in the Baroque style of his teacher **Lully, François Couperin le Grand**, and the Belgian **Jean-Baptiste Loeillet** (1680-1730).

B. The ornamented rococo style, which appeared in works of **François Couperin**, became increasingly prominent in the next generation of composers which included **Jean-Baptiste Senaillé** (1687-1730), **Jacques Aubert** (1689-1753), **Charles Dieupart** (c. 1670-1740), **Rameau, Leclair,** and **Michel Blavet** (1700-1768).

C. **François Couperin le Grand** (1668-1733)
1. **Couperin,** the first true representative of the rococo, was clavecinist to Louis XIV and Louis XV, teacher of the royal family, organist of the Chapelle Royale and the church of St. Gervais. He was the most famous member of a musical family which was prominent from 1626 to 1860 as organists, clavecinists, and composers.
2. **Couperin** knew and admired the Italian style. His trio sonatas, written in the style of **Corelli,** were the earliest and most important ones in France. He used *basso continuo,* sometimes requiring as many as three clavecins.
   a. This facile style is subtle and animated; his melodies are expressive, and his ornamentation highly individualistic.
3. *Concerts Royaux,* Paris, 1722 *(CE,* v. 7)
   a. The four "Royal Concerts" are suites which were played at the chamber music concerts of Louis XIV. They include preludes, echoes, airs, and in addition various dance movements—allemandes, sarabandes, gavottes, menuets with trio, and gigues.
   b. The *Concerts* are mostly written in two parts, a melody and figured bass. A third part was sometimes indicated and occasionally almost completely written out *(Second Concert, Echos).* The third part, which may have been improvised, is usually "realized" in performances today.
   c. In the preface, **Couperin** has indicated that the *Concerts* are not for clavecin alone, but include the violin, oboe, viol, and bassoon. The keys are arranged by tones a fifth apart: G, D, A, E.
4. *Les Goûts-réünis,* 1724 *(CE,* v. 8)

a. The "United Tastes" consist of a series of trio *Concerts* for "all kinds of instruments" and continuo.

    1) No. 7 in G minor is Italian in style, and No. 9 in E major has an Italian title, *Ritratto dell'amore* (Portrait of love). The influence of **Corelli** is found in the second movement, *L'Enjouement.*

    2) **Couperin** stated, in regard to the French and Italian styles, that he had "always esteemed things of merit irrespective of author or nation." In various movements, especially Nos. 6 and 7, he has successfully imitated **Corelli's** style, but the varied rhythms, counterpoint, freedom, facile and expressive melodies, and ornaments are typical of **Couperin.**

b. *Le Parnasse ou l'Apothéose de Corelli, grande Sonade en Trio,* 1724 (*CE,* v. 10)

    1) This musical apotheosis, the last piece of the *Goûts-rëünis,* attempts to join French and Italian styles and consists of a series of seven movements depicting **Corelli's** reception on Mount Parnassus:

        1. **Corelli** at the foot of Mount Parnassus asks the Muses to receive him.

        2. **Corelli** expresses his joy at the reception given him on Parnassus and continues with those accompanying him.

        3. **Corelli** drinks at the fountain of Hypocrène.

        4. Enthusiasm of **Corelli** caused by the waters of Hypocrène.

        5. **Corelli** falls asleep while his companions play the slumber music which follows.

        6. The Muses awaken **Corelli** and place him beside Apollo on Parnassus.

        7. The thanks of **Corelli.**

5. *Apothéose de Lully,* 1725 (*CE,* v. 10)

  a. A large-scale work in honor of **Lully,** whom **Couperin** said was "the greatest man in music whom the preceding century had produced." French and Italian music are again in rivalry and **Couperin** reveals again his complete mastery of the two styles.

    1) Although written for violins, **Couperin** suggests that it may be performed on two clavecins or on any appropriate group of instruments.

    2) The 13 movements begin with **Lully** in the Elysian Fields. Apollo descends to offer **Lully** his violin and to take him to Parnassus, where he is entertained by **Corelli** and the Muses. Apollo persuades **Lully** and **Corelli** that the union of French taste should make music perfect, and **Lully** and **Corelli** alternate in playing solos and accompaniments to show this union. This work concludes with the "Peace at Parnassus," a *Sonade en trio* in four movements. The first movement is a French overture and the others are in Italian style.

6. *Les Nations,* 1726 (*CE,* v. 9)

  a. "The Nations" is for two treble and one bass instrument with continuo. It consists of four suites (*ordres*) with a lengthy *sonade* to open each suite entitled 1) *La Françoise,* 2) *L'Espagnole,* 3) *L'Impériale,* 4) *La Piémontoise.* Three of these *sonades* in the Italian *da chiesa* manner had originally been written in 1692 under different titles.

D. **Jean-Baptiste Loeillet** (1680-1730)

  1. **Loeillet** wrote sonatas for flute, oboe, and violin, flute trios, and clavecin pieces (*M* 8). He was a progressive composer, and his works show the influence of the Italian concerto style.

  2. *XII Sonates à une flûte et basse continue,* Op. 1, 2, 3, 4, 1705-1715 (*HM,* vols. 43, 162, 165, 166, 176, 181), 48 sonatas for flute or oboe and continuo.

E. **Jean-Philippe Rameau** (1683-1764)

  1. **Rameau's** greatest achievements as a composer were in the field of opera. He summed up his philosophy of music in the statement that the "expression of thought, sentiment and passions should be the true goal of music."

  2. *Pièces de Clavecin en Concert,* 1741

    a. These pieces consist of 16 short movements in five *Concerts* for clavecin and accompanying instruments. These include violin or traverse flute, tenor viol, or a second violin. The importance of the clavecin in these works is shown by **Rameau's** comment that "these pieces when played on the clavecin alone leave nothing to be desired; indeed, one would never suspect that they were capable of any other adornment." There is, however, some interdependence between clavecin and strings. Techniques include runs in triplets, uneven arpeggios, crossing of hands, and rushing scales before the cadence.

    b.   *La Livri,* First Concert, No. 2 (*SS,* 720)
       1)   This rich-textured *tombeau* is dedicated to Comte de Livri.
    c.   *La Forqueray,* Fifth Concert, No. 1 (*SS,* 722)
       1)   This elaborate fugue was possibly presented to Jean-Baptiste Forqueray, a composer and viol player, on his wedding day.

  F. **Jean-Marie Leclair** (1697-1749) (*NagMA,* v. 209)
    1. **Leclair,** a pupil of **Giovanni Battista Somis,** is the outstanding representative of the French violin school and, along with **Jacques Aubert,** wrote the first French concertos which were strongly indebted to Italian models. **Leclair** used an advanced violin technique with unusual agility in bowing, double stops, high positions, and ornamentation.
    2. *Second livre de Sonates pour le Violon et pour la Flûte traversière avec la Basse continue,* Op. 2, *c.* 1728 (*PAM,* v. 27)
      a. *Aria* (*GMB,* No. 294)
    3. *Troisième livre de sonates à violon avec la basse continue,* Op. 5, 1734 (*RRMB,* vols. 4, 5)
      a. *Sonata,* Op. 5, No. 12, first movement (*HAM,* No. 278; *RRMB,* v. 5)

III.   **Clavecin Music**

  A. Clavecin (harpsichord) music was the most representative music of the French Late Baroque. Composers include **Louis Marchand** (1669-1732), **Louis-Claude d'Aquin** (1694-1764) (*MMF,* Ser 1, v. 24), and **François Couperin,** the greatest of French clavecinists.
  B. The clavecin pieces, all in the same key, resembled the form of a suite (*ordre*). Although they began with a few dance movements in the character of the allemande, courante, and sarabande, they also included a considerable number of imaginative and descriptive pieces.
  C. **François Couperin le Grand** (1668-1733)
    1. **Couperin's** clavecin music forms a musical portrait of his time. Picturesque titles were used for characters, ideas, types, and descriptions. He used typical small forms, short phrases, repetitions in various registers, and often elaborate ornamentation.
    2. *Pièces de Clavecin,* v. I, 1713; v. II, 1716; v. III, 1722; v. IV, 1730 (*CE,* vols. 2–5; *MMF,* Ser. 1, v. 9; *LP,* vols. 21-24; *AM,* v. 26, p. 92)
      a. These 27 *ordres* in four volumes are collections of from 4 to 20 compositions. Each *ordre* is often in the same key, with some use of the opposite mode and related keys; some form miniature scenes, such as *Les Folies françoises* (*CE,* v. 4; *MMF,* Ser. 1, v. 9, Book 3, p. 5)
        1) *La Galante,* Book 2, Ordre 12, No. 3 (*CE,* v. 3; *MM,* p. 170)
        2) *La Rossignol en amour* (The nightingale in love), Book 3, Ordre 14, No. 1; (*CE,* v. 4; *HAM,* No. 265a)
        3) *Soeur Monique,* Book 3, Ordre 18, No. 3 (*CE,* v. 4; *HAM,* No. 265b)
        4) *La Fleurie ou La tendre Nanette,* Book 1, Ordre 1, No. 16 (*CE,* v. 2; *GMB,* No. 264,1)
        5) *La Ténébreuse* (The mysterious), Book 1, Ordre 3, No. 1 (*CE,* v. 2; *GMB,* No. 264,2)
        6) *L'Auguste,* Book 1, Ordre 1, No. 1 (*CE,* v. 2; *MSO,* v. 1, p. 116)
    3. *L'Art de toucher le clavecin,* 1716, revised edition, 1717 (*CE,* v. 1; *MMF,* Ser. 2, v. 23; *B* 3)
      a. This "method" includes observations on teaching, developing technique, style, performance practice, a complete table of ornaments, and many examples of fingering from his own works. The book was known to **Bach,** as were **Couperin's** clavecin works.

D. **Jean-Philippe Rameau** (1683-1764)

1. **Rameau**, an outstanding French musician of his time, was a composer, organist, clavecinist, and theorist.

2. *Traité de l'harmonie*, 1722 (*MMF*, Ser. 2, v. 3; *B* 12b, Ser. 3, v. 1; *B* 12f) (*SR*, 564)

   a. In this treatise **Rameau** developed a new system of music theory on which modern theory is founded: 1) chord building is by thirds; 2) a chord and its inversion is classified as the same chord, and 3) the fundamental bass consists of an imaginary bass line made up of the roots of the chords.

3. Other theoretical treatises by **Rameau** are *Démonstration du Principe de l'Harmonie*, 1750 (*MMF*, Ser. 2, v. 4; *B* 12b, Ser. 3, v. 3) and *Nouvelles Réflections sur la Démonstration du Principe de l'Harmonie*, 1752.

4. **Rameau** also revived, and later discarded, the so-called "dualistic theory" of **Zarlino**, which is that the minor triad is an exact mirror of the major triad, reading down with the same intervals as ascending (g'–b'–d''; descending g'–e-flat'–c').

5. **Rameau** composed three collections of clavecin pieces, most of which are *genre* pieces with descriptive titles.

   a. *Premier Livre de pièces de clavecin*, 1706 (*CE*, v. 1, pp. 1-18)

   b. *Pièces de clavecin*, 1724 (*CE*, v. 1, pp. 19-59; *MMF*, Ser. 1, v. 7)

   1) This collection and the following one include important prefaces on fingering and ornaments. **Rameau** shows his interest in harmony rather than in melody in these pieces and, in this regard, was opposed by **Rousseau** (1712-1778), who believed melody was more important than harmony.

   2) *Tourbillons* (Whirlwinds) (*MSO*, v. 1, p. 115)

   c. *Nouvelles Suites de pièces de clavecin*, *c.* 1728 (*CE*, v. 1, pp. 60-103; *MMF*, Ser. l, v. 13)

   1) Accompanying this book is **Rameau's** *Méthode de la mecanique des doigts* (Method of fingering) which he later expanded into his *Dissertation sur les différentes méthodes d'accompagner pour le clavecin ou l'orgue*, 1732 (*MMF*, Ser. 2, v. 118).

IV. **Organ Music**

A. **François Couperin le Grand** (1668-1733)

1. **Couperin** became organist at Saint-Gervais, Paris, in his 18th year and remained there until his death. He was also organist at the Chapelle Royale and music master to the royal family.

2. *Pièces d'orgue consistantes en deux Messes*, 1690 (*AMO*, v. 5; *LO*, vols. 1, 2; *M* 4)

   a. The two organ Masses were brought out in manuscript copies with a printed title page which stated that they were composed by his uncle, "**François Couperin, Sieur de Croüilly**." However, it is generally considered that the Masses were composed by the younger **François le Grand**. The Masses, especially the first, reach a high point of elegance, expression, and in the fusion of sacred and secular styles in French organ music of the Late Baroque.

3. [*Messe pour les Paroisses*]

   a. The first organ Mass is for use in parish churches (*Paroisses pour les Festes Solemnelles*). It consists of versets based on the chants of Mass IV for the first and last movements of the Kyrie, and the first movements of the Gloria, Sanctus-Benedictus, and Agnus Dei. All the other versets are freely composed. A brilliant Offertoire and the Deo gratias are also included.

4. [*Messe pour les Couvents*]

   a. The second organ Mass is for use in the smaller abbey churches (*Couvents de Religieux et Religieuses*). The order of the first Mass is followed, but all the versets are freely composed, and an Elévation is added in place of the Benedictus.

B. **Jean-François Dandrieu** (1682-1738)

1. Successor to **Lebègue** at Saint-Merry, Paris, at Saint-Barthélemy, and the Chapelle Royale.

2. *Premier livre de pièces d'orgue*, 1735 (*AMO*, v. 7; *M* 5)
   a. Contains six suites of pieces in different tones, each beginning with an *Offertoire*. Following each suite are six versets for the *Magnificat* on the same tone.
3. *Noëls, O filii, Chansons de Saint-Jacques, Carillons*
   a. It is possible that at least part of this collection was composed by **Dandrieu's** uncle, **Pierre** (*c.* 1600-1733).

C. **Louis Marchand** (1669-1732)
1. Successor to **Nivers** at the Chapelle Royale and organist at Saint-Honoré, Paris.
2. *Pièces choisies, Livre premier, c.* 1700 (*AMO*, vols. 3, 5; *LO*, v. 1)
   a. Contains two suites, couplets (versets) for the *Te Deum*, and several more groups of pieces. His music reaches a higher level than many of the Late Baroque French organist-composers.

D. **Gaspard Corrette** (*c.* 1680-*c.* 1733)
1. *Messe du 8.ᵉ ton pour l'orgue à l'usage des Dames Religieuses*, 1703 (*M* 2)
   a. Contains nine free-composed versets for the Ordinary, two *Graduels*, an *Offerte* and two *Elévations*.

E. **Michel Corrette** (1709-1795), son of **Gaspard**
1. His works include two books of organ music and instruction books for clavecin, violin, cello, flute, harp, guitar, and mandolin.
2. *Premier livre d'orgue*, 1737 (*M* 3)
   a. Contains four groups of six versets each for the tones of the *Magnificat*. One set of versets, in three sharps, **Corrette** described as "very useful for nuns."
3. *Nouveau livre de Noëls avec un Carillon. Pour le Clavecin ou l'orgue, c.* 1740 (*M* 3)
   a. Contains 19 *Noëls* for clavecin or organ, arranged in four suites with a *Carillon*. **Corrette** includes notes on registration and tempo, and gives directions for playing the *Noëls* on the keyboard alone, and with strings, flutes, and harpsichord in "concerto" style.

F. **Guilain [Wilhelm] Freinsberg** (*fl.* 1700)
1. This German musician, a friend of **Marchand**, settled in Paris where he taught clavecin.
2. *Pièces d'orgue pour le Magnificat*, 1706 (*AMO*, v. 7)
   a. This book contains four suites of seven versets each which show the influence of **Marchand**.

G. **Pierre du Mage** (1676-1751)
1. Born in Beauvais, **du Mage** studied with **Marchand** in Paris. He became organist at the convent church of Saint-Quentin, and later at the Cathedral of Laon.
2. *Premier livre d'orgue*, 1708 (*AMO*, v. 3; *M* 7)
   a. Contains a suite of eight pieces in the first mode (Dorian). The suite concludes with a *Grand jeu* in the style of a French overture.

H. **Louis-Nicolas Clérambault** (1676-1749)
1. Organist to the king, organist and master of the clavecin at Saint-Cyr, and organist at Saint-Sulpice, Paris.
2. *Premier livre d'orgue contenant deux Suites du Iᵉʳ et du IIᵉ ton dédié à Monsieur Raison*, 1710 (*AMO*, v. 3; *LO*, v. 2; *M* 1)
   a. Each of the two suites contains seven secular pieces in different styles. These include *Duos* and *Trios* in *galant style*, and expressive monothematic *Fugue*, an ostinato figure in the *Récits de Cromorne et Cornet séparé*, and a *Récit de Nazard* in the style of an Italian *siciliano*.

I. **Louis-Claude d'Aquin** (1694-1772)
1. One of four organists at Notre Dame, Paris, **d'Aquin** was a brilliant virtuoso, skillful improviser, and famous composer of variations on *Noëls*.
2. *Nouveau livre de Noëls pour l'orgue et le Clavecin dont le plupart peuvent s'executer sur les violons, flûtes, hautbois, etc., c.* 1740 (*AMO*, v. 3; *LO*, v. 2; *CO*, v. 1; *M* 6ab)
   a. **d'Aquin** was the last important composer of the 18th-century French organ school.

V. Opera

A. *Opéra-ballet,* a new operatic form, developed during the period between the death of **Lully** in 1687 and **Rameau's** first opera in 1733. Opera composers of this period, still under the influence of **Lully,** include **Colasse, Destouches,** and **Campra.**

B. *Opéra-ballet* consisted largely of ballet in order to give opportunity for dancing and stage effects. There was no unified plot. Many Italian characteristics appeared, such as the use of Italian settings, arias, some use of the da capo form, and Italian harmonic devices.

    1. **Pascal Colasse** (1647-1709)
       a. *Thétis et Pelée,* 1689 (*COF,* v. 9)
       b. *Les saisons* (The seasons), 1695 (*COF,* v. 8)
    2. **André Destouches** (1673-1749)
       a. *Issé,* 1697 (*COF,* v. 10)
       b. *Omphale,* 1701 (*COF,* v. 11)
       c. *Les éléments,* 1721 (*COF,* v. 14) with **Michel-Richard de Lalande** (1657-1726)

C. **André Campra** (1660-1744)

    1. **Campra** was one of the most remarkable dramatic composers of his day, although his position in French opera has been eclipsed by **Lully** and **Rameau.**
    2. *L'Europe galante,* 1697 (*COF,* v. 4)
       a. **Campra's** first *opéra-ballet* with prologue and four *entrées* was designed for public performance with professional dancers. It consists principally of divertissements (dances) with airs, ballets, elaborate stage effects, and little plot.
    3. *Les Festes vénitiennes,* 1710 (*COF,* v. 5; *LP,* v. 19)
       a. This very successful *opéra-ballet* contains a prologue and three (later expanded to five) *entrées* with arias in the Italian style (called *ariette*). They make some use of the da capo form, florid vocal lines, and harmonic materials influenced by the Italians.
       b. *Chaconne,* the final dance of the third *entrée* (*TEM,* 270).
       c. *Quelle audace!* (What audacity!), a recitative between the singing master and the student, Leontine, a soprano (*GMB,* No. 261).

D. **Jean-Philippe Rameau** (1683-1764)

    1. **Rameau** began his career as a serious opera composer at the age of 50 with *Hippolyte et Aricie,* Paris, 1733. This opera started a violent discussion between "Lullistes" and "Ramistes." The "Lullistes" considered **Rameau** a traitor to French music because of what they thought was his Italian style. He wrote a long preface to his *opéra-ballet, Les Indes galantes* (The gallant Indies), Paris, 1735 (*COF,* v. 34), in which he expressed his sincere admiration for **Lully,** but the "Lullistes" were not satisfied.
    2. **Rameau's** finest serious operas were written before his appointment as composer to Louis XV in 1745. After that time his operas became lighter and more characteristically rococo. He used large forms, da capo arias with florid passages, and dramatic choruses. His harmonic style is rich, clear, and varied, and he made frequent use of diminished 7ths, chromatic alterations, and remote modulations.
    3. Instrumental music included as many as 47 or more players and was an important feature of **Rameau's** operas.
       a. His early overtures were generally in the standard French form, sometimes thematically connected with the opera. In later operas he developed program overtures, which led into the opera without a break, and experimented with other types of overtures.
       b. Short programmatic symphonies were incorporated into the operas, illustrating scenes on the stage (earthquakes, storms). Dances, played by the orchestra and sometimes sung, are numerous and varied.
    4. Opera had already begun to decline in **Rameau's** time, due partly to poor librettos and a plot which served only to carry the divertissements.
    5. *Hippolyte et Aricie,* 1733 (*CE,* v. 6; *COF,* v. 33)

6. *Castor et Pollux*, Paris, 1737 (*CE*, v. 8; *COF*, v. 30)
    a. The theme of the typical French overture (p. 1) is used in the finale (p. 322). A dramatic chorus (p. 63), chromatic lines (p. 62), and a large chaconne form (pp. 337-355) are other features.
    b. *Gavotte* in rondeau (*GMB*, No. 296, 2)
    c. *Ma voix puissant maître du monde* (My voice, powerful master of the world) (*GMB*, No. 297)
    d. *Séjour de l'éternelle paix* (Abode of eternal peace) (*CE*, v. 8, p. 219; *MM*, 174)
7. *Dardanus*, Paris, 1739 (*CE*, v. 10; *COF*, v. 31)
    a. The Prologue has examples of dance airs and Italian style arias (*ariette* or *air gracieux*). There is an extended scene for chorus, soloists, and orchestra (p. 310).
    b. *Sommeil* (Slumber song) (*HAM*, No. 277) is instrumental music to accompany a dream scene.
    c. *Mars, Bellone, guidez nos coupe* (Mars, Bellona, guide our onslaught) (*GMB*, No. 297)
8. *Le Temple de la Gloire*, Paris, 1745 (*CE*, v. 14)
    a. *Ramage des oiseaux* (Warbling of the birds) (*HAM*, No. 276)

E. *Opéra comique*
1. *Opéra comique* had its beginning in vaudeville comedies which developed in the time of **Lully**.   These comedies were performed with spoken dialogue to which was added popular tunes (*vaudevilles*) with new texts.
2. The vaudeville comedies, known as *opéra comique* after about 1715, were often a satire on serious opera.
    a. Under the influence of the Italian *opera buffa,* original music was later substituted for borrowed airs but spoken dialogue continued to be used. The *opéra comique* ended with a "vaudeville final," a strophic song with refrain.
3. **Jean-Jacques Rousseau** (1712-1778)
    a. Literary genius, famous philosopher, amateur musician, and author of papers and books on music (*MMF*, Ser. 2, v. 31), **Rousseau** made his most important contribution with his *Dictionnaire de Musique*, Paris and Amsterdam, 1768.
    b. In the later 18th century there was a reaction against artificiality and a "return to nature," and there was continued rivalry between grand and popular opera, and between the French and Italian styles in what was called the *Guerre des Bouffons* (War of the buffoons). King Louis XV favored the music of **Lully** and **Rameau**, and the Queen favored the music of the Italian buffoons (*opera buffa*) as did **Rousseau**. In this controversy was **Rousseau's** most important writing, *Lettre sur la musique française,* Paris, 1753 (*SR*, 636-654).
    c. *Le Devin du village* (The village soothsayer), Fontainebleau, 1752
        1) The simple libretto, based on a pastoral theme, as well as the music is by **Rousseau**. The opera is in the Italian *opera buffa* style, but the music is continuous without spoken dialogue. **Rousseau** produced this *opéra-comique* for the king in Fontainebleau, then later in Paris where it remained in the repertoire until 1829 with more than 400 performances.
        2) *Allons danser sous les ormeaux* (Let us dance under the elms) (*HAM*, No. 291)

VI. **Cantata and Motet**

A. Most French Baroque composers made some contributions to church music, but there were few significant works.
B. **André Campra** (1660-1744) (*CS*, vols. 6, 9, 17, 32, 56, 63)
C. **François Couperin** (1668-1733)
1. *Leçons des Ténèbres* (Lessons for Holy Week), 1713-1715 (*LP*, v. 8; *CS*, vols. 3,4)
    a. The *Leçons* are based on Latin texts from Jeremiah and interspersed with Hebrew phrases. The first two are for solo voice and the third is for two solo voices accom-

panied with viol and organ continuo.
- b.   Elaborate ornamentation, long suspensions, chromaticism, cross relations, bold harmonies and key changes create works of dramatic power. They include recitative, arioso, and aria, and make some use of canon.
- 2.   Motets (*LP*, v. 45)
  - a.   The motets, similar to the cantata, contain arias, recitatives, and instrumental ritornellos. **Couperin** makes little use of the chorus in these motets.
- D.   **Jean-Philippe Rameau** (1683-1764)
  - 1.   *Laboravi clamans* (I am weary with my crying) (*CMA*, 337)
    - a.   This contrapuntal one-movement motet for five voices and organ continuo was used by **Rameau** in his *Traité de l'harmonie* as an example of fugue. It is based on Psalm 69:3.

SELECTED BIBLIOGRAPHY

Books

1.   Brunold, Paul. *François Couperin,* tr. J. B. Hanson. Paris: Lyrebird Press, 1949.
2.   Cauchie, Maurice. *Thematic Index of the Works of François Couperin.* Monaco: Lyrebird Press, 1949.
3.   Couperin, François. *L'Art de toucher le clavecin,* ed. and tr. Margery Halford. Port Washington, New York: Alfred Publishing Co., 1974.
4.   Dandrieu, Jean-François. *Principes de l'accompagnement de Clavecin, c.* 1719. Geneva: Minkoff Reprint, 1972. (Facsimile)
5.   Farrar, C. R. *Michel Corrette and Flute-playing in the Eighteenth Century.* New York: Institute of Mediaeval Music, 1970.
6.   Girdlestone, Cuthbert. *Jean-Philippe Rameau, His Life and Works.* London: Cassell, 1957. (Reprint, New York: Dover Publications, 1969)
7.   Mellers, Wilfrid. *François Couperin and the French Classical Tradition.* London: Dennis Dobson, 1950; New York: Roy Publishers, 1951.
8.   Mather, Betty Bang. *Interpretation of French Music from 1676-1775 for Woodwind and Other Performers, Additional Comments on German and Italian Music.* New York: McGinnes & Marx, 1973.
9.   Raguenet, François. *A Comparison between the French and Italian Musick and Opera's translated from the French; With some Remarks, To which is added A Critical Discourse upon Opera's in England, and a Means proposed for their Improvement.* London, 1709. (Facsimile, Farnborough, Hantshire, England: Gregg International Publishers, 1968)
10. Rameau, Jean-Philippe.
  - a.   *Code de musique pratique,* 1760   (*MMF*, Ser. 2, v. 5)
  - b.   *Complete Theoretical Writings*   (*MMF*, Ser. 3, vols. 1, 2, 3)
  - c.   *Démonstration du principe de l'harmonie,* 1750   (*MMF*, Ser. 2, v. 4)
  - d.   *Génération harmonique,* 1737   (*MMF*, Ser. 2, v. 6)
  - e.   *Nouveau système de musique théorique,* 1726   (*MMF*, Ser. 2, v. 7)
  - f.   *Traité de l'harmonie réduite à ses principes naturels; divisé en quatre livres,* 1722   (*MMF*, Ser. 2, v. 3)
  - g.   *Treatise on Harmony,* tr. Philip Gosset. New York: Dover Publications, 1971.
11. Rousseau, Jean-Jacques. *Traités sur la musique.* Geneva, 1781. (Facsimile, *MMF,* Ser. 2, v. 31)
12. Tunley, David. *The Eighteenth Century French Cantata.* London: Dobson, 1974.

Articles

1. Beechey, Gwilym. "Daquin and His Keyboard Music," *Organ* 52, No. 208 (1973), p. 184.
2. Brofsky, Howard. "Notes on the French Concerto," *JAMS* 19 (1966), p. 87.
3. Brenet, Michel. "French Military Music in the Reign of Louis XIV," *MQ* 3 (1917), p. 340.
4. Cauchie, Maurice. "The High Lights of French Opéra Comique," *MQ* 25 (1939), p. 306.
5. Dahms, Walter. "The 'Gallant' Style of Music," *MQ* 11 (1925), p. 356.
6. Donington, Robert. "The Problem of Inequality," *MQ* 53 (1967), p. 503.
7. Foster, Donald H. "The Oratorio in Paris in the 18th Century," *Acta Mus* 47 (1975), p. 67.
8. Fleury, Louis. "The Flute and Flutists in the French Art of the Seventeenth and Eighteenth Centuries," *MQ* 9 (1923), p. 515.
9. Neumann, Frederick. "The dotted note and the so-called French style," *Early Music* 5 (1977), p. 310.
10. ——————"François Couperin and the Downbeat Doctrine for Appoggiaturas," *Acta Mus* 41 (1969), p. 71.
11. ——————"External Evidence and Uneven Notes," *MQ* 52 (1966), p. 114.
12. ——————"Ornament and Structure," *MQ* 56 (1970), p. 153.
13. ——————"The French 'inégales,' Quantz, and Bach," *JAMS* 18 (1965), p. 313.
14. Richards, James E. "Structural Principles in the Grand Motets of Michel-Richard de Lalande (1657-1726)," *JAMS* 11 (1958), p. 119.
15. Sachs, Curt. "Bach and Blavet," *MQ* 30 (1944), p. 84.
16. Savage, Roger. "Rameau at Covent Garden," *Early Music* 5 (1977), p. 499.
17. Vene, Ruggero. "The Origin of *Opera Buffa*," *MQ* 21 (1935), p. 33.
18. Verba, E. Cynthia. "The Development of Rameau's Thoughts on Modulation and Chromatics," *JAMS* 26 (1973), p. 69.
19. Tiersot, Julien. "Concerning Jean-Jacques Rousseau, The Musician," *MQ* 17 (1931), p. 341.
20. ——————"Rameau," *MQ* 14 (1928), p. 77.

Music

1. Clérambault, Louis-Nicolas. *Premier livre d'orgue,* ed. Norbert Dufourcq. Paris: Schola Cantorum, 1954.
2. Corrette, Gaspard. *Messe du 8ᵉ ton pour l'orgue.* Paris: Schola Cantorum.
3. Corrette, Michel. *Premier Livre d'orgue* and *Nouveau livre de Noëls,* ed. Gwilym Beechey. Madison: A-R Editions, 1974.
4. Couperin, François.
    a. (CE) *Oeuvres complètes.* Paris: Editions de l'Oiseau-lyre, 1932-1933.
    b. *Pièces d'orgue* (two masses), ed. Paul Brunold. Monaco: Editions de l'Oiseau-lyre, 1949.
5. Dandrieu, Jean-François. *Noëls,* 4 volumes. Paris: Schola Cantorum, 1955-1956.
6. d'Aquin, Louis-Claude.
    a. *Nouveau livre de Noëls.* Paris: Schola Cantorum, 1955.
    b. *Nouveau livre de Noëls.* Mainz: Schott.
7. du Mage, Pierre. *Livre d'orgue,* ed. Felix Raugel. Paris: Schola Cantorum, 1952.
8. Loeillet, Jean-Baptiste. *Werken voor clavicembel. Monumenta Musicae Belgicae,* v. 1. Antwerp, 1932. (*Lessons for the harpsichord or spinet* and *Six suits of lessons for the harpsichord or spinet.*)
9. Rameau, Jean-Philippe. *Oeuvres complètes,* 18 volumes. Paris: Durand, 1895-1913.

12.   The first page of **Couperin's** *Les Folies françoises*,
from the first edition of the *Pièces de clavecin*, III (1722).

OUTLINE X

MUSIC IN GERMANY

LATE BAROQUE BEFORE AND CONTEMPORARY WITH BACH

Introduction — Italian Opera in Germany and Austria — German Opera
Oratorio and Passion Music — Secular Cantatas — Odes — Continuo Songs
Orchestra and Chamber Music — Harpsichord and Clavichord Music — Organ Music
Protestant Church Music — Catholic Church Music
Bibliography of Books — Articles — Music

I. Introduction

    A. The composers of the Late Baroque in Germany were strongly influenced by Italian and French styles. The Italian concerto and sonata, the French overture, dance suite, ornamentation, and programmatic tendencies were adapted to the typical German solid harmonic and contrapuntal style. **J. S. Bach** (*Outline XI*) achieved a synthesis of the three styles.

II. Italian Opera in Germany and Austria

    A. Italian opera was sung in the musical centers of Germany and Austria, and native German opera was not established until the Late Baroque.
    B. **Francesco Conti** (1681-1731)
        1. A celebrated theorboist, **Conti** performed at the Vienna court from 1701 and was appointed court composer in 1713. He wrote 16 operas, the most successful being *Don Chisciotte*, 1719, after Cervantes' *Don Quixote*.
        a. *Menuet*, from *Griselda*, Vienna, 1725 (*GMB*, No. 274)
    C. **Johann Adolph Hasse** (1699-1783)
        1. Highly acclaimed throughout Europe, **Hasse** conducted most of his 94 operas in Dresden .
        2. *Arminio*, Milan, 1730 (*EDM*, vols. 27, 28; *AM*, v. 45, p. 133)
        3. *Il Ruggiero* or *L'Eroica Gratitudini*, Milan, 1771 (*M 8*)
    D. **Karl Heinrich Graun** (1704-1759)
        1. **Graun** began his career as a tenor at Brunswick where he learned operas by **Lotti** and other Venetians. In 1740 he was commissioned by Frederick the Great of Prussia to direct the new opera house in Berlin, where he composed most of his 36 operas.
        2. *Montezuma*, Berlin, 1755 (*DdT*, v. 15)
        a. The opera is based on the conquest of Mexico by Cortez and is set to a libretto by King Frederick.
        b. *Godi l'amabile* (Enjoy the friendly present moment) (*HAM*, No. 282)
        1) This is a cavatina which became very common in place of the da capo aria.
    E. **Agostino Steffani** (1654-1728)
        1. **Steffani**, the most oustanding Italian opera composer in Germany, wrote 18 operas. These combined elements of the German (counterpoint), French (overture), and Italian (da capo aria) styles. He exerted a strong influence on **Reinhard Keiser** and on **Handel**, his successor at the court of Hanover (*DTB*, v. 11).
        2. **Steffani**'s French overtures are modeled after **Lully** and are some of the first to contain trio sections in the fast movements. In the arias, "motto" beginnings are common.
        3. *Alarico*, Munich, 1687 (*DTB*, v. 21; *AM*, v. 45, p. 54)
        4. *Tassilone*, Düsseldorf, 1709 (*DRM*, v. 8)
        5. *Henrico Leone*, Hanover, 1689
        a. Overture (*NagMA*, v. 141); *Un balen* (A flash of uncertain hope) (*HAM*, No. 244)

F. **Johann Joseph Fux** (1660-1741)
1. Known today principally as a theorist (*Gradus ad Parnassum,* Vienna, 1725) (*MMF,* Ser. 2, v. 24; *CE,* Ser. 7, v. 1), this Austrian composer and organist became court composer in 1698 and head *Kapellmeister* in 1715, successor to **Marc Antonio Ziani.**
2. Fux wrote 18 operas (*CE,* Ser. 5, vols. 1, 2), 10 oratorios (*CE,* Ser. 4, v. 1), and other church music (*CE,* Ser. 1, 2, 3). The operas are conservative and, as might be expected, many contrapuntal devices are used in the choruses, ensembles, and extended da capo arias.
3. *Costanza e fortezza* (Constancy and fortitude), Vienna, 1723 (*DTÖ,* vols. 34, 35; *SCMA,* v. 2; *AM,* v. 45, p. 69)
    a. *Saprei morir* (I die with pleasure) (*DTÖ,* vols. 34-35, p. 171; *GMB,* No. 272)

III. **German Opera**

A. **Sigmund Theophil Staden** (1607-1655)
1. **Staden,** a composer and organist, wrote the first native German opera, both libretto and music.
    a. *Seelewig* (The Soul), Nuremberg, 1644
        1) A spiritual pastoral with an allegorical plot, this opera is in the monodic style for solo voices and figured bass with short instrumental preludes and interludes.
        2) *Die schwanke Nachtigall* (The wavering nightingale) (*GMB,* No. 195)
B. The term *"singspiel"* was used at first for both serious and comic operas. After 1750 the term was generally applied to comic operas with some spoken dialogue. The English ballad opera by **Charles Coffey,** *The Devil to Pay,* 1731, played an important part in the development of the *singspiel.*
C. German opera was produced during the last part of the 17th century and early 18th century at the courts of Brunswick, Wolfenbüttel, and Weissenfels, and in the cities of Leipzig and Hamburg. The second public opera house in Europe (the first in Venice, 1637) opened in Hamburg in 1678 and flourished for the next sixty years.
D. **Johann Wolfgang Franck** (*fl.* 1679-1686)
1. *Die drey Töchter Cecrops* (The three daughters of Cecrops), Hamburg, 1679 (*DTB,* v. 38)
E. **Johann Sigismund Kusser** (1660-1727)
1. **Kusser** spent eight years in Paris where he was a friend of **Lully** and acquired an experience in French music. He wrote eight operas and some orchestral suites.
2. *Erindo,* Hamburg, 1693 (*M 10; GMB,* No. 250)
F. **Georg Kaspar Schürmann** (1672-1751)
1. *Ludovicus Pius,* Brunswick, 1726 (*PAM,* v. 17)
G. **Reinhard Keiser** (1674-1739)
1. The foremost opera composer of his time in Germany, **Keiser** wrote over 120 operas (only 25 are extant) during his 45 years in Hamburg.
2. He was a master of orchestration, melody, and dramatic expression. He used French overtures, ariosos, da capo arias, continuo arias of the popular *singspiel* type, and solo and ensemble recitatives, choruses, and ballets. Italian influence is seen in his use of the concerto style with unison passages and rapid bass lines. The overtures and dance suites show French influence.
3. *Der hochmütige, gestürtzte und wieder erhabene Croesus* (The haughty, fallen, and again exalted Croesus), 1711 (*DdT,* vols. 37-38)
    a. In the revised edition of 1730, the ballets are omitted and the French overture is substituted for the Italian type.
    b. *Kleine Vöglein* (Little bird), from Act II, scene 1 (*DdT,* vols 37-38, p. 84; *GMB,* No. 269). The ritornello of this soprano and tenor duet employs the *zuffolo,* a primitive shepherd flute played by a shrill-sounding *schalmei.*

      c. *Hoffe noch* (Hope yet) (*DdT,* vols. 37-38, p. 17; *TEM,* 277)
    4. *Der geliebte Adonis* (The beloved Adonis), Hamburg, 1697
      a. *Fahret wohl* (Farewell, beloved eyes), aria   (*HAM,* No. 267)
    5. *Der lacherliche Prinz Jodelet* (The ridiculous Prince Jodelet), Hamburg, 1726 (*PAM,* v. 17)
  H. **Georg Philipp Telemann** (1681-1767)
    1. **Telemann,** a friend of **J. S. Bach** and one of the most famous musicians of his time, composed numerous works, including cantatas, operas, Passions, and orchestral, chamber, harpsichord, and organ music. **Telemann** and **Johann Mattheson** (1681-1764) were the last German opera composers of the Hamburg School. He composed some 40 operas in the "gallant" style of the 18th century.
    2. *Pimpinone* or *Die ungleiche Heirat* (The unequal marriage), Hamburg, 1725 (*EDM,* v. 6; *AM,* v. 45, p. 88)

IV. Oratorio and Passion Music

  A. During the decline of native German opera about 1730, composers turned to the writing of semi-secular oratorios, Passions, and cantatas which provided the principal opportunities for high quality dramatic music.
    1. The oratorical Passion interspersed the Biblical Passion narrative with other verses of Scripture, hymns, and various sacred texts. These works were operatic rather than devotional and focused more toward the concert hall than the church. This form flourished from about 1650 to 1750 and developed into the Passion proper around 1700.
    2. The text most frequently used was the famous Passion poem by **Barthold Heinrich Brockes** (1680-1747) of Hamburg, *Der für die Sünde der Welt gemarterte und sterbende Jesus* (That for the sin of the world Jesus was wounded and died), 1712. The Evangelist's texts are paraphrased in poetry rather than being straight Scripture, and allegorical figures are added.
    3. The text was used by **Keiser** in 1712, **Telemann** and **Handel** in 1716, **Mattheson** in 1718, **Stölzel** in 1727, and many others. It became popular to piece together parts of this text with chorales and Gospel texts such as **Bach** did in his *St. John Passion.*

V. Secular Cantatas

  A. Solo cantatas developed from the Italian aria whether in simple arioso or embellished coloratura style supported by a bass.
  B. **Georg Philipp Telemann** (1681-1767)
    1. *Ino,* Hamburg, 1765 (*DdT,* v. 28, p. 121)
      a. *Ino* is a dramatic monologue for soprano on a Greek mythological theme. There is no *secco* recitative, but the expressiveness of the accompanied recitatives and arias are heightened by dramatic use of the orchestra.

VI. Odes

  A. The odes, like the cantatas, were often commissioned for special occasions of honor or celebration.
  B. **Georg Philipp Telemann** (1681-1767)
    1. *Die Donnerode* (The thunder ode), Hamburg, 1756 (*CE,* v. 22, p. 3)
      a. Based on Psalms 8 and 29, this dramatic ode in two parts is written for five soloists, four-part chorus, and a large orchestra. Almost every movement is marked with an expressive word: *e.g.* the opening chorus "how is Thy name so great?" is marked *"munter"* (lively) and succeeding movements *"freundlich"* (friendly), *"demütig"* (humbly), and *"kraftig"* (powerful).
      b. Considerable text painting is apparent: *e.g.* against the text "The voice of the Lord

breaks the cedars of Lebanon" the strings use a rapid repeated note figure containing a major seventh suggesting a storm (*CE*, v. 22, p. 43).
  2. *Das befreite Israel* (The liberation of Israel) (*CE*, v. 22, p. 97)
    a. Based on Exodus 15, this ode dramatizes the deliverance of Israel from the Egyptians.

VII. Continuo Songs

  A. **Philipp Heinrich Erlebach** (1657-1714)
    1. *Harmonische Freude musikalischer Freunde* (Harmonic happiness of musical friends), Nuremberg, 1697, 1710 (*DdT*, vols. 66-67; *AM*, v. 45, p. 66)
      a. This large collection of morality and political songs in all voices exhibits a variety of styles. The 50 songs of volume I are accompanied with two violins and continuo, and the 25 songs of volume II are accompanied by various instruments and continuo.
  B. **Johann Krieger** (1651-1735) (*NagMA*, vols. 174, 175)
    1. *Neue musikalische Ergötzlichkeit* (New musical entertainment), Frankfort and Leipzig, 1684, in three parts, this collection contains sacred, political and theatrical songs.
      a. *Die Losung ist: Geld* (The solution is: Money) (*GMB*, No. 235)
  C. **Georg Philipp Telemann** (1681-1767)
    1. *Sing-, Spiel-, und Generalbassübungen* (Singing, Playing, and Thorough-bass Exercises), Hamburg, 1734
    2. *Oden*, Hamburg, 1741 (*DdT*, v. 57)
      a. Twenty-four continuo songs under the title of "Odes."
  D. **Sperontes:** Pseudonym of **Johann Sigismund Scholze** (1705-1750)
    1. **Sperontes** was an amateur musician in Leipzig through which the Pleisse river flows.
    2. *Die singende Muse an der Pleisse* (The singing muse on the Pleisse), Leipzig, 1736 (*DdT*, vols. 35-36; *M* 14)
      a. This is a collection of 100 German songs the music of which is mostly adapted from keyboard pieces and French songs.
      b. *Menuet: Liebste Freiheit* (Beloved freedom), No. 23 (*GMB*, No. 289,1)
      c. *Murky: Ach, wenn kommt der frohe Tag?* (Ah, when will the happy day come?) No. 46 (*GMB*, No. 289,2)

VIII. Orchestra and Chamber Music

  A. **Johann Sigismund Kusser** (Cousser), **Georg Muffat**, and **Johann Fischer** were pupils of **Lully**, and all show his influence. **J. K. F. Fischer** and **G. P. Telemann**, in their suites, also wrote in the lighter French style, the so-called "rococo."
  B. The French overture in three sections, used as a prelude to the suite, was introduced by **Kusser**. The fugal movement in the overture became considerably more contrapuntal than in the overtures of **Lully**. As it became more important, the whole suite was called an "Ouverture."
  C. Dance movements, as with the French composers, were frequently program pieces, but the sections were longer, more varied, and the dances did not follow any particular order. Composers from south Germany (**Fux** and others) followed Italian models in their orchestra music, but emphasized counterpoint.
  D. Solo concertos show the influence of **Vivaldi** and were written in large numbers by **Telemann** (*EDM*, v. 11), **Graupner** (*DdT*, v. 30), and his pupil **Fasch**, all contemporaries of **J. S. Bach.**
  E. Chamber music was written by most well-known Late Baroque composers in Germany. They generally followed the model of **Corelli**, but with the typical serious German fugal style. In trio sonatas the gamba frequently replaced the second violin of the Italian trio sonata.
  F. **Johann Sigismund Kusser** (1660-1727)

1.   *Composition de musique suivant la méthode française,* Stuttgart, 1682
     a.   These six sets of dances open with an *Ouverture. Ouverture* IV (*NagMA,* v. 100)
G.   **Georg Muffat** (1645-1704)
   1.   *Florilegium Musicum* (Musical Garlands), vol. I, Augsburg, 1695 (*DTÖ,* v. 2);
        vol. II, Passau, 1698 (*DTÖ,* v. 4; *AM,* v. 45, p. 48)
      a.   These 15 suites which include 112 compositions often begin with an *Ouverture*
           and have programmatic titles for the movements.
      b.   The two Prefaces (*SR,* 442-448) include interesting discussions on the contrast of
           French and German performance practices. A table of ornaments is in volume II.
   2.   *Concerti Grossi,* Passau, 1701 (*DTÖ,* v. 23)
      a.   These six *concerti,* Nos. 2, 4, 5, 10, 11, 12, were not composed for the church or
           the dance, but "for the express refreshment of the ear" (*SR,* 449-452).
      b.   Inspired by **Corelli,** these *concerti* were first played in **Corelli's** home. An enigmatic
           title for each, and an additional six *concerti,* suggests that they were performed "on
           highly distinguished occasions at various times and places" (No. 2, *Cor vigilans;*
           No. 8, *Coronatio Augusto*).
   3.   *Exquisitioris Harmoniae Instrumentalis* (Exquisite harmonies for instruments),
        Passau, 1701 (*DTÖ,* v. 89)
   4.   *Armonico Tributo* (Harmonic tributes), Salzburg, 1682 (*DTÖ,* v. 89)
      a.   These five five-part *sonate da camera* for two violins, two violas, and continuo
           open with a *sonata* movement. The last sonata includes a fugue and closes with a
           passacaglia.
H.   **Johann Fischer** (1646-1721)
   1.   *Tafelmusik* (Table music), Hamburg, 1702   (*HM,* v. 17)
      a.   For four string instruments, with or without continuo, this group of dances is in
           Lully's style and begins with a three-part *Ouverture* (*grave—allegro—grave*).
I.   **Philipp Heinrich Erlebach** (1657-1714)
   1.   Sonatas for two violins and continuo, 1694   (*HM,* v. 117)
J.   **Johann Philipp Krieger** (1649-1725)
   1.   *Lustige Feldmusik*
      a.   Suites for four wind instruments (oboes and bassoons).
K.   **Johann Kaspar Ferdinand Fischer** (1650-1746)
   1.   *Le Journal de printemps consistant en airs, & balets à 5 parties, & les trompettes à
        plaisir,* Opus I, Augsburg, 1695 (*DdT,* v. 10)
      a.   These eight suites open with an *Ouverture* and in addition to the regular dance
           movements also include examples of the *Brandle* (2/2), *Traqenard* (2/2), *Amener*
           (3/4), *Canarie,* and *Echo* (4/4).
L.   **Johann Joseph Fux** (1660-1741)
   1.   *Concentus Musico-Instrumentalis in Septem Partittas,* Nuremburg, 1701 (*DTÖ,* v.
        47; *AM,* v. 34, p. 59; *HM,* vols. 30, 51)
      a.   The first suite in 16 movements is an eight-part *Serenade* for strings, two oboes,
           and two trumpets. Five suites follow, three with four-part strings only and two
           with a pair of oboes added.
      b.   The seventh *Partitta* is a *Sinfonia* à 2 for oboe, flute, and continuo. In one move-
           ment the flute plays an Italian air in 6/8 time simultaneously with an oboe playing
           a French air in 4/4 time.
M.   **Georg Philipp Telemann** (1681-1767) (*NagMA,* vols. 16, 23, 47, 50, 51, 131, 151, 167,
     177; *AM,* v. 36, p. 42)
   1.   *Musique de Table partagée en Trio Productions,* Hamburg, 1733 (*DdT,* vols. 61-62;
        CE, vols. 12, 13, 14)
      a.   The *Productions* are three suites each containing an *Ouverture* à 7, a *Quartet,* a
           Concerto à 7, a *Trio,* a *Solo* and a *Conclusion* à 7, but with a variety of string and
           wind instruments.

2. *Concerto* (*DdT*, v. 29-30, p. 103)
   a. This solo violin concerto, after the style of **Vivaldi**, is accompanied with an orchestra of strings, two flutes, two oboes, two trumpets, and timpani.
3. *Der getreue Musikmeister* (The faithful music master)
   a. The first music periodical, which had four pages, to appear regularly every two weeks. It includes both vocal and instrumental compositions and several of **Telemann's** sonatas appeared first in this periodical.
   b. Four *sonate da camera* for flute and continuo (*HM*, v. 6; *NagMA*, vols. 8, 163)
   c. Sonatas and pieces for melody instruments and continuo (*HM*, vols. 7, 8, 11)
   d. *Sonata* in C for two flutes and continuo (*HM*, v. 10)
     1) After the opening movement, each movement is titled with the name of a lady.
4. *Gulliver Suite* (*HM*, v. 11, p. 11)
   a. Based on Oliver Swift's *Gulliver's Travels,* 1726, this work is the product of **Telemann's** humor and wit, presented visually as well as audibly.
   b. After the *Intrada* is the *Lilliput Chaconne* (3/32) in 128th notes.
   c. The *Brobdingnagian Gigue* (24/1) is in long giant-size note values.
   d. "Reverie of the Laputans upon awakening" with abrupt staccato notes suggesting the awakening is followed by the "Loure of the well-bred Houyhnhms" played simultaneously with "Furie of the ill-bred Yahoos."
5. *Six Quatuors à violon, flute, viole, ou violoncelle et basse continue,* c. 1735 (*NagMA,* vols. 10, 24)
   a. *Soave* (*HAM*, No. 271)
6. *Die Kleine Kammermusik* (*HM*, v. 47)
   a. Six partitas of six movements each, for violin and continuo.
7. 12 *Fantasies* for violin alone, 1735 (*CE*, v. 6)
   a. *Fantasie* No. 4 (*CE*, v. 6, p. 34; *TEM*, 297)

N. **Christoph Graupner** (1683-1760) (*M* 7a, vols. 1, 2, 3, 4; *HM*, vols. 120, 121)
  1. *Concerto* for two flutes, two oboes and strings (*DdT*, vols. 29-30, p. 196)

O. **Gottfried Heinrich Stölzel** (1690-1749)
  1. *Concerto* for four instrumental choirs: two brass choirs with timpani, one woodwind choir, and strings. (*DdT*, vols. 29-30, p. 221)

P. **Johann Friedrich Fasch** (1688-1758)
  1. *Sonata à Flûte à bec, Hautbois, Violino, Cembalo* (*HM*, v. 26)
  2. *Concerti grossi* (*EDM*, v. 11, p. 74)

Q. **Dietrich Buxtehude** (1637-1707)
  1. *VII. Suonate à due Violino & Violadagamba, con Cembalo,* Vol. I and II, Hamburg, 1696
   a. A series of 14 *sonate da chiesa* (*DdT*, v. 11; *NagMA*, v. 117)

R. **Johann Pachelbel** (1653-1706)
  1. *Musikalische Ergötzung* (Musical recreation), Nuremberg, 1695 (*HM*, vols. 54, 55, 56)
   a. These are six *Partie "verstimbte stükh tzu 2 Violin und Bass"* (mistuned, *scordatura,* pieces for two violins and bass.

IX. **Harpsichord and Clavichord Music**

A. The term "clavier" (keyboard) was sometimes used to designate any one of the three keyboard instruments, harpsichord, clavichord, or organ. With the more definite separation in style between harpsichord and organ music, the term commonly indicated the harpsichord and/or sometimes the clavichord.
B. The principal forms of harpsichord music were the sonata (influenced by the Italian church sonata and French program music) and the suite (influenced by the French overture and dance movements). The term "partita" (*partie*) was used to signify either a series of variations or a suite. The term "overture" (*ouverture*) was also used for the suite.

C.   **Johann Kuhnau** (1660-1722)
   1.   **Kuhnau** was **Bach's** predecessor at St. Thomas' Church, Leipzig, where he became organist in 1684 and cantor in 1701. He founded the *Collegium Musicum,* a semi-public concert organization, in 1688 in Leipzig.
   2.   *Neue Clavierübung,* Part I, Leipzig, 1689; Part II, Leipzig, 1692 (*DdT,* v. 4)
        a.   Both parts of the "New Keyboard Practice" contain seven suites in seven keys; Part I in major and Part II in minor.
   3.   *Frische Clavierfrüchte oder Sieben Suonaten* (Fresh clavier fruits), Dresden and Leipzig, 1696 (*DdT,* v. 4, p. 96)
        a.   These seven "sonatas" are in four or five movements of varying types and order. Included is a chaconne, fugue, and an aria.
   4.   *Musikalische Vorstellungen einiger Biblischer Historien nebst Auslegung in sechs Sonaten* (Musical presentation of sundry Biblical stories together with explanations in six sonatas), Leipzig, 1700 (*DdT,* v. 4, p. 114)
        a.   The influence of French program music is seen in these six highly descriptive, and sometimes amusing, keyboard sonatas based on Biblical stories: 1) The combat of David and Goliath; 2) Saul cured by David with the aid of music; 3) Jacob's wedding (*AM,* v. 36, p. 30); 4) Hezekiah who was deathly sick and regained his health; 5) Gideon, the Savior of Israel; 6) Jacob's death and burial.
D.   **Johann Kaspar Ferdinand Fischer** (*c.* 1665-1746)
   1.   *Musikalisches Blumenbüschlein* (Little musical blooming bush), Op. 2, Augsburg, 1698, a republication of *Les Pièces de clavissen* (*M* 4a)
        a.   This work is a collection of eight suites, but the usual order of the suite is not maintained, and various other dances are substituted.
        b.   Suite V is a prelude and aria with eight variations (*M* 4a, p. 18). Suite VIII is a prelude and chaconne only (*M* 4a, p. 30).
        c.   Suite III in A minor (*M* 4a, p. 12; *HAM,* No. 248)
   2.   *Ariadne musica neo-organoedum,* Op. 4, 1702; republished in Augsburg, 1715 (*LO,* v. 7; *M* 4a, p. 75; *AM,* v. 19, p. 54)
        a.   This set of 20 preludes and fugues in 19 different keys was the model for **Bach's** *Well-Tempered Clavier,* Book I, 1722, which includes all 24 keys. **Bach** borrowed themes from the *Ariadne musica* for his *Well-Tempered Clavier* and *Inventions.* As the title suggests, **Fischer**'s work is to "guide" the young organist through a "labyrinth" of modern keys.
        b.   The general order of keys is the ascending scale, first minor, then major, except for the key of C which opens the collection in major and closes it in minor. Joined at the end are five *Ricercar* based on chorales for various festivals of the church year.
        c.   Prelude and Fugue in A (*M* 4a, p. 83; *HAM,* No. 247)
   3.   *Blumen-Strauss,* Augsburg, 1732 (*M4b; AM,* v. 19, p. 55)
        a.   The "Musical Banquet," a large collection of pieces, is organized into eight groups, each of which contain a prelude, six fugues, and a finale. The preludes and finales are homophonic or toccata-like in contrast to the short fugues.
   4.   *Musikalischer Parnassus oder ganz neu unter dem Nahmen der IX Musen* (Musical Parnassus or completely new under the names of nine Muses), Augsburg, 1738 (*M* 4a, p. 35)
        a.   Each of the nine suites is in a different key, and each has a title of a Greek muse.
        b.   No. 4 (*M* 4a, p. 46) begins with a *Toccatina;* No. 7 (*M* 4a, p. 57) begins with a *Tastada;* No. 9 (*M* 4a, p. 65) opens with a *Toccata* and closes with a *Passacaglia* of 22 variations.
E.   **Johann Krieger** (1651-1735)
   1.   *Sechs musicalische Parthien,* Nuremberg, 1697 (*DTB,* v. 30)
        a.   These six suites follow the usual suite form (allemande, courante, sarabande, gigue), closing with an optional movement. The suites do not have preludes, but the first

suite begins with an extended fantasia which might be an independent work.

    2.   *Anmuthige Clavierübung* (Pleasant clavier practice), Nuremberg, 1698 (*DTB*, v. 30)

        a.   A collection of nine preludes, seven fugues, five ricercars, two toccatas, a ciacona, and a fantasia.

        b.   Ricercar (*DTB*, v. 30, p. 36; *HAM*, No. 249a); *Fuga* (*DTB*, v. 30, p. 46; *HAM*, No. 249b)

F.   **Johann Pachelbel** (1653-1706)

    1.   *Hexachordum Apollinis Sex Arias Exhibens Organo pneumatico, vel clavato cymbalo* (The six strings of Apollo, six arias presented for pneumatic organ or clavicembalo), Nuremberg, 1699 (*DTB*, v. 2)

        a.   This unusual work is a series of six *arias*, each in the form of a theme and variations. The keys ascend in order: d, e, F, g, a, F.

    2.   Other harpsichord works include chorales, fantasias, suites, and fugues.

        a.   *Suite ex gis* (*HAM*, No. 250)

G.   **Georg Böhm** (1661-1733)

    1.   **Böhm's** works for harpsichord and clavichord include 11 suites and one minuet (*CE*, vols. 1, 2) The suites are among **Böhm's** finest keyboard works. They consist mainly of the usual Late Baroque four-movement suite: allemande, courante, sarabande, gigue.

        a.   Suite No. 2 in D (*CE*, v. 1, p. 31)

            1)   The suite consists of an overture, air, rigaudon, trio, rondeau, minuetto, chaconne.

H.   **Gottlieb (Theophil) Muffat** (1690-1770)

    1.   A distinguished organist, **Gottlieb** was the son of **Georg Muffat** and a pupil of **Fux**.

    2.   *Componimenti Musicali per il cembalo,* Augsburg, c. 1735 (*DTÖ*, v. 7)

        a.   These "Musical Compositions" contain six suites and a *ciaccona* with 38 variations. The suites are the French type in eight or more varied movements and begin with an *ouverture*, prelude, or fantasia in toccata style.

        b.   The Preface contains important information regarding harpsichord playing and ornaments.

        c.   *Final* (*DTÖ*, v. 7, p. 20; *HAM*, No. 280)

        d.   *Ouverture,* No. 1 (*DTÖ*, v. 7, p. 11; *GMB*, No. 292)

    3.   *12 Toccaten und 72 Versetl,* Vienna, 1726 (*DTÖ*, v. 58; *MMF*, Ser. 1, v. 18)

        a.   Toccata and one fugue, No. 1 (*DTÖ*, v. 58, p. 1; *MMF*, Ser. 1, v. 18, p. 1; *LO*, v. 5, p. 30)

I.   **Georg Philipp Telemann** (1681-1767)

    1.   *Fantaisies pour le Clavessin: 3 Douzaines,* 1733

        a.   The 36 *Fantaisies* show strong influence of both French and Italian styles. **Telemann's** style is not essentially contrapuntal or profound, but his music has the life and charm of the rococo style.

        b.   The first and third dozen *Fantaisies* have Italian markings and French markings appear in the second dozen. Much use is made of sequence, repetition, and syncopation.

J.   **Johann Mattheson** (1681-1764)

    1.   One of the most versatile musicians of his time, **Mattheson** was a composer of operas, oratorios, cantatas, keyboard music, and sonatas, and was an organist, harpsichordist, singer, musical director, cantor, and writer on musical subjects.

    2.   *Pièces de Clavecin,* Vols, I and II, London, 1714 (*MMF*, Ser. 1, v. 5)

        a.   The clavecin pieces consist of a collection of 12 suites in two books. After an opening movement (*Toccatine,* No. 2; *Fantaisie,* No. 5; *Symphonie,* No. 10; *Ouverture,* No. 12), the standard suite movements are often expanded with "doubles" and other movements are added.

        b.   Suite No. 4 contains a second courante à la Françoise (*MMF*, Ser. 1, v. 5, p. 15).

X.   **Organ Music**

A.   The composition of German organ music, which had been strongly influenced by the Netherlander **Sweelinck** (1562-1621), and to a lesser extent by the Italian **Frescobaldi** (1583-1643), reached a remarkably high level during the Baroque, culminating in **J. S. Bach**.

B.   German organs in the Baroque were complete instruments, many of them with three or four manuals and independent pedal.

   1.   The principal north German builder of the late 17th century was **Arp Schnitger** (1648-1718) who is said to have built or rebuilt upwards of 150 organs. **Schnitger's** work is characterized by distinctive tone colors and mixtures which might be very brilliant or only serve to strengthen the unison tone.

   2.   The 18th-century organs by the north-central builder, **Gottfried Silbermann** (1683-1753) were generally more mild than the **Schnitger** organs since **Silbermann** was strongly influenced by the sounds of the classical French organ.

C.   North German Protestant composers include **Buxtehude, Böhm, Lübeck,** and **Bruhns**. They wrote in free style and in the larger forms, which include the prelude, fugue, toccata, and chorale fantasia.

D.   Central German composers include **Pachelbel, Johann Christoph Bach, J. Krieger, Buttstedt** (*M* 2), and **J. G. Walther**. They wrote in smaller forms, particularly the chorale prelude and chorale variation.

E.   The south German and Austrian organists are represented by **Georg Muffat, Gottlieb Muffat,** and **F. X. A. Murchhauser**. The Catholic composers did not use the chorale, but wrote ricercars, canzonas, versets, and toccatas.

F.   There are four principal types of settings of the Protestant organ chorale (any work for organ based on a chorale melody). Most composers wrote all types of organ chorales (often called "chorale preludes") but certain types are characteristic of the composers. Many organ chorales overlap in treatment and there are other possible classifications.

   1.   Chorale variation (*partita*)

     a.   A few or all stanzas of the text are represented by a variation. **Pachelbel, Böhm, Buxtehude, J. Krieger, Buttstedt,** and **Johann Gottfried Walther** wrote organ chorales of this type. Dance rhythms were sometimes used by **Buxtehude** and others for chorale variations.

   2.   Chorale fantasia

     a.   A free virtuoso type of extended treatment of the chorale melody, which was often broken into fragments. **Buxtehude, Bruhns, Böhm, Reinken,** and **Lübeck** wrote organ chorales of this type.

   3.   Chorale fugue

     a.   The first phrase of the chorale melody may be treated in fugal style, followed by the entire chorale melody used as a *cantus firmus*, often in the bass.

     b.   Another type, known as "motivistic," treats a fragment of each phrase of the chorale melody in diminution as a fughetta. This is followed by the chorale melody, usually in the soprano.

     c.   The chorale motet treats each phrase of the chorale contrapuntally in a series of fugal expositions. Chorale fugues were written by **J. C. Bach, Pachelbel, Zachow** (*DdT*, vols. 21-22), and **J. G. Walther**.

   4.   Chorale prelude

     a.   The chorale prelude proper was intended to be played before the congregation sang the chorale. The chorale appears in the upper voice and is usually unornamented (melody chorale). **Buxtehude, Pachelbel,** and **J. G. Walther** were composers of the true chorale prelude.

G.   **Dietrich Buxtehude** (1637-1707)

   1.   **Buxtehude**, who exerted a profound influence on **J. S. Bach**, was born in Helsingborg, a Danish town at that time. He was influenced by the music of **Sweelinck** and, indirectly, the Italian school of **Frescobaldi**. In 1668 he succeeded **Franz Tunder** as

organist and treasurer of the *Marienkirche* in Lübeck.

    b.   **Buxtehude's** organ music includes preludes and fugues (often free toccatas in many sections), chaconnes, a passacaglia, canzonettas, toccatas, organ chorales, and settings of the *Te Deum* and *Magnificat*.

    c.   His style is bold and imaginative and his preludes and fugues, toccatas, and chorale fantasias are brilliant and full of virtuoso flourishes for manuals and pedals.

        1)   Fugues are often in three parts, the second and third themes evolved from the first, and include free recitative-like interludes. Fugue subjects are frequently angular, and wide leaps are characteristic.

        2)   Prelude and Fugue in E (*M* 3c, v. 2, p. 79; *LO*, v. 6, p. 17; *HAM*, No. 234)

        3)   Prelude and Fugue in E minor (*M* 3c, v. 2, p. 52; *GMB*, No. 249)

        4)   Prelude and Fugue in D minor (*M*, 3c, v. 2, p. 108; *LO*, v. 6, p. 26)

    d.   **Buxtehude** wrote various types of organ chorales, from the extended chorale fantasia, such as *Nun freut euch* (*M* 3c, v. 3, p. 66), to simple chorale preludes, such as *Nun komm, der Heiden Heiland* (Now come, Saviour of the world) (*M* 3c, v. 4, p. 48; *TEM*, 237) or *In dulci jubilo* (*M* 3c, v. 4, p. 33; *MSO*, v. 1, p. 104), or chorales in motet style, such as *Vater unser in Himmelreich* (*M* 3c, v. 4, p. 50; *HAM*, No. 190b).

        1)   The chorale *Auf meinen lieben Gott* (*M* 3c, v. 3, p. 37) is used as the basis of a suite with dance rhythms, a device also used by **Pachelbel**.

H.   **Johann Nicolaus Hanff** (1630-1706)

   1.   **Hanff** is known as a composer of a few organ chorales which belong to the **Buxtehude** type of expressive ornamented chorale. The figurations in the melody express the mood or *affect* of the text.

    a.   *Erbarm' dich mein, o Herre Gott* (Have mercy on me, O Lord God) (*RGO*, v. 2, p. 199)

    b.   *Helft mir Gott's Güte preisen* (Help me praise God's goodness) (*RGO*, v. 2, p. 200)

I.   **Johann Pachelbel** (1653-1706)

   1.   **Pachelbel**, the most important composer of the central German School, was born in Nuremberg. He was organist at churches and courts in Vienna, Eisenach, Erfurt, Stuttgart, and Gotha, and was organist at St. Sebald's, Nuremberg, from 1695. His son, **Carl Theodore**, came to the United States in 1730 and was active in Boston, Newport, Rhode Island, New York, and Charleston.

   2.   **Pachelbel** wrote fugues, toccatas, chaconnes, and fantasias in "free" style, ricercars, and various types of organ chorales (*DTB*, v. 6).

    a.   Toccata in E minor (*DTB*, v. 6; *MM*, 157; *M* 13, v. 1, p. 21)

    b.   Chaconne in D minor (*DTB*, v. 6; *RGO*, v. 2, p. 134; *M* 13, v. 1, p. 46)

   3.   **Pachelbel** used three types of organ chorale settings: 1) chorale fugue; 2) chorale prelude; 3) a combination of both types.

    a.   Many of his organ chorales are in the "motivistic" style of the chorale fugue (*Vater unser in Himmelreich*) (*DTB*, v. 6; *M* 13, v. 3, p. 8; *HAM*, No. 190c). Sometimes only the first line of the chorale melody is treated thematically, and the remaining interludes are unrelated to the chorale melody which follows.

    b.   Chorale prelude *Ach Herr, mich armen Sünder* (Ah, Lord, I a poor sinner) (*DTB*, v. 6; *M* 13, v. 3, p. 18; *GMB*, No. 243)

    c.   The third type of organ chorale is original with **Pachelbel**. It consists of an introductory fugal exposition, usually on the first line of the chorale, followed by a *cantus firmus* setting with the complete chorale melody in the bass (*Vom Himmel hoch*) (*DTB*, v. 6; *M* 13, v. 2, p. 20)

   4.   Fughettas on the *Magnificat* (*DTÖ*, v. 17)

    a.   This collection of 94 fughettas was written for the services at St. Sebald's and replaced the even-numbered verses of the *Magnificat*. Although now grouped in various numbers for each tone, the original plan ordered 64 *Magnificats* in two volumes, four on each tone.

  b. Magnificat No. 4 on Tone V (*DTÖ*, v. 17, p. 58; *HAM*, No. 251)
  c. Magnificat No. 2 on Tone II (*DTÖ*, v. 17, p. 27; *LO*, v. 6, p. 34)
  d. Magnificat No. 8, on Tone VII (*DTÖ*, v. 17, p. 84; *LO*, v. 6, p. 36)

J. **Georg Böhm** (1667-1733)

  1. **Böhm** was born in Hohenkirchen, Thuringia, and from 1698 was organist at the *Johanneskirche*, Lüneberg. He exerted a strong influence on **Bach**, especially in the use of French ornaments and the chorale variation.

  2. His works include preludes, fugues, and organ chorales (*CE*, v. 1, 2).

    a. The preludes are short works of an improvisatory character similar to **Buxtehude's** in style. The fugues are more extended, with short subjects, non-modulatory episodes, and tonal answers. They are without countersubjects or stretti and often conclude with a coda in free style.

    b. The organ chorales are of several types: 1) chorale fugue; 2) chorale prelude, usually with ornamented melody; 3) chorale variation (*partita*) in harpsichord style.

K. **Johann Gottfried Walther** (1684-1748)

  1. **Walther** was a pupil of **Johann Bernhard Bach** in Erfurt and a distant relative of **J. S. Bach**. He was appointed town organist in Weimar in 1707 and became a court musician in 1720. In Weimar, during the tenure of **J. S. Bach** (1708-1717), they were closely associated.

  2. **Walther** was a master of the chorale fugue and chorale variation. He wrote five preludes and fugues (*DdT*, vols. 26-27, p. 253; *M* 17) and arranged for organ 13 concertos by **Albinoni, Torelli, Meck, Taglietti, Gentili, Gregori,** and **Telemann** (*DdT*, vols. 26-27, p. 285).

    a. Three variations on the chorale *Wie soll ich dich empfangen* (How shall I receive Thee) (*DdT*, vols. 26-27, p. 229; *GMB*, No. 291).

  3. **Walther** wrote the first bio-bibliographical encyclopedia of music, *Musicalisches Lexicon oder Musikalische Bibliothek,* Leipzig, 1732, which includes a short biography of **Bach** (p. 64) and a list of his works published up to that time (*BR*, 46).

L. **Georg Muffat** (c. 1645-1704)

  1. **Muffat** studied in Paris while **Lully** was there and later visited Vienna, Prague, and Rome (1680) where he became acquainted with **Corelli**. He was organist of the Strassbourg cathedral and later to the Archbishop of Salzburg (1678) and the Bishop of Passau (1690).

  2. *Apparatus Musico-organisticus,* Augsburg, 1690 (*M* 12)

    a. This collection consists of twelve toccatas, a *ciacona,* a passacaglia, and concludes with the *Nova Cyclopeias Harmonica,* a series of variations.

      1) The *Nova Cyclopeias Harmonica* consists of a short *aria* and a set of eight variations on the melody *Ad malleorum ictus allusio* (With the allusion of the blow of a hammer). Some imitation on the sound of forge hammers is suggested in the music.

    b. The toccatas are made up of several contrasting slow and fast movements in different styles. These include fugue, free imitations, brilliant passages, and quiet chordal sections. The various sections often conclude on the dominant which leads on into the succeeding section.

    c. *Passacaglia* (*HAM*, No. 240)

      1) This unusual work, a combination of variation and rondeau forms, consists of 24 variations without a ground bass. Each variation is repeated and the theme is repeated at the end of every five variations (Nos. 6, 12, 18, 24).

    d. Toccata XI (*LO*, v. 5, p. 22)

XI. **Protestant Church Music**

  A. The cantata had its beginnings in the Middle Baroque with the dramatic concerto style of **Schütz** and the chorale concerto style of **Tunder**. These styles were incorporated into a new form in the Late Baroque, known, for the first time, as the "church cantata." The

cantata was the principal type of Protestant church music in Germany.
B.   This new cantata grew out of the "reforms" of the orthodox Lutheran pastor, **Erdmann Neumeister** (1671-1756), who published five cycles (1700-1717) of poetic cantata texts. These texts were used either to replace the scriptural texts, or to serve as commentaries.
  1.   The texts were set to recitatives and arias in Italian operatic style. This aroused the violent opposition of the Pietists whose church music consisted only of simple sacred songs. With **Neumeister's** "reforms," the cantata with chorales was often replaced by a free setting of the text without the use of a chorale melody. Composers using **Neumeister's** texts for church cantatas were **Philipp Krieger, Johann Kuhnau,** and **Zachow.**
C.   **Dietrich Buxtehude** (1637-1707)
  1.   The traditional *Abendmusiken* at the *Marienkirche*, Lübeck, originated by **Franz Tunder** in the 1640's, were continued by his son-in-law, **Buxtehude,** when he became organist in 1668. These concerts took place annually on the last two Sundays in Trinity and the last three Sundays in Advent. The varied concerts included cantatas, chorales, organ and chamber music. Among the musicians who attended the programs were **Handel** and **Mattheson** together in 1703, and **Bach** in 1705.
  2.   **Buxtehude's** cantatas (*DdT*, v. 14), numbering more than 120, are based on free poetic texts and are in conservative Italian style. They are of the *concertato* type, without recitatives or da capo arias, and often have accompanied ariosos and instrumental ritornellos.
  3.   *Eins bitte ich vom Herrn* (One request I make of the Lord) (*DdT*, v. 14, p. 15)
    a.   This *Abendmusiken* cantata for the twenty-fifth Sunday in Trinity opens with an instrumental *Sonatina* and is followed by seven verses of solo soprano arias and choruses alternating with ritornellos.
  4.   *Liebster Jesu* (Dearest, Lord Jesus)   (*DdT*, v. 14, p. 23; *HAM*, No. 235)
  5.   *In dulci jubilo*, 1685 (*CMA*, 381)
    a.   This Christmas chorale cantata is for three voices, two violins, and continuo. The chorale melody, somewhat elaborated, remains in the soprano throughout.
D.   **Georg Böhm** (1661-1733)
  1.   **Böhm** wrote nine cantatas, a motet, and a *Sanctus*. Two cantatas are based on Psalm texts (*CE*, v. 1, pp. 45, 69), and one is a series of variations on *Nun komm der Heiden Heiland* (*CE*, v. 1, p. 89). **Böhm** also wrote in the older *concertato* style which contrasted vocal and instrumental groups, or even two vocal groups.
  2.   *Das Himmelreich ist gleich einem Könige* (Heaven is like a King) (*CE*, v. 1, p. 1) is a concerto type cantata with a variety of forms: opening instrumental *sonata*, arias, concerted chorale settings on *Wachet auf, ruft uns die Stimme* (Wake, a voice is calling), and several chorale stanzas.
E.   **Johann Pachelbel** (1653-1706)
  1.   **Pachelbel** used the chorale variation and *concertato* style in his cantatas (*DTB*, v. 10).
  2.   *Was Gott tut, das ist wohlgetan* (What God doeth is done well)   (*DTB*, v. 10)
F.   **Johann Philipp Krieger** (1649-1725)
  1.   **Krieger** was a very progressive and prolific cantata composer and was strongly influenced by the Italian operatic style in his recitatives and arias. He also wrote cantatas in the chorale variation form (*DdT*, vols. 53-54).
G.   **Johann Kuhnau** (1660-1722)
  1.   **Kuhnau** wrote chorale cantatas (*DdT*, vols. 58-59) including recitatives, *secco* and *accompagnato*, ariosos, arias, and choruses accompanied with strings and continuo.
  2.   *Gott, sei mir gnädig nach deiner* (God, be merciful to me), 1705 (*DdT*, vols. 58-59, p. 224)
  3.   *Ich freue mich im Herrn* (I rejoice in the Lord), 1712 (*DdT*, vols. 58-59, p. 321)
H.   **Friedrich Wilhelm Zachow** (1663-1712)
  1.   *Das ist das ewige Leben* (This is eternal life)   (*DdT*, vols. 22-23, p. 3)
I.   **Christoph Graupner** (1683-1760)

1. *Herr die Wasserströme erheben sich* (Lord, the waters extol Thee) (*DdT*, vols. 51-52, p. 173)
   a. Written in the "gallant" style, this cantata makes use of both *secco* and *accompagnato* recitatives, muted strings, and some text painting.

J. **Georg Philipp Telemann** (1681-1769)
1. *Der Tag des Gerichts* (The day of judgment), 1761 (*DdT*, v. 28)
   a. An elaborate four-act oratorio based on the events surrounding the apocalyptic day of judgment. Expressive recitatives, arias, ariosos, and choruses of various groups are supported by a large orchestra. A variety of expression marks are indicated.
   b. Chorus of the blessed (*DdT*, v. 28, p. 101; *HAM*, No. 272)
      1) Against the four-part chorus singing "Holy is our God." the apostle John, a bass, sings "The Lamb which was slain is worthy to receive adoration, praise, and thanks."

K. **Johann Mattheson** (1681-1764)
1. Oratorio: *Die heylsame Geburth und Menschwerdung unsers Herrn* (The holy birth and incarnation of our Lord), Hamburg, 1715
   a. *Fürchtet euch nicht* (Fear not) (*GMB*, No. 267)

XII. **Catholic Church Music**

A. **Johann Joseph Fux** (1660-1741)
1. Fux wrote several settings of the Ordinary of the Mass (*DTÖ*, v. 1) and also wrote motets for the Proper (*DTÖ*, v. 3).
2. *Missa S. Caroli* (*Canonica*) (*DTÖ*, v. 1, p. 67)
   a. This unusual four-part *a cappella* setting is of the complete Ordinary. As Fux proceeds through the Mass he uses every conceivable arrangement of canon.
      1) The *Kyrie* opens with canon at the ninth; *Christe*, canon at the octave; *Kyrie*, canon at the seventh; three sections of the *Gloria* are in canon at the sixth, fifth, and fourth; the *Credo* is in canon at the third and the second. At the word *"Et resurrexit"* Fux, on each successive phrase of the text, descends from canon at the ninth to the unison. The *Sanctus* is set with canon at the twelfth, octave, fifth, and unison simultaneously.
3. Motets (*DTÖ*, v. 3)
   a. Fux wrote 27 *a cappella* motets for four or five voices on the texts of the Proper of the Mass. He suggests that the parts be doubled with organ alone, instruments, or organ and instruments. Plainsong *incipits* are common.
   b. Fux also wrote a number of solo motets on Latin antiphon and hymn texts accompanied with strings and continuo, or with other instruments added (*DTÖ*, vols. 101-102, pp. 77-127).

SELECTED BIBLIOGRAPHY

Books

1. Barbour, J. Murray. *Trumpets, Horns and Music.* East Lansing: Michigan State University Press, 1964.
2. Buelow, George J. *Thorough-Bass Accompaniment according to John David Heinichen.* Berkeley: University of California Press, 1966.
3. Cannon, Beekman C. *Johann Mattheson, Spectator of Music.* New Haven: Yale University Press, 1947.
4. Petzoldt, Richard. *Georg Philipp Telemann,* tr. Horace Fitzpatrick. New York: Oxford University Press, 1974.

5.   Woodward, Henry. "Musical Symbolism in the Vocal Works of Johann Pachelbel," in *Essays on Music in Honor of Archibald Thompson Davison.* Cambridge: Department of Music, Harvard University, 1957.

Articles

1.   Buszin, Walter E. "Dietrich Buxtehude (1637-1707). On the Tercentenary of his Birth," *MQ* 23 (1937), p. 465.
2.   Grout, Donald J. "German Baroque Opera," *MQ* 32 (1946), p. 545.
3.   Lenneberg, Hans. "Johann Mattheson on Affect and Rhetoric in Music," with selected portions of *Der Vollkommene Capellmeister,* 1739, *Journal of Music Theory* 2 (Apr. 1958), p. 47; (Nov. 1958), p. 193.
4.   Russell, Theodore. "The Violin 'Scordatura'," *MQ* 24 (1938), p. 84.
5.   Sheldon, David A. "Johann Friedrich Fasch: Problems in Style Classification," *MQ* 58 (1972), p. 92.
6.   Smithers, Don L. "The baroque trumpet after 1721," *Early Music* 5 (1977), p. 177.

Music

1.   Böhm, Georg. (*CE*) *Sämtliche Werke,* 4 vols. Wiesbaden: Breitkopf & Härtel, 1952.
2.   Buttstedt, Johann Heinrich. *Das Erbe deutscher Musik,* v. 9 (organ chorales).
3.   Buxtehude, Dietrich
    a.   (*CE*) *Werke,* 8 vols. Klecken: Ugrino, 1925-
    b.   *Ausgewählte Werke,* ed. Walter Haacke. Wiesbaden: Breitkopf & Härtel.
    c.   *Sämtliche Orgelwerke,* 4 vols., ed. Josef Hedar. Copenhagen: Wilhelm Hansen Musik-Forlag, 1952.
4.   Fischer, Johann Kaspar Ferdinand
    a.   *Sämtliche Werke für Klavier und Orgel,* ed. E. von Werra. Leipzig, 1901. (Reprint, New York: Broude Brothers, 1965).
    b.   *Blumenstrauss,* ed. Rudolf Walter. Altötting: Coppenrath.
5.   Fux, Johann Joseph. (*CE*) *Sämtliche Werke.* Graz: Johann-Joseph—Fux Gesellschaft, 1959-
6.   Graun, Karl Heinrich. *Der Tod Jesu. Collegium Musicum,* Ser. 2, v. 5.
7.   Graupner, Christoph. *Ausgewählte Werke,* vols. 1-4. Kassel: Bärenreiter.
8.   Hasse, Johann Adolf. *Il Ruggiero,* or *L'Eroica Gratitudini. Concentus Musicus,* v. 1. Köln: Arno Volk Verlag, 1973.
9.   *Keyboard Music of the Baroque and Rococo,* ed. Walter Georgii. Köln: Arno Volk Verlag, n. d.
10.   Kusser, Johann Sigismund. *Das Erbe deutscher Musik, Landschaftsdenkmale* 9, v. 3.
11.   Mattheson, Johann
    a.   *Cleopatra* (opera). *Das Erbe deutscher Musik,* v. 69.
    b.   *Der Vollkommene Capellmeister. Documenta musicologica,* Ser. 1, v. 5. Kassel: Bärenreiter, 1951-
    c.   *Das Lied des Lammes* (Passion oratorio). *Collegium Musicum,* Ser. 2, v. 3.
12.   Muffat, Georg. *Apparatus musico-organisticus,* ed. Rudolf Walter. Altötting: Coppenrath, 1957.
13.   Pachelbel, Johann. *Ausgewählte Orgelwerke,* ed. Karl Matthaei. Kassel: Bärenreiter, 1934.
14.   Scholze, Johann Sigismund ("Sperontes"). *Die singende Muse an der Pleisse,* Leipzig, 1736. (Facsimile, Leipzig: VEB Deutscher Verlag für Musik, 1964).
15.   Telemann, Georg Philipp
    a.   (*CE*) *Musikalische Werke,* 20 vols. Kassel: Bärenreiter.
    b.   48 Organ Chorales, ed. Alan Thaler. *Recent Researches in the Music of the*

Baroque Era, v. 2. New Haven: A-R Editions.

16. Theile, Johann. *Passionmusik. Denkmäler deutscher Tonkunst,* v. 17. Leipzig: Breitkopf & Härtel, 1892-1931.

17. Walther, Johann Gottfried. *Ausgewählte Orgelwerke,* 3 vols., ed. Heinz Lohmann. Wiesbaden: Breitkopf & Härtel, 1966.

13.   No. 47, *Aria,* from **Speronstes's,**
Singende Muse an der Pleisse (1736).

14.   *Toccata XII*, from the first edition of **Georg Muffat's**
Apparatus musico-organisticus (1690).

OUTLINE XI

JOHANN SEBASTIAN BACH (1685-1750)

Life of Bach — Organ Music — Harpsichord and Clavichord Music
Chamber Music — Orchestral Music — The Musical Offering — The Art of Fugue
Church Cantatas — Secular Cantatas — Oratorios
Passion Music — Motets — Magnificat — Mass in B Minor — Spiritual Songs
Appendix (First editions, Facsimiles, Reviews and Criticisms, Publications)
Bibliography of Books — Articles — Music

I. **Life of Bach (1685-1750)**

1685-1695   Eisenach. Born March 21, the son of **Johann Ambrosius Bach** (1645-1695), a musician in the service of the Town Council of Eisenach.

1695-1700   Ohrdruf. After his parents' deaths, Bach lived with his older brother, **Johann Christoph** (1671-1721), a pupil of **Pachelbel.**

1700-1703   Lüneberg. **Bach** received a scholarship in St. Michael's Church School. There he learned of the north German style from **Jan Adam Reincken** and **Vincent Lübeck** in Hamburg, the French style from **Georg Böhm** in Lüneberg, and heard the music of **Couperin** at the French court in Celle. In 1702 he applied for the position of organist at the Jacobikirche in Sangerhausen but failed to receive the appointment. He was in Weimar for a few months in 1703 as a violin player in the private chamber orchestra of **Johann Ernst,** brother of the Duke.

1703-1707   In August, 1703, **Bach** was appointed to his first organ position at the Neuekirche. He visited the north German city of Lübeck during Advent in 1705 (*BR,* 51) and remained there four months. He learned the vocal and organ music of **Buxtehude,** who became his chief model for the north German style.

1707-1708   Mühlhausen. **Bach** married his second cousin, **Maria Barbara Bach,** in Dornheim, just after he moved to Mühlhausen. He succeeded **Johann Georg Ahle** as organist at the Church of St. Blasius and in 1708 was asked to make suggestions for improving the organ (*BR,* 58). He resigned on June 25, 1708, largely because of the conflict between the Pietists, who were opposed to the use of elaborate church music, and the orthodox Lutherans (*BR,* 60). During this early period (1700-1708) he composed organ and harpsichord music and his first published work, *Gott ist mein König,* cantata No. 71 (parts only). St. Blasius's Church was **Bach's** last position as a church organist.

1708-1717   Weimar. He was appointed court organist and, in 1714, concertmaster of the 18-piece chamber orchestra of Duke **Ernst August.** He began his second creative period under strong Italian influence and wrote large compositions for organ (preludes, fugues, toccatas). He also composed some cantatas, mostly solo, to "reform" texts. In 1714 he refused the invitation to become organist at the Frauenkirche in Halle. His interest in Italian concerted and chamber music resulted in many keyboard transcriptions, particularly from **Vivaldi,** and he also used themes by **Corelli, Legrenzi,** and **Albinoni.** He became famous as an organ virtuoso (*BR,* 223, 231, 236) and was engaged to inspect new organs (*BR,* 64, 71, 72, 430). In Weimar, his relative and colleague was the distinguished organist, composer, and scholar, **Johann Gottfried Walther.** Walther's *Musicalisches Lexicon,* 1732 (*BR,* 46), contains the first published biography of **Bach.**

1717-1723   Cöthen. **Bach** became Capellmeister of the Court of Prince Leopold. The Court belonged to the Reformed Church, and **Bach** was not required to compose church music or to play the organ. Prince Leopold, an excellent musician, maintained a chamber orchestra, and **Bach** devoted himself largely to the composition of instrumental music. This included chamber music, keyboard music, particularly for instruction, and concertos. He went to Leipzig in 1717 to inspect the organ in the Paulinerkirche (*BR*, 76). In 1720 **Maria Barbara** died and was buried when **Bach** was away with Prince Leopold. He married **Anna Magdalena Wülcken** in 1721 (*BR*, 431). In 1720 he applied for the position of organist at the Jakobikirche, Hamburg, but was not accepted (*BR*, 79).

1723-1750   Leipzig. **Bach** succeeded **Johann Kuhnau** as cantor at the St. Thomas School and became director of music at other Leipzig churches. **Georg Philipp Telemann, Christoph Graupner**, and **Georg Friedrich Kauffmann** were offered the position but had declined, and **Johann Friedrich Fasch** refused to apply. The church authorities wanted a cantor who was identified with the modern Italian style and considered **Bach** too conservative (*BR*, 88). This fourth, last, and greatest period of **Bach's** life was devoted mainly to great choral works: Masses, Passions, the *Magnificat, Christmas Oratorio*, and cantatas. He also wrote harpsichord and organ music and, in his last years, the *Musical Offering* and *Art of Fugue*. During the Leipzig period he made several journeys to Dresden and inspected organs in various places (*BR*, 127, 173, 174). His last journey was to Potsdam to play for **Frederick the Great**, 1747 (*BR*, 176). **Bach's** relations with the Leipzig authorities were never satisfactory, and he was continually involved in quarrels with the Consistory, University (with which he was semi-officially connected), the municipality, and with his last rector, **August Ernesti**. Of **Bach's** 20 children, only nine survived him. His most famous sons were **Wilhelm Friedemann** and **Carl Philipp Emanuel**, children by **Maria Barbara**, and **Johann Christoph Friedrich** and **Johann Christian**, children by **Anna Magdalena**. Bach died on July 28, 1750, in his sixty-sixth year.

Bach acquired his musical education principally by studying and copying music of his forerunners and contemporaries. He learned organ style in his youth from **Jan Adam Reincken** (pupil of **Sweelinck**), **Dietrich Buxtehude**, and **Georg Böhm**.

He came to know music by the Italian composers **Giovanni Palestrina, Girolamo Frescobaldi** (*Fiori musicali*), **Domenico Scarlatti, Giovanni Legrenzi, Arcangelo Corelli, Tomaso Albinoni, Francesco Bonporti, Antonio Vivaldi** (violin concertos), and **Antonio Caldara**.

Among the French he knew the music of **François Couperin, Charles Dieupart, Nicolas de Grigny** (*Livre d'Orgue*), **André Raison** (Passacaglia), **Jean-Baptiste d'Anglebert**, and possibly **Jean-Baptiste Lully**.

Bach knew music of the following German composers: **Heinrich Schütz, Johann Theile** (the teacher of **Buxtehude** and **Zachow**), **Johann Jakob Froberger, Johann Caspar Kerll, Johann Joseph Fux, Johann Pachelbel, Johann Kuhnau, Christoph Graupner, Georg Philipp Telemann, Johann Kaspar Friedrich Fischer, George Frideric Handel** (whom he never met), **Nikolaus Bruhns, Nikolaus Strungk**, and **Johann Kayser (Kaiser)**.

II.   Organ Music

A.   **Bach** composed over 200 works for organ. These represent, however, only about seven percent of his complete works. Most of his organ music is suitable for use in church and is written in the conventional forms of his predecessors and contemporaries: organ chorale, prelude, fugue, fantasia, toccata, passacaglia, trio, and concerto arrangements. The organ chorale includes about half of all the organ works. Very few preludes and fugues show any thematic relationship. They were often put together according to key by editors.

1.   About a third of **Bach's** organ music was preserved in his own autograph. This includes the *Orgelbüchlein* (*S*. 599-644); Eighteen Chorale Preludes (*S*. 651-668); Six Trio Sonatas (*S*. 525-530); Passacaglia (*S*. 582); Preludes and Fugues in G major (*S*. 541),

A major (variant) (*S.* 536); B minor (*S.* 544); E minor (*S.* 548); and C major
(*S.* 547); Fugue in C minor (*S.* 575); Canonic Variations on *Vom Himmel hoch*
(*S.* 769); and two organ chorales, *Valet will ich dir geben* (*S.* 735) and *Wie schön
leuchtet der Morgenstern* (*S.* 739). The Concerto in G major (*S.* 592); Concerto in
A minor (*S.* 593); and the incomplete Pedal Etude in G minor (*S.* 598) are also
preserved in autograph.

2. Organ works published in **Bach's** lifetime are the *Clavierübung*, Part III, Leipzig, 1739
(*S.* 552 and 669-689); Schübler Chorales, Zella, 1747 (*S.* 645-650); and the Canonic
Variations on *Vom Himmel hoch*, Nuremberg, 1748 (*S.* 769).

3. There are about 120 organ chorales extant. The majority of these are in four collections arranged by **Bach** himself: *Orgelbüchlein, c.* 1717; *Clavierübung,* Part III, 1739;
Schübler Chorales, 1747; Eighteen Chorale Preludes, 1750.

4. Editions of music referred to include the complete edition of the **Bach** works, *Bach-
Gesellschaft* (*BG*) and a newly revised edition in process of publication, *Neue Ausgabe
Sämtlicher Werke* (*NB*). The editions of organ music include G. Schirmer (vols. 1–5
edited by Widor and Schweitzer, vols 6–8 by Schweitzer and Nies-Berger) (*GS*) and
Peters (*PE*). Three separate collections have been published by Peters: Little Organ
Book, No. 3946; Six Chorales [Schübler] and Eighteen Chorales, No. 3947; Third
Part of the *Clavierübung*, No. 3948. Pertinent references in *The Bach Reader* (*BR*)
are included. Other references include those from the thematic index of the complete
Bach works by **Wolfgang Schmieder**, *Bach-Werke Verzeichnis* (*S.*).

    a. There are a number of doubtful works which have been attributed to **Bach** (see
B 11, 14).

B. Lüneberg,.1700-1703; Arnstadt, 1703-1707; Mühlhausen, 1707-1708

1. During this early period **Bach** wrote chorale partitas (variations), chorale fantasias,
preludes, fugues, and toccatas (*GS*, v. 1; *PE*, v. 5).

2. **Bach** was in the process of mastering his art, but these early works, in spite of their
immaturity, show unmistakable signs of **Bach's** genius. The influence of **Böhm's**
French ornamentation and **Buxtehude's** brilliant, rhapsodic style is evident.

3. Four Chorale Partitas

    a. **Bach's** chorale variations reflect the earlier techniques of **Georg Böhm** (1667-1733),
organist at the Johanneskirche, Lüneberg.

    b. There are variations in from two to five parts, many for manuals alone, and a number
with an independent pedal. The number of variations often agrees with the number
of stanzas in the chorale text, but rarely seem to reflect the affect (mood) of the
words.

    c. *Christ, der du bist der helle Tag* (Christ, Thou art the light of day) (*S.* 766) (*BG,*
v. 40, p. 107; *GS*, v. 8, p. 78; *PE*, v. 5, p. 60)

    d. *Ach, was soll ich Sünder machen* (Ah, what shall I a sinner do?) (*S.* 770) (*BG,* v.
40, p. 189; *GS*, v. 8, p. 114; *PE*, v. 9) (This work is of doubtful authenticity.)

    e. *O Gott, du frommer Gott* (*S.* 767) (*BG*, v. 40, p. 114; *GS*, v. 8, p. 84; *PE*, v. 5,
p. 68)

    f. *Sei gegrüsset, Jesu gütig* (Be Thou welcome, blessed Jesus) (*S.* 768) (*BG*, v. 40, p.
122; *GS*, v. 8, p. 92; *PE*, v. 5, p. 76)

        1. This important set of eleven variations was revised at various times and probably
reached its definitive form during **Bach's** Weimar period (1708-1717). The first
youthful variations are for manuals alone; the last five include an independent
pedal part and anticipate the mature mastery of **Bach's** later works.

4. Prelude and Fugue in C minor (*S.* 549) (*BG*, v. 38, p. 3; *GS*, v. 1, p. 4; *PE*, v. 4,
p. 36). Arnstadt or possibly Lüneberg.

    a. The Prelude consists of a long pedal solo and manual flourishes. The Fugue, with
its repeated tonic and dominant entries, contrapuntal weaknesses, loose construction, and lack of polyphonic use of the pedal, shows **Bach** in the process of mas-

tering the fugue form.

5. Fugue in G minor (*S.* 578) (*BG*, v. 38, p. 116; *GS*, v. 2, p. 104; *PE*, v. 4, p. 7; *NS*, 153; *AM*, v. 19, p. 68)

C. Wiemar, 1708-1717; Cöthen, 1717-1723

1. Strong Italian influence is seen in a number of his works. These include the arrangements of **Vivaldi** concertos; the Allabreve (*S.* 589) (*BG*, v. 38, p. 131; *GS*, v. 1, p. 18; *PE*, v. 8, p. 74); fugues on themes by **Corelli** (*S.* 579) (*BG*, v. 38, p. 121; *GS*, v. 1, p. 114; *PE*, v. 4, p. 46) and **Legrenzi** (*S.* 574) (*BG*, v. 38, p. 94; *GS*, v. 1, p. 10; *PE*, v. 4, p. 36); and the Canzona (*S.* 588) (*BG*, v. 38, p. 126; *GS*, v. 2, p. 71; *PE*, v. 4, p. 54) on a theme of **Frescobaldi** (**Bach** is said to have owned a copy of the *Fiori musicali.*)

2. Five Concertos, arrangements of violin concertos of Vivaldi and Prince **Johann Ernst**.

   a. Concerto No. 1 in G major (*S.* 592) (*BG*, v. 38, p. 149; *GS*, v. 5, p. 2; *PE*, v. 8, p. 2) is arranged from Prince **Ernst** or possibly **Telemann**.
   Concerto No. 2 in A minor (*S.* 593) (*BG*, v. 38, p. 158; *GS*, v. 5, p. 12; *PE*, v. 8, p. 10) is arranged from **Vivaldi** Concerto, Op. 3, No. 8.
   Concerto No. 3 in C major (*S.* 594) (*BG*, v. 38, p. 171; *GS*, v. 5, p. 26; *PE*, v. 8, p. 22) is from **Vivaldi** Concerto, Op. 7, Book 2, No. 5.
   Concerto No. 4 in C major (*S.* 595) (*BG*, v. 38, p. 196; *GS*, v. 5, p. 52; *PE*, v. 8, p. 44) is arranged from a concerto by Prince **Ernst**.

   b. Concerto No. 5 is arranged from **Vivaldi** Concerto, Op. 3, No. 11 and has been attributed to and published under the name of **Friedemann Bach**.

3. Virtuoso concert pieces, *c.* 1709

   a. These works include many brilliant manual and pedal passages and were probably composed especially for recitals. The Toccata, Adagio and Fugue is in Italian concerto form, combined with the north German toccata. The principal section of the Toccata is in *concerto grosso* style with two themes alternating as solo and tutti.

   b. Prelude and Fugue in D major (*S.* 532) (*BG*, v. 15, p. 88; *NB*, Ser. 4, v. 5, p. 58; *GS*, v. 2, p. 57; *PE*, v. 4, p. 16)

   c. Toccata and Fugue in D minor (*S.* 565) (*BG*, v. 15, p. 267; *GS*, v. 2, p. 84; *PE*, v. 4, p. 27)

   d. Toccata, Adagio and Fugue in C major (*S.* 564) (*BG*, v. 15, p. 253; *GS*, v. 2, p. 32; *PE*, v. 3, p. 72)

4. Prelude and Fugue in **A** minor, 1709 (*S.* 543) (*BG*, v. 15, p. 189; *NB*, Ser. 4, v. 5, p. 186; *GS*, v. 4, p. 62; *PE*, v. 2, p. 54)

   a. The influence of **Buxtehude** is seen in the scale passages, arpeggios, trills, and manual and pedal cadenzas.

5. Passacaglia in C minor (*S.* 582) (*BG*, v. 15, p. 289; *GS*, v. 4, p. 91; *PE*, v. 1, p. 76; *SS*, 371; *NS*, 158)

   a. This great work consists of an eight-measure theme followed by 21 variations including a fugue. Although Forkel stated that the Passacaglia was originally written for pedal harpsichord, it is pure organ music except for variations 14 and 15.

   b. The first half of the theme is borrowed from a brief *Trio en Passacaille* (*AMO*, v. 2) by **André Raison** (1650-1720), organist at St. Etienne du Mont, Paris.

   c. The first 10 variations have the theme in the pedal, the next five (11–15) introduce the theme in the upper voices without pedal (except variation 12), and in the last five variations the theme returns to the pedal.

   d. The variations are frequently unified thematically and/or rhythmically. Variations 10 and 11, the exact center of the Passacaglia, are in double counterpoint at the octave.

   e. An increase in the rhythmic movement, from quarter notes to sixteenth notes, takes place from the first statement of the theme to variation 6. Variations 6–16 are unified by being based on sixteenth-note patterns.

    f.   Variation 17 is based on a triplet rhythm, 18 on the rhythm of variation 4, and 19 and 20 return to the sixteenth-note pattern. The added part and the higher pitch increase the volume without the addition of stops.

    g.   The fugue uses the first four measures of the Passacaglia theme as a subject. The second subject, which enters immediately, is one measure in length, repeated in sequence. The third idea is actually only one beat long. The entire material of the four voices is derived from these three contrasting ideas. In order to preserve the striking character of the themes, the answers to the two subjects are real.

    h.   The fugue is in three sections (meas. 1–29; meas. 29–65; meas. 65–117), and coda (meas. 117–124). There are five entries of the subject in the first section, three entries in the second section (which is mostly in three voices with frequent use of major keys) and four entries in the third section which culminates in a dramatic Neapolitan-sixth chord just before the coda. Possibly **Bach** improvised a cadenza at this point.

6.   Fantasia and Fugue in G minor, *c.* 1720 (*S.* 542) (*BG*, v. 15, p. 177; *NB*, Ser. 4, v. 5, p. 167; *GS*, v. 4, p. 40; *PE*, v. 2, p. 20)

    a.   The rhapsodic "fantasia" is in north German toccata style. It is noteworthy for its powerful suspensions and striking modulations. The fugue theme, based on a Netherland folksong, was well-known in **Bach's** time and was printed in a compressed form by **Mattheson** in his *General-Bass-Schule*.

7.   *Orgelbüchlein* (*S.* 599-644) (*BG*, v. 25², pp. 3-60; *GS*, v. 7, pp. 2-60; *PE*, v. 5; *PE*, No. 3946)

    a.   The Little Organ Book, *c.* 1717, was planned to include 164 chorale preludes, but only 45 were completed. The first part, fairly complete, contains settings of hymns for the Church Year; the second part for the Christian Life.

    b.   **Bach's** purpose, stated in the title, was to give the beginner instruction in working out a chorale in various ways and at the same time acquire facility in playing the pedals (*BR*, 75). The organ chorales are mostly on a small scale, and most of them were intended to be played before the singing of the chorale.

    c.   An understanding of the organ chorales requires a knowledge of the words, and **Bach's** principles in the use of accompanying motives. These motives, in general, only have meaning when associated with the text, or part of it. **Bach** uses accompanying motives in three ways: 1) representing pictorially the meaning or mood of the words, sometimes for a particular verse as in *Durch Adams Fall* (*S.* 637); 2) abstractly, but usually contributing to the general meaning of the hymn as in *Alle Menschen müssen sterben* (*S.* 643); 3) based on pictorial representation, but also used abstractly as in *Vom Himmel kam der Engel Schaar* (*S.* 607).

    d.   Types of organ chorales in the *Orgelbüchlein*.

        1)   Ornamented chorale

            a)   *O Mensch, bewein' dein Sünde gross* (O man, bewail thy grievous sin) (*S.* 622)

            b)   *Wenn wir in höchsten Nöthen sein* (When we are in utmost need) (*S.* 641)

            c)   *Das alte Jahr* (The old year) (*S.* 614)

        2)   Chorale canon

            a)   *In dulci Jubilo* (In sweet jubilance) (*S.* 608), a double canon in which both the accompaniment and the chorale are in canon at the octave.

            b)   *Gottes Sohn ist kommen* (Once He came in blessing) (*S.* 600)

            c)   *Christ, du Lamm Gottes* (Christ, the Lamb of God) (*S.* 619)

        3)   Simple chorale. Chorale in the soprano with little or no ornamentation.

            a)   *Christ lag in Todesbanden* (Christ lay in bonds of death) (*S.* 625)

            b)   *Der Tag, der ist so Freudenreich* (This day, so rich in joy) (*S.* 605)

            c)   *Ich ruf' zu dir* (I call to Thee) (*S.* 639)

            d)   *Vater unser im Himmelreich* (Our Father Who art in heaven) (*S.* 636)

D.   Leipzig, 1723-1750

1. Organ music of the Leipzig period consists of six trio sonatas, three collections of organ chorales, five preludes and fugues, and the variations on *Vom Himmel hoch da komm' ich her.*

2. Six Trio Sonatas, *c.* 1727 (*S.* 525-530) (*BG,* v. 15, pp. 3-78; *GS,* v. 5, pp. 58-142; *PE,* v. 1, pp. 2-74)

   a. These sonatas "for two claviers and pedal" were, according to Forkel, written for **Bach's** eldest son, **Friedemann,** to help him become a great performer (*BR,* 346). Some of the movements were taken from earlier works, but all are in strict three-voice polyphony. Most of them are in three movements, fast–slow–fast.

3. Eighteen Chorales (*S.* 651-668) (*BG,* v. 25^2, pp. 79-146; *GS,* v. 8, pp. 15-77; *PE,* v. 6, p. 7; *PE,* No. 3947)

   a. These large scale organ chorales were collected, revised, and some composed during **Bach's** last years. They include chorale fugues, chorale fantasias, and chorale preludes. These types appear as ornamented chorales, chorales in **Pachelbel** style, *cantus firmus* chorales with the chorale in the bass, and trios. A few are descriptive, but most of them are abstract compositions.

   b. *Nun komm' der Heiden Heiland* (Now come, Saviour of the nation) (*S.* 659)
      1) An ornamented chorale with interludes somewhat in **Pachelbel's** motivistic style.

   c. *O Lamm Gottes, unschuldig* (O Lamb of God, guiltless) (*S.* 656)
      1) Three stanzas of the hymn are set with the chorale in soprano, alto, and bass. The third stanza is pictorially represented in the music.

   d. *Vor deinen Thron tret' ich hiermit* (Before Thy throne I stand) (*S.* 668)
      1) The manuscript of **Bach's** last chorale, also set to the text *Wenn wir in höchsten Nöthen sein* (When we are in deepest need), was partly in **Bach's** own hand and the remainder dictated to his son-in-law **Altnikol.** The chorale was added at the end of **Bach's** incomplete *Art of Fugue.* The simple chorale melody is presented with interludes in **Pachelbel** style, and there is much use of imitation by inversion and augmentation. The final cadence is an unusual succession of 6/4 chords.

4. Catechism Chorales (*S.* 669-689) (*BG,* v. 3, pp. 184-241; *NB,* Ser. 4, v. 4, pp. 16-91; *GS,* v. 7, pp. 61-112; *PE,* v. 6, p. 7)

   a. **Bach's** first organ works to appear in print were 21 " Preludes on the Catechism and other Hymns," published as the third part of the *Clavierübung,* Leipzig, 1739. They are divided into seven sections: 1) Trinity, including the *Kyrie* (three large and three small settings), and three settings of *Allein Gott;* 2) Ten Commandments, 3) Creed; 4) Lord's Prayer; 5) Baptism; 6) Penitence; 7) Holy Communion.

   b. It is sometimes referred to as an "Organ Mass" because of the inclusion of preludes on the *Kyrie, Gloria, Credo,* and *Pater noster.*

   c. Each chorale, except *Allein Gott in der Höh',* is set twice: 1) a longer form to illustrate the greater catechism of the adults, and 2) a shorter form to illustrate the lesser catechism of the children. The longer chorales represent various types of treatment; the shorter ones are mostly simple fughettas for manuals without pedals. The collection is preceded by the Prelude in E-flat major and concludes with the fugue in E-flat major (*St. Anne*). Four two-part pieces (duets), for use during Communion, are also included.

   d. *Kyrie, Gott Heiliger Geist* (*S.* 671)
      1) A *cantus firmus* organ chorale. The accompanying polyphony is based on the theme in diminution and inversion. The extraordinary coda is unusually dissonant, even for **Bach.**

   e. *Wir glauben all'* (We all believe in one God) (*S.* 680)
      1) A three-part fugue with an independent ostinato-like bass representing steadfastness of faith.

   f. *Christ unser Herr zum Jordan kam* (Christ our Lord came unto the Jordan) (*S.* 684)

     1)   A descriptive prelude with a flowing melody in the left hand.

   g.   *Aus tiefer Noth* (Out of the depths do I cry unto Thee) (*S.* 686)

     1)   A massive six-part chorale-fugue with double pedal.

5.   Schübler Chorales, Zella, 1747 (*S.* 645-650) (*BG*, v. 25^2, pp. 63-76; *GS*, v. 8, pp. 2-14; *PE*, v. 7, pp. 72, 84, 76, 33; v. 6, p. 4; v. 7, p. 16; *PE*, No. 3947)

   a.   The "Six Chorales of Various Sorts" were published by **Bach's** pupil, **Johann Georg Schübler**. They are all organ transcriptions of movements from **Bach's** Leipzig church cantatas, except No. 2, *Wo soll ich fliehen hin*, which is unknown and may be an original composition.

   b.   Four of the chorales are in three parts (Nos. 1, 2, 5, 6), and two (Nos. 3, 4) are in four parts. The transcriptions follow the vocal and instrumental parts of the original closely, but lack the supporting harmonies of the figured-bass in the original.

   c.   The sources of the Schübler Chorales are as follows: No. 1 (Cantata No. 140); No. 2 (Cantata unknown); No. 3 (Cantata No. 93); No. 4 (Cantata No. 10); No. 5 (Cantata No. 6); No. 6(Cantata No. 137).

6.   Canonic Variations on *Vom Himmel hoch da komm ich her* (From Heaven above to earth I come) (*S.* 769) (*BG*, v. 40, p. 137; *NB*, Ser. 4, v. 2, p. 98; *GS*, v. 8, p. 106; *PE*, v. 5, p. 92)

   a.   "A few Canonic Variations on the Christmas Chorale 'From Heaven Above to Earth I Come' for the Organ with 2 manuals and Pedal" were published in Nurnberg by Balthazar Schmid (*n.d.*).

   b.   The original edition of the Canonic Variations was probably published shortly after **Bach's** election to the Mizler Society in June, 1747. The autograph score, which was presented to the Society also exists, and there are a number of differences in notes and the order of the five variations.

   c.   The chorale melody appears in different voices in the variations while another part is in canon with it at varying intervals and in augmentation and inversion. The last few measures, in five parts, use all four lines of the chorale together, with canonic imitation in diminution.

7.   Leipzig Preludes and Fugues

   a.   The great architectural preludes and fugues of the Leipzig period are expanded in form, with some characteristics of the Italian concerto style in alternating expositions and interludes.

   b.   The Fugue in E minor (Wedge) (*S.* 548; *BG*, v. 15, p. 236; *NB*, Ser. 4, v. 5, p. 94; *GS*, v. 3, p. 84; *PE*, v. 2, p. 64) and the earlier Fugue in C minor (*S.* 537) (*BG*, v. 15, p. 129; *NB*, Ser. 4, v. 5, p. 47; *GS*, v. 3, p. 20; *PE*, v. 3, p. 55) have da capo sections.

   c.   Prelude and Fugue in G major, 1724-1725 (*S.* 541) (*BG*, v. 15, p. 169; *NB*, Ser. 4, v. 5, p. 146; *GS*, v. 4, p. 30; *PE*, v. 2, p. 7)

     1)   This is one of the few works in which there is some thematic connection between the prelude and fugue. A particularly fine stretto in various intervals concludes the fugue.

   d.   Prelude and Fugue in E-flat major (*St. Anne*) (*S.* 552) (*BG*, v. 3, Prelude, p. 173, Fugue, p. 254; *NB*, Ser. 4, v. 4, Prelude, p. 2, Fugue p. 105; *GS*, v. 3, p. 61; *PE*, v. 3, p. 2)

     1)   The Prelude of this great work, based on three themes, is placed at the beginning and the Fugue at the end of the Catechism Chorales (*Clavierübung III*). The Prelude is in north German toccata style with fugal sections. The Fugue is in three sections, often interpreted as a symbol of the Trinity, with each section a complete fugue with its own theme. The theme of the first fugue, identical with the beginning of **Croft's** hymn-tune known as "St. Anne," appears in varied rhythms in the second and third fugues. At no time do the three fugue themes appear together.

   e.   Prelude and Fugue in B minor (*S.* 544) (*BG*, v. 15, p. 199; *NB*, Ser. 4, v. 5, p. 198; *GS*, v. 4, p. 76; *PE*, v. 2, p. 78)

1) The Prelude is possibly **Bach's** last work in this form. Formally, melodically, harmonically, rhythmically, and expressively it is one of his great organ compositions. The Fugue, based on a simple diatonic subject, is in three large divisions with tutti and solo contrasting sections.

III.   Harpsichord and Clavichord Music

A.   Lüneberg, Arnstadt, Mühlhausen, 1700-1708
  1. **Bach** composed keyboard music throughout most of his life, often for purposes of instruction. The *cembalo* (harpsichord) was often designated or implied, but many works, because of their nature, were undoubtedly intended for the clavichord, an instrument preferred by **Bach** for expressive music.
      a. The early clavier works (*BG,* v. 36; *NB,* Ser. 5, v. 10) include fantasias, preludes, fugues, toccatas, two capriccios, and a sonata.
  2. *Capriccio sopra la lontananza del suo fratello dilettissimo* (Capriccio on the Departure of His Beloved Brother), 1704 (*S.* 992) (*BG,* v. 36, p. 190; *NB,* Ser. 5, v. 10, p. 3)
      a. This piece is a secular counterpart of **Kuhnau's** *Biblische Historien.* It is a programmatic piece on the departure of **Bach's** brother, **Johann Jacob,** who was leaving for Sweden to become an oboist in the army band of Charles XII. The movements describe 1) his friends trying to dissuade him from the journey, 2) dangers, 3) general lament (chaconne bass), 4) leave-taking of his friends, 5) air of the postilion, 6) the postilion's horn call (fugue).
  3. Sonata in D major (*S.* 963) (*BG,* v. 36, p. 19; *NB,* Ser. 5, v. 10, p. 32)
      a. A church sonata, based on the sonatas from **Reincken's** *Hortus musicus.* There is a descriptive movement imitating a clucking hen and a cuckoo.
B.   Weimar, 1708-1717
  1. During this period **Bach's** music for solo harpsichord consisted principally of 16 arrangements, mostly of violin concertos (*BG,* v. 42). There are six concertos arranged from **Vivaldi,** and some of the remaining have not been definitely identified.
      Concerto No. 1 in D (*S.* 972) from **Vivaldi,** Op. 3, No. 9 (*Tomo,* 414)
      Concerto No. 2 in G (*S.* 973) from **Vivaldi,** Op. 7, Book 2, No. 2 (*Tomo,* 449)
      Concerto No. 3 in D minor (*S.* 974) from **Marcello,** oboe concerto
      Concerto No. 4 in G minor (*S.* 975) from **Vivaldi,** Op. 4, No. 6 (*Tomo,* 423)
      Concerto No. 5 in C (*S.* 976) from **Vivaldi,** Op. 3, No. 12 (*Tomo,* 417)
      Concerto No. 7 in F (*S.* 978) from **Vivaldi,** Op. 3, No. 3 (*Tomo,* 408)
      Concerto No. 9 in G (*S.* 980) from **Vivaldi,** Op. 4, No. 1 (*Tomo,* 418)
      Concerto No. 11 in B-flat (*S.* 982) from Duke **Johann Ernst**
      Concerto No. 13 in C (*S.* 984) from Duke **Johann Ernst**
      Concerto No. 14 in G minor (*S.* 985) from **Telemann**
      Concerto No. 16 in D minor (*S.* 987) from Duke **Johann Ernst**
C.   Cöthen, 1717-1723
  1. This period was devoted mostly to compositions for clavier and chamber music. Many clavier works were written for the instruction of his family and pupils. These include **Friedemann's** and **Anna Magdalena's** Little Clavier Books, preludes, Inventions, and the Well-tempered Clavier, Book I. Other clavier works include the six "English" and six "French" suites, toccatas, and the Chromatic Fantasy and Fugue.
  2. *Clavier-Büchlein vor Wilhelm Friedemann Bach* (begun in 1720) (*BG,* v. 45; *NB,* Ser. 5, v. 5) (*BR,* 79)
      a. This instruction book contains explanations of clefs and ornaments, examples of fingering, 15 two-part *Praeambula* (Inventions), 14 three-part *Fantasia* (Sinfonias), 17 Preludes, and other short pieces.
  3. **Anna Magdalena's** *Clavierbüchlein,* completed in Leipzig, 1725 (*BG,* v. 43; *NB,*

Ser. 5, v. 4, p. 47) (*BR*, 97)

a.   This is a miscellaneous collection of pieces by **Bach** and a few other composers (**Böhm, Dieupart, Couperin**). It includes early versions of two Partitas and two French Suites, dance movements, chorales, and arias (*Bist du bei mir*). An earlier *Clavierbüchlein*, 1722, exists in part (*BG*, v. 45; *NB*, Ser. 5, v. 4, p. 3) (*BR*, 84).

4.   Well-Tempered Clavier, I, 1722 (*S.* 846-869) (*BG*, v. 14; *NS*, 207)

a.   **Bach** used the term *clavier* (keyboard) to designate any keyboard instrument, the harpsichord, or clavichord, and sometimes the organ (*Clavierübung*), never specifically the clavichord. Sometimes the reference was to the harpsichord or clavichord and did not include the organ. The title "Well-Tempered" (*Wohl-Temperirte*) Clavier does not mean a *clavier* tuned in "equal" temperament, but one "well-tuned." In order to play in all 24 keys without retuning, the usual mean-tone tuning of the time must have approached equal temperament.

b.   The first set of 24 Preludes and Fugues "through all the tones and semitones" was written "for the Use and Profit of young Musicians Desirous of learning, as well as for the Pastime of those already Skilled in this Study" (*BR*, 85, 447-448). There is a prelude and fugue in every major and minor key.

c.   The Preludes, over a third of which were originally written for the instruction of **Friedemann**, have little or no thematic relationship with the fugues. They consist of many types and styles, each based on a characteristic motif. These include the etude (Nos. 2, 5), toccata (No. 7), saraband (No. 8), solo with accompaniment No. 10), invention (Nos. 3, 9, 11), fugue, with three themes in triple counterpoint (No. 19), trio with two upper parts in imitation and a free-running bass (No. 24).

d.   The Fugues are mostly monothematic and include a wide variety of styles or types, from the *ricercar* (No. 4, 22) to an elaborate theme using all twelve notes of the scale with modulations (No. 24). The Fugues are unified by the use of material taken from the subject (Nos. 5, 16, 19, 22), or counter-subject (Nos. 11, 12), or both (No. 8). The subjects always have strong themes, and counter-subjects and counterpoints are of primary importance, giving to each fugue a special character. There are fugues with no counter-subject (Nos. 1, 15, 19), two counter-subjects (Nos. 3, 4, 21); several stretti (Nos. 1, 4, 6, 8); unusual order of entry of the voices in the exposition (Nos. 12, 14); inversion of the subject and answer in the modulatory section (Nos. 6, 14, 20, 22); pedal points (Nos. 1, 2, 20); real answers (Nos. 1, 5, 10); tonal answers (Nos. 2, 7, 16); augmentation No. 8); many episodes (Nos. 3, 7, 15); and counter-expositions (Nos. 11, 19).

5.   Inventions, 1723 (*S.* 772-801) (*BG*, v. 3, pp. 1-42; *NB*, Ser. 5, v. 3) (*BR*, 86)

a.   On the title page of his manuscript of the Inventions, **Bach** wrote that the Inventions would be an "honest guide for lovers of the clavier, and especially those desirous of learning." They would first "learn to play clearly in two voices" and later in three parts and "above all develop a singing style." The Inventions would also give the student a "strong foretaste of composition" and teach him to develop thematic ideas.

b.   In the Little Clavier Book that **Bach** began in 1720 for the instruction of his eldest son, **Wilhelm Friedemann**, he included early versions of the two-part *Praeambula* (Inventions) and three-part *Fantasias* (Sinfonias). These were later incorporated into one collection.

c.   The Inventions, in their original order, followed an interesting key scheme in common with many other collections by **Bach** (C, d, e, F, G, a, b, B-flat, A, g, f, E, E-flat, D, c). The technique of developing motifs is especially well illustrated in the first six two-part Inventions, and all of the Inventions reveal **Bach's** complete mastery of form and counterpoint.

6.   Suites

a.   **Bach** wrote two sets of six keyboard suites, so-called "English" and "French" while he was at Cöthen (1717-1723). He did not give the names "English" and

"French" to the suites, and the names are not an indication of their style. The standard suite of **Bach** consists of Allemande–Courante–Sarabande–Gigue. The dance movements are in binary form, either with both sections of the same length, or with the second section expanded. Optional dances, which originated in late 17th-century French ballet, are usually more dance-like, and are not as completely stylized as are the older standard dance movements.

  b.   Six "English" Suites (*S.* 806-811) (*BG,* v. 45, p. 3)

    1) The "English" Suites (A, a, g, F, e, d) have preludes in Italian style, except for No. 1, and show the influence of the *concerto grosso,* especially Nos. 2 and 3. Other movements show a mastery of the French style. The suites include the usual dance movements, with a "double" (simple ornamented variation) for some of the courantes and sarabandes. Optional dances are the Anglaise, bourrée, gavotte, musette, minuet, passepeid, and rondeau. The harmonic modulations are found in the sarabande for Suite No. 3.

  c.   Six "French" Suites (*S.* 812-817) (*BG,* v. 45, p. 89)

    1) The "French" Suites (d, c, b, E-flat, G, E) appear in an early form in **Anna Magdalena's** first Clavier Book, 1722. The first suite and part of the second were revised in her Little Clavier Book, 1725 (*BG,* v. 45 gives the various versions of the suites). These suites are without preludes and represent the complete fusion of Italian, French, and German styles. The optional movements include the minuet, air, gavotte, bourrée, loure, and polonaise. **Bach** used both the French type of *courante* (Nos. 1, 3) and the faster Italian *corrente* (Nos. 2, 4, 5, 6). Expressive sarabandes are found in the first, fifth, and sixth suites.

  7. Chromatic Fantasy and Fugue in D minor, *c.* 1720 (*S.* 903) (*BG,* v. 36, p. 71)

    a. This brilliant "free fantasy" is in the style of the great "G minor Fantasia" for organ (*S.* 542) (*BG,* v. 15, p. 177; *GS,* v. 4, p. 40; *PE,* v. 2, p. 20). It is unique among **Bach's** clavier works and was popular in his own day. Among the unusual harmonic devices are enharmonic modulations.

  8. Toccatas in F-sharp minor and C minor, *c.* 1720 (*S.* 910) (*BG,* v. 3, p. 331) (*S.* 911) (*BG,* v. 3, p. 322)

    a. **Bach** uses the variation-ricercar style in the F-sharp minor toccata and the concerto style in the rhapsodic toccata in C minor.

D. Leipzig, 1723-1750

  1. *Clavierübung I, II, IV* contain the first harpsichord music of **Bach's** to be published, and it represents his most mature style. The Well-tempered Clavier II and the Fantasy in C minor complete the comparatively few keyboard works written in Leipzig.

  2. Six Partitas (*Clavierübung I,* 1731) (*S.* 825-830) (*BG,* v. 3, pp. 46-136; *NB,* Ser. 5, v. 1, pp. 2-113) (*BR,* 105)

    a. **Bach** gave the name "partita" to these suites (B-flat, c, a, D, G, e), a term which had been used earlier by **Kuhnau** for the suites in his *Clavierübungen,* 1689, 1692. The introductory movements have the titles of *Praeludium, Sinfonia, Fantasia, Ouverture, Praeambulum,* and *Toccata.* The dance movements are completely stylized, and unusual suite movements included are rondeau and caprice (No. 2); burlesca and scherzo (No. 3). **Bach** uses the French *courante* (Nos 2, 4) and the Italian *corrente* (Nos. 1, 3, 5, 6). Partita Nos. 3 and 6 were elaborated from earlier versions in **Anna Magdalena's** Little Clavier Book, 1725.

  3. Partita in B minor (*Clavierübung II,* 1735 (*S.* 831) (*BG,* v. 3, p. 154; *NB,* Ser. 5, v. 2, p. 20) (*BR,* 133)

    a. Originally this partita was designated as an "Ouverture in the French manner, for a Harpsichord with two Manuals." It begins with an adagio and fugal allegro and omits the allemande. There are many *"Galanterien"* such as gavottes, passepeids, bourrées, and, following the gigue, an echo.

4. Italian Concerto (*Clavierübung II,* 1735) (*S.* 971) (*BG,* v. 3, p. 139; *NB,* Ser. 5, v. 2, p. 3)

    a. The "Concerto after the Italian taste" is in F major and was published with the Partita in B minor. It was **Bach's** only harpsichord work in this form and represents the transfer of the Italian orchestral concerto form to the keyboard. The three movements are Allegro–Andante–Presto. The concerto was praised by **Bach's** critic, **Johann Adolph Scheibe** (*BR,* 234).

5. Aria with 30 Variations (*Clavierübung IV,* 1742) (*S.* 988) (*BG, v. 3, p. 263; NB,* Ser. 5, v. 2, p. 69) (*BR,* 171)

    a. The "Goldberg Variations" were written on a chaconne bass taken from a sarabande in G major in **Anna Magdalena's** Little Clavier Book, 1725. The work begins and ends with the Aria, and every two free variations are followed by a variation in canon. The canons are treated in every interval from unison (No. 3) to the ninth (No. 27). The free variations use a variety of forms, including the fugue (No. 10); overture (No. 16); sonata (No. 25); and dance (No. 26). The final variation (No. 30) is a polyphonic *quodlibet* in which two popular songs are combined with the chaconne theme.

6. Well-Tempered Clavier II, 1744 (*S.* 870-893) (*BG,* v. 14, p. 91) (*BR,* 172, 435)

    a. The second part of the Well-Tempered Clavier, "consisting of Preludes and Fugues through all the tones and semitones," includes many works from early and late periods arranged, as in the first part, in the systematic order of keys. Some of the pieces were transposed in order to fit them into the key scheme. The second set of Preludes and Fugues was not written primarily for instruction, and it shows a wide variety of treatment and an expansion of forms and ideas (No. 5 in D; No. 9 in E).

7. Fantasy in C minor, *c.* 1738 (*S.* 906) (*BG,* v. 36, p. 145)

    a. Written in the Neapolitan keyboard style using the two-part form of **Scarlatti.**

IV. Chamber Music

A. Most of **Bach's** chamber music was composed at Cöthen (1717-1723). It includes sonatas for harpsichord and one instrument, and unaccompanied solo sonatas for violin and for cello. The Brandenburg Concertos and Orchestral Suites are sometimes considered as chamber music, because of their relatively small instrumentation.

B. Sonatas with harpsichord and one instrument

  1. **Bach** broke away from the established custom of indicating the harpsichord part in ensemble music by a figured bass. The harpsichord is usually written out in two parts (adagios are harmonic), forming a trio with the other instrument. He wrote very few chamber works for one instrument and figured bass, or in the Italian trio sonata form. The *Musical Offering* has an outstanding trio sonata, however.

  2. Six Sonatas for Harpsichord and Violin (*S.* 1014-1019) (*BG,* v. 9, p. 69; *NB,* Ser. 6, v. 1, p. 83; *AM,* v. 45, p. 115)

    a. In these sonatas (b, A, E, c, f, G) the harpsichord part is written out, except for a few passages with figured bass when the violin is not playing (Sonatas 1, 2, 5, 6).

    b. The violin sonatas are generally in the four-movement form of the church sonata. The flute sonatas are in the three-movement form of the concerto. The concerto da capo form is used in the first version of the Sonata in G (No. 6), both in the first movement and in its repetition at the end of the sonata.

  3. Three Sonatas (G, e, c), for violin and harpsichord (figured bass). No. 1 (*S.* 1021) (*NB,* Ser. 6, v. 1, p. 65); No. 2 (*S.* 1023) (*BG,* v. 43, p. 31; *NB,* Ser. 6, v. 1, p. 73; *AM,* v. 45, p. 113); No. 3 (*S.* 1024) may not be by **Bach.**

  4. Three Sonatas (b, E-flat, A), for harpsichord (part written out) and flute (*S.* 1030-

1032)   (*BG*, v. 9, p. 3; *NB*, Ser. 6, v. 3, p. 33)

5. Three Sonatas (C, e, E), for flute and harpsichord (figured bass). (*S.* 1033-1035)
   (*BG*, v. 43, p. 3; *NB*, Ser. 6, v. 3, p. 11)
6. Three Sonatas (G, D, g), for harpsichord (part written out) and gamba (*S.* 1027-
   1029) (*BG*, v. 9, p. 175)
7. Sonata (suite in A minor), for flute alone (*S.* 1013) (*NB*, Ser. 6, v. 3, p. 1)

C. Solo Sonatas (unaccompanied), 1720
   1. *Sei Solo à Violino senza Basso accompagnato* (*S.* 1001-1006) (*BG*, v. 27, p. 3;
      NB, Ser. 6, v. 1, p. 3)
      a. These six solo violin sonatas alternate between sonata and partita: *Sonata* I in
         G minor; *Partia* I in B minor; *Sonata* II in A minor; *Partia* II in D minor;
         Sonata III in C major; *Partia* III in E major.
      b. The solo violin sonatas "senza Basso accompagnato" consist of three church
         sonatas (*sonata*) and three chamber sonatas (*partia* or suites).
      c. The sonata-suites are technically difficult and often complex works. They are
         conceived polyphonically, with much use of multiple stops. The polyphony is
         often suggested by dividing the single line between the two implied parts.
      d. The Sonata in C (No. 3, *S.* 1005) has an extended fugue as the second movement.
         Bach's transcription for organ (*S.* 539) (*GS*, v. 2, p. 77; *PE*, v. 3, p. 42) of the
         fugue from the Sonata in G minor (No. 1) shows the type of polyphony **Bach**
         implied in the violin fugue. The Sonata in A minor (No. 2) was arranged by
         Bach for harpsichord (*S.* 964). The theme from the fugue of this sonata was
         quoted by **Mattheson** (*BR*, 230). The Partita in D minor (No. 2) concludes with
         the great Chaconne. Partita in E (No. 3) makes use of bariolage.
   2. Six Solo Violoncello Suites (*S.* 1007-1012) (*BG*, v. 27, p. 59)
      a. Solo music for the violoncello is comparatively rare. **Bach's** unaccompanied
         cello sonatas (G, d, C, E-flat, c, D) are all in chamber sonata (suite) form. Each
         begins with a Prélude which is followed by dance movements. The sixth suite
         was written for a "violoncello à cinque cordes," possibly the violoncello piccolo,
         but not the viola pomposa. Multiple stops are not used as frequently as in the
         solo violin sonatas, but the single line is often divided into parts. In the fifth
         suite, the "A" string is tuned to "G."

V. Orchestral Music

A. **Bach's** principal orchestral works (about 30 in all) consist of concertos for harpsichord, for violin, for two violins, the Brandenburg Concertos, and the Orchestral
   Suites (*Ouvertures*).
B. Concertos for harpsichord (*S.* 1052-1065) (*BG*, vols. 17, 21, 31, 42)
   1. The 13 harpsichord concertos were written for the *Collegium Musicum* in Leipzig.
      They are for from one to four harpsichords with string accompaniment and are
      mostly arrangements of **Bach's** own works.
   2. There are seven for one harpsichord of which several are arranged from **Bach's**
      violin concertos (d, E, D, A, f, F, g) (*S.* 1052-1058) (*BG*, v. 17); three for two
      harpsichords, of which the first and third are arranged from **Bach's** concertos for
      two violins (c, C, c) (*S.* 1060-1062) (*BG*, v. 21); two for three harpsichords
      (d, C) (*S.* 1063-1064) (*BG*, v. 31); and one for four harpsichords which is an
      arrangement of **Vivaldi's** Concerto for four violins, Op. 3, No. 10 (A minor) (*S.*
      1065) (*BG*, v. 43).
C. Concertos for violin (*S.* 1041-1043) (*BG*, v. 21)
   1. **Bach** wrote three violin concertos: two for one violin (a, E) (*S.* 1041-1042)
      and one for two violins (D minor) (*S.* 1043). The first movement of the violin
      concerto in E major, as in many of **Bach's** concertos, uses the da capo form. The

first movement of the concerto in A minor suggests the later sonata form. The first and last movements of the double violin concerto are in typical concerto form.

D. Concerto in A minor (*S.* 1044) (*BG,* v. 17, p. 223) for harpsichord, flute, and violin.

   1. This concerto was arranged from older works. The first (Allegro) and last (Alla Breve) movements are expanded from a Prelude and Fugue in A minor for harpsichord (*S.* 894).   The slow (Adagio) movement was arranged from the organ Trio Sonata No. 3 in D minor (*S.* 527) (*BG,* v. 15, p. 26; *GS,* v. 5, p. 84; *PE,* v. 1, p. 24).

E. Brandenburg Concertos, 1721 (*S.* 1046-1051) (*BG,* v. 19) (*BR,* 82)

   1. In 1721, while he was at Cöthen, **Bach** sent six concertos (F, F, G, G, D, B-flat) "for several instruments" to the Margrave of Brandenburg with a typical, but amusingly humble, dedication.

      a. Each concerto is scored for a unique combination, with emphasis on wind instruments. Each one includes strings and continuo with harpsichord. All but Nos. 1 and 3 (only a Phrygian cadence separates the two Allegros in No. 3) are in the three-movement form of **Vivaldi:**   fast—slow—fast.

      b. The Allegros are in a rondo-like form, alternating the tutti-ritornello with the concertino (solo group). The middle sections are in nearly related keys. The concertino episodes are modulatory. The closing tutti is usually a restatement of the first tutti, and sometimes the second and next to last sections are related. The solo (concertino) group may introduce a new theme or use motives from the tutti. The principal theme may be introduced by the solo group.

      c. The second, fourth, and fifth concertos are in *concerto grosso* form with three or four solo instruments. The first, third, and sixth concertos are for instrumental groups which are contrasted with each other, sometimes giving way to a solo instrument.

   2. Concerto No. 1 in F (*S.* 1046) (*BG,* v. 19, p. 3; *AM,* v. 23, p. 76) 2 corni di caccia, 3 oboes, bassoon, "violino piccolo concertato" (tuned a minor third higher than the violin), strings and continuo (the violone and, in general, the cello and bassoon double the bass line of the continuo.

      a. This concerto has the largest instrumentation and is the only one with four movements. The first movement is based on three motifs: 1) meas. 1, corno II; 2) meas. 1, oboe I; 3) meas. 6, oboes and bassoon. This movement was later used in Cantata No. 52.

      b. In the Adagio (d), the theme is given to the oboe, violino piccolo, and basses in turn. It is later used in canonic imitation.

      c. The third movement (Allegro) is in three-part form with new material in the second section and a da capo for the third section. **Bach** arranged this movement with chorus in a secular cantata (No. 207).

      d. The fourth movement is a Menuetto with three interludes: 1) a trio for two oboes and bassoon, 2) a *Polacca* (early example) for strings, 3) a trio for two horns and three oboes in unison.

   3. Concerto No. 2 in F (*S.* 1047) (*BG,* v. 19, p. 33; *MSO,* 126; *NS,* 171) Concertino: clarino trumpet, flute (recorder), oboe, "violino concertato." Tutti: 5 strings and continuo.

      a. The first movement begins with a triad motif in typical concerto style. Each of the four instruments in the unusual concertino introduces a new theme (meas. 9), with the tutti concluding the phrase. The new theme is used later in fugal entries.

      b. Andante (d), for flute, oboe, violin, and continuo (with cello). This movement, for the solo instruments, is based on a short motif, treated in imitations.

      c. Allegro. A free fugue in which the exposition is developed by the concertino instruments. The tutti provides accompaniments and also episodes connecting the fugal sections. The theme appears in the bass at the end of the second exposition (meas. 72). Further episodes, partial recapitulations, and a final tonic pedal point, with the trumpet playing the first four measures of the theme, conclude the concerto.

4. Concerto No. 3 in G (S. 1048) (BG, v. 19, p. 59). 3 violins, 3 violas, 3 cellos "col Basso per il Cembalo"

   a. Scored for three groups of equally balanced solo strings, without accompanying parts. The strings are opposed to each other individually and in groups, and sometimes they all play in unison. The concerto has only two movements. The first Allegro is separated from the second Allegro by a Phrygian cadence. Bach possibly improvised a slow movement on the harpsichord at this point.

   b. The extensive first Allegro begins with a tutti (meas. 1-8) in three-part harmony, which is followed by two-part harmony, and then all parts in unison. This thematic material is developed by the solo instruments, various groups, and the tutti. An episode (meas. 78) introduces a new theme with the main theme, and a third theme in the violas, suggesting a triple fugue.

   c. The second Allegro is in two-part form. The first part is repeated, and the second part includes two repetitions of the first part in different keys.

5. Concerto No. 4 in G (S. 1049) (BG, v. 19, p. 85). "Violino principale, due flauti d'echo" (2 recorders), ripieno violins, viola, violone, violoncello, and continuo.

   a. Often called a violin concerto because of the virtuosity required. The violin is contrasted with the recorders and string tutti and is also used as a concertino instrument.

   b. The first movement (Allegro) is in five sections: A–BCB–A. Section I (meas. 1-82) has thematic material given to the violin and two recorders; II features the violin; III (meas. 156-235) the recorders and later the violin, accompanied by recorders and strings; IV (meas. 235-344) uses both new and old material; V (meas.) 345-427) is a recapitulation of section I.

   c. The second movement (Andante in e) uses the two recorders and the violin as a concertino in the style of a Corelli concerto grosso. The same theme alternates between the tutti and solo. There are five sections: A–BCB–D (the last section is slightly related to section A).

   d. The third movement (Presto) is, like Concerto No. 2, a free fugue, but here the tutti has the exposition and the concertino instruments play the episodes. The form is three-part with Coda: I (meas. 1-87); II (meas. 87-188); III (meas. 188-219); Coda (meas. 219-244).

6. Concerto No. 5 in D (S. 1050) (BG, v. 19, p. 127). Concertino: flute, violin, "cembalo concertato" (Harpsichord solo). Tutti: violin, viola, cello, violone (there is no part for the second violin).

   a. The first original keyboard concerto to be composed. The first movement (Allegro) is in three sections. Section I (meas. 1-8) contrasts the tutti with the concertino. The concertino uses independent material and also the first theme of the tutti. Section II (meas. 32-110) works out the opening motif of the first section and introduces a new theme (meas. 71). Section III (meas. 110-227) is a recapitulation of the first section and includes a remarkable cadenza for the solo harpsichord (65 measures).

   b. The second movement (Affettuoso in b), for the solo instruments and bass, is based on a short theme given to the concertino (flute, violin, harpsichord).

   c. The third movement, in gigue rhythm, combines fugal style with the da capo form. The fugal section (meas. 1-78) is repeated in the recapitulation (meas. 233-310). The middle section (meas. 79-232) introduces a song-like theme (meas. 79-86) which is based on the fugue theme. There is a short harpsichord cadenza in canon at the octave (meas. 163).

7. Concerto No. 6 in B-flat (S. 1051) (BG, v. 19, p. 167). 2 violas (viole da braccio), 2 gambas (viole da gamba), violoncello, violone, and continuo.

a.   This concerto, with its unusual instrumentation (the violins are omitted) often uses the two violas and gamba as a concertino group in the solo sections.

b.   The first movement (Allegro) begins with the two violas in a close canon at the unison, accompanied by other instruments (meas. 1-16). The solo sections introduce new motifs treated in imitation.

c.   The second movement (Adagio, E-flat) omits the gambas. The theme is developed by the two violas over a continuous quarter-note accompaniment in the cello, supported by the violone. Near the end of the movement (meas. 40) the theme appears in the bass. The Adagio concludes with a cadence on the dominant of G minor.

d.   The third movement (Allegro), in a gigue rhythm, is in strict da capo form. The solo sections use new themes and material from the tutti.

F.   Orchestral Suites (*Ouvertures*)

1.   The first two suites, in C major and B minor, are for woodwinds and strings, and were composed at Cöthen. The third and fourth suites, both in D major, include trumpets and timpani. They were probably composed at Leipzig between 1727 and 1736 for the *Collegium Musicum* which **Bach** conducted (*BR*, 149).

2.   Each of the four suites, or "Ouvertures" as they were commonly called, begins with an extended French overture.

a.   The movement is divided into three parts with the fast fugal section separating the two slow sections. Unusual features include the extended last slow section, the repetition of the first slow section, the fugal section with the last slow section, and the use of the concerto idea in the fugal section.

b.   The wide variety of dance movements which follow the first movement include bourrées, gavottes, menuets, and one courante, forlane, passepied, sarabande, polonaise, gigue, rondeau, badinerie (banter), air, and rejouissance (rejoicing).

1)   About half of the dance movements have variations (doubles), after which the first dance is repeated. The movements of each suite are in the same key, except in two instances.

3.   Suite No. 1 in C (*S.* 1066) (*BG*, v. 31^1, p. 3; *NB*, Ser. 7, v. 1, p. 3), for 2 oboes, bassoon, strings, and continuo.

a.   The second gavotte (double), as was often the custom, is scored as a trio for wind instruments. The term "trio" came to be used for the middle section of the minuet and other movements, even when scored for more than three instruments.

b.   The use of the three wind instruments sometimes suggests the concertino of the *concerto grosso*.

4.   Suite No. 2 in B minor (*S.* 1067) (*BG*, v. 31^1, p. 24; *NB*, Ser. 7, v. 1, p. 27), for flute, strings, and continuo.

a.   The flute is used as a virtuoso solo instrument and also in unison with the first violin. The rondeau is in the style of a gavotte. The numerous repetitions of the first section and episodes suggests the rondo form of **Haydn**. The sarabande is a canon at the twelfth between the two outer voices. The double of the polonaise has the original melody in the bass with the flute playing a counterpoint above it.

5.   Suite No. 3 in D (*S.* 1068) (*BG*, v. 31^1, p. 40; *NB*, Ser. 7, v. 1, p. 49; *NS*, 211), for 2 oboes, 3 trumpets, timpani in D and A, strings, and continuo.

a.   The first movement, Vivace (indicated by **Bach** "viste" for "vite"), is in fugato style with three counter-subjects.

b.   The second movement, in four parts, is the famous "Air" (arranged by **August Wilhelmj**, 1848-1908, as "Air on the G String").

c.   The gavotte is one of **Bach's** most popular movements. The theme is used in inversion in the second section.

6.   Suite No. 4 in D (*S.* 1069) (*BG*, v. 31^1, p. 66; *NB*, Ser. 7, v. 1, p. 81), for

3 oboes, 3 trumpets, timpani in D and A, strings, and continuo.

    a.   This suite has the largest instrumentation of any of the four suites. The trumpets, oboes, and strings are frequently contrasted with each other in concerto style as in the opening measures of the Overture. The entire Overture is used as an introduction to Cantata No. 110 (*Unser Mund*), with chorus added to the second section.

VI. **The Musical Offering, Leipzig, 1747** (*S.* 1079) (*BG,* v. 31^2, p. 3; *NB,* Ser. 8, v. 1, p. 14) (*BR,* 178-179, 182)

    A.   When **Bach** visited the court of Frederick the Great at Potsdam in May, 1747, he improvised a three-part fugue (*ricercar*) on the king's theme, possibly on one of the new **Silbermann** pianofortes. After he returned to Leipzig he worked out the theme in every conceivable way and had the entire composition engraved. He dedicated the work to Frederick (May, 1747) and sent the king a special copy.

        1.   The *Musical Offering* was engraved by **Bach's** pupil, J. G. Schübler, as the manuscripts were sent to him, which resulted in four groups of pieces in no logical order.

    B.   The *Musical Offering* may be symmetrically divided into five parts: 1) *Ricercar a 3;* 2) 5 Canons; 3) Trio Sonata; 4) 5 Canons; 5) *Ricercar a 6.* There are 16 movements in all. The instrumentation is specified in only a few movements (Trio sonata, 3 canons).

    C.   Both of the *ricercari* were originally written in keyboard notation, but the six-part *Ricercar* was published in open score. Some canons were written in abbreviated notation and as puzzle canons. Hans David has published a complete analysis of the work and the music (*B* 6).

    D.   Movements of the Musical Offering (*Musikalisches Opfer*)

        1.   *Ricercar a 3* (three-part fugue)

            a.   The king's theme is divided into three parts, which are often developed separately: 1) the minor triad and diminished 7th; 2) chromatic lines; 3) concluding group. The acrostic on the word "ricercar" was inscribed on the king's copy before the three-part fugue – *R*egis *I*ussu *C*antio *E*t *R*eliqua *C*anonica *A*rte *R*esoluta ("At the Command of the King, the Theme and Remainder Resolved in Canonic style").

        2.   Five canons in three parts

            a.   The first group of canons have the king's theme in one part as a *cantus firmus,* accompanied by the other two parts in canon. The first canons in each group of five are called *canon perpetuus,* but all of the canons except the modulating, retrograde, and canonic fugue, are led back to the beginning and may be repeated.

            b.   Canon at the double octave. The king's theme is in the middle of two canonic parts.

            c.   Canon at the unison, for two violins. The king's theme is in the bass.

            d.   Canon in contrary motion. The king's theme is in the upper voice. The inversion is almost exact.

            e.   Canon in augmentation and contrary motion.

               1)   "As the notes grow so may the King's Fortune." **Bach** wrote this inscription to accompany this complicated canon. The antecedent begins in the lower voice, and the consequent appears in the upper voice in augmentation and in contrary motion.

            f.   Modulating canon (Circle canon)

               1)   "And as the modulation rises, so may the King's Glory." This canon at the fifth moves up by step in both canonic parts until the original tonality is reached. The king's theme, slightly varied, is in the upper voice. The keys (c, D, E, F-sharp, G-sharp, B-flat, c) follow the whole-tone scale.

        3.   *Sonata a 3* for flute, violin, and *basso continuo.*

            a.   This work is **Bach's** most important trio sonata. It is in the usual four movements of the church sonata: Largo–Allegro–Andante–Allegro.

            b.   The Largo (C minor) is in two sections (AA–BA'BA'). Only the opening part of the king's theme is used and appears in the continuo.

c. The fugal Allegro (C minor) is in three-part da capo form, divided into five sections: I (meas. 1-45); II (meas. 46-88); III (meas. 89-159); IV (meas. 160-206); V (meas. 207-249). The third section forms the middle part of a large three-part form. The fourth and fifth sections are a recapitulation of the first and second sections (AB–C–A'B'). The king's theme appears for the first time at the beginning of the second section. It always accompanies the first subject and is not developed.

d. In the Andante (E-flat) the king's theme is suggested in the melodic lines. The movement is in two parts. The first part (meas. 1-17) consists of five short divisions which are rearranged in the second part (meas. 18-30). Alternating "forte" and "piano" groups were indicated by **Bach** in the original edition.

e. The final Allegro (C minor) is a fugue on the king's theme varied. There are four sections: I (meas. 1-38); II (meas. 38-61); III (meas. 61-77); IV (meas. 77-113).

4. Five canons

a. The king's theme is used in canon for the first time.

b. *Canon perpetuus* (mirror canon). The king's theme, in altered form, is used in a two-part canon in contrary motion, accompanied by a figured bass.

1) The canonic line is presented twice, once in C minor and once in G minor (meas. 19). The one in G minor is a tonal inversion of the one in C minor. The answer is real, so that the first E-flat appears as E-natural in the inversion. The second pair of entries uses the third degree of G minor (B-flat) as the pivot of the inversion. The second pair of entries is an inversion of the first pair of entries and is therefore a mirror.

c. Retrograde canon. The two voices begin at the same time, with one going forward from the beginning and the other backward from the end.

d. Canon in contrary motion. The triad beginning of the king's theme is filled in chromatically.

e. Four-part canon. The only canon with more than two canonic parts. The king's theme, in a varied form, is stated at the octave in each of the four parts (A-T-B-S).

f. Canonic fugue. The king's theme is answered in canon at the fifth above (*epidiapente*), accompanied by an unfigured bass. The entrance (meas. 39) in the subdominant is answered by the tonic. The theme is in the bass in measure 59.

5. *Ricercar a 6* (six-part fugue)

a. The king's theme, slightly varied, is the subject. The answer is tonal.

b. There are five sections: I (meas. 1-39), exposition and first episode; II (meas. 39-52), material derived from the theme, which enters in measure 48; III (meas. 52-62) begins the second part of the fugue, with material derived from the chromatic part of the theme. A transition (meas. 62-65) leads to the next section. IV (meas. 66-82), the subject enters with two accompanying counterpoints. V (meas. 83-103) begins with the trio motif and uses material derived from the theme and new counterpoints.

VII. **Art of the Fugue** (*S.* 1080) (*BG*, v. 25¹, Rust; *BG*, v. 47 Gräser) (*BR*, 198)

A. This is the last great work of **Bach**, who died before its completion. It ends abruptly just after **Bach** had introduced, for the first time, the theme on the letters B–A–C–H (in German nomenclature B is B-flat and H is B-natural). **Johann Walther** had pointed out in his *Musicalisches Lexicon*, 1732, that the letters in **Bach's** name made a musical theme.

1. The Art of Fugue is a musical composition of extraordinary effectiveness, as well as a compendium of the art of fugal writing.

2. The work was partly engraved before **Bach's** death, and the chorale prelude "*Wenn wir in höchsten Nöten sein*," one of the Eighteen Chorales (where it is called "*Vor deinen Thron*"), was added by the engraver at the end of the work.

3.   The exact order that **Bach** intended for the fugues is not certain and editions vary.

B.   The Art of Fugue consists of 14 (some editions list 16) fugues (*contrapuncti* (*AM*, v. 19, p. 76) and four canons, all in the key of D minor. They are based on one short subject, varied melodically and rhythmically, but in double, triple. and quadruple fugues new subjects are added.

1.   The music was written and published in open score except for the four canons for harpsichord and the mirror fugue (No. 13), arranged by **Bach** for two harpsichords. Opinions differ as to the order of the fugues and as to what instruments should be used for the performance of the fugues. It is possible that **Bach** intended them primarily for keyboard.

C.   The Art of Fugue begins with a group of fugues in which the theme appears in its original form and inverted (Nos. 3, 4). The music becomes more involved as it develops and the emotional tension increases.

1.   The subject is used in stretto (Nos. 5, 6); augmentation and diminution (No. 7); in a triple fugue (Nos. 8, 11); in a double fugue (Nos. 9, 10); and in mirror (Nos. 12, 13). The unfinished fugue at the end was intended to be a quadruple fugue, as the three subjects could all be combined with the original subject of the work. D. F. Tovey and others have attempted to complete the work. Note: Fugue numbers refer to the work as found in the *Bach-Gesellschaft*.

VIII.   Church Cantatas

A.   **Bach** composed nearly 300 cantatas between 1704 and 1745, of which about 200 are extant. He used the term *Stück* (piece), *Concerto,* or *Motetto* for most of his choral cantatas and *Cantata* for works for solo voice, following the Italian tradition.

1.   The cantatas were orchestrated for a wide variety of instrumental combinations, and the organ was generally used with the continuo.

a.   The harpsichord is sometimes used with the continuo in performances today, and there is some evidence that **Bach** may have used it with the organ as an additional support for the singers.

2.   The instruments (except the continuo) and the voices were treated as of equal importance.

3.   The cantata, which usually lasted from 20 to 30 minutes, was the "principal music" for the main Service. It was performed after the Creed on Sundays and Holy Days, except during Lent and the last three Sundays in Advent.

a. In cantatas which were divided into two parts, the second part was sung after the sermon.

B.   The numbers given to the cantatas are not in the chronological order of composition, but correspond to their publication in the *Bach-Gesellschaft* edition and Schmieder.

1.   The approximate dates of the cantatas (except for the few **Bach** dated) are determined by watermarks in the paper which may correspond with dated compositions, the changes in **Bach's** handwriting, the publication date of the text, the transposition of the parts for the instruments up to the high pitch of the organ at Weimar (a minor third above the other instruments), and the transposition of the organ parts in Leipzig down a whole tone (the organs there were tuned a whole tone above the other instruments).

C.   Instruments used in the cantatas include various types of flutes, oboes, horns, trumpets, timpani, and strings. Other instruments include lute, *glöckchen* (bells), harpsichord, and organ. The usual strings include the violin, viola, violoncello, and violone (bass viol), and these are the basis for the orchestration of the majority of the cantatas. **Bach** wrote to the Town Council of Leipzig in 1730 requesting a total of at least 18 instrumentalists (*BR*, 121).

D.   Early cantatas (1704-1711)

1. The early cantatas show the influence of **Buxtehude**, **Böhm**, **Pachelbel**, and **Kuhnau**. They include arias (frequently based on ostinato-like figures), ariosos (accompanied recitatives with instrumental ritornellos), and choruses in concertato style (alternating choral and instrumental groups).
   a. Recitatives accompanied by figured bass only were not used.
2. Texts of the early cantatas were based on verses from the Bible, chorale texts (hymns), and sometimes original poetry.
   a. **Bach** "was governed strictly by the content of the words" and suited his music to the mood and meaning of the text (*affetto*).
3. **Bach's** first cantata (No. 15) was written in Arnstadt in 1704 and revised in 1735 in Leipzig.
4. *Gott ist mein König* (God is my King) (*S.* 71) (*BG*, 18, p. 3) (*BR*, 57), described by **Bach** on the title page as a "Congratulatory Church Motetto," was performed on February 4, 1708, for the festival service which began the new year of the Town Council in Mühlhausen.
   a. It is the earliest cantata by **Bach** to be preserved in its original form and was the only one published (parts only) during his lifetime. It is a brilliant example of the concertato style. Other cantatas written in Mühlhausen include Nos. 131 and 196.
5. *Gottes Zeit ist die allerbeste Zeit* (God's time is the best time), No. 106, Weimar 1711? (*BG*, v. 23, p. 149)
   a. This cantata, often called *Actus tragicus*, is one of the finest of **Bach's** early cantatas and was probably written for a funeral service. It is scored for the unusual combination of 2 recorders, 2 gambas, and continuo. The text is taken from the Bible and church hymns.
   b. The cantata, similar in many respects to *Gott ist mein König*, is based on the idea (portrayed in musical symbolism) of the conflict between the Old Testament fear of death ("It is the old decree") and the New Testament joy of death ("Yea come, Lord Jesus").
   c. The cantata begins with an extraordinary *Sonatina* for 2 recorders, 2 gambas, and continuo. During the course of the work, three chorale tunes, all treated symbolically, are introduced. The first, *Ich hab mein Sach* (I have cast my care on God), is played by the recorders during the singing of the great fugal chorus "It is the old decree." The second chorale, "In peace and joy I now depart" (**Luther's** burial hymn), is sung by the altos over the words of Jesus, "Today shalt thou be with Me in Paradise," and the third chorale, the last stanza of "In Thee, Lord, have I put my trust," begins the final section, which returns to the key of E-flat.
E. Weimar cantatas (1708-1717)
   1. **Bach** wrote about 20 cantatas during the Weimar period and revised a number of them later. Between 1712 and 1714 he began to use the "reform" text of Pastor **Erdmann Neumeister** and particularly those by the more conservative **Salomon Franck**.
      a. These texts, in general, consisted of six or seven stanzas of free poetry based on the Bible (often the Gospel of the Day), or chorale texts.
         1) **Neumeister** often based his cantata texts on the theme of the sermon which followed the singing of the cantata.
      b. The recitatives and da capo arias were in the style of the Italian operatic forms. Choruses and chorales, if used at all, were placed at the beginning and the end.
   2. *Nun komm der Heiden Heiland* (Come, Redeemer of our race), No. 61, Advent, 1714. Text by **Neumeister**. (*BG*, v. 16, p. 3; *NB*, Ser. 1, v. 1, p. 3) (*BR*, 70; *BM*, 206)
      a. **Bach** used the chorale tune in the unusual opening chorus, which is in the style of a French overture (*grave–gai–grave*). The bass recitative "Behold I stand" is an example of descriptive writing. The final "Amen" is a chorale fantasia on the last half of the chorale melody *Wie schön leuchtet der Morgenstern*.
      b. This cantata was probably the one performed by **Bach** in Leipzig on December

2, 1714. On the back of the cantata **Bach** had noted down the Order of Service on that day (*BR*, 70).

3.　Other cantatas to texts by **Neumeister** include No. 142 (*BG*, v. 30, p. 19); No. 160 (*BG*, v. 32, p. 171); No. 18 (*BG*, v. 2, p. 229; *NB*, Ser. 1, v. 7, p. 109); No. 59 (*BG*, v. 12^2, p. 153; *NB*, Ser. 1, v. 13, p. 67).

4.　*Ich hatte viel Bekümmernis* (My spirit was in heaviness), No. 21. Trinity season, 1714. Text by **Salomon Franck**. (*BG*, v. 5^1, p. 1)

　a.　This cantata is in two parts which were separated by the sermon in performance. The *Sinfonia*, for oboe and violin with continuo, is followed by the first of two choruses written in the older concertato style. The reiteration of the text in the first chorus was criticized by **Mattheson** (*BR*, 229).

　　1)　The subjective feeling of the cantata and the contrasting ideas are realized in the first two choruses by sudden changes in tempo and dynamics and by the strong contrasts between the solo and tutti sections.

　b.　**Bach** used the newer operatic da capo aria and instrumental forms in the solo sections with unusual skill.

　c.　The next to last chorus introduces a chorale and the final **Handelian** chorus is a brilliant choral fugue with **Bach's** "festival orchestra" which added trumpets and timpani to the woodwinds, strings, and continuo.

5.　*Komm, du süsse Todesstunde* (Come, sweet hour of death), No. 161. Trinity season, 1715. Text by **Salomon Franck**. (*BG*, v. 33, p. 3)

　a.　The Passion chorale, a favorite with **Bach**, symbolizes the yearning for death and release from earthly troubles. The chorale melody appears in the organ part in the opening alto aria and at the end, where it is in a harmonized setting with a flute obbligato.

　　1)　**Bach** also used the Passion chorale (*Herzlich tut mich verlangen*) in cantatas No. 25, 135, 153, 159, and five times in the *St. Matthew Passion*.

6.　*Nach dir, Herr, verlanget mich* (For Thee, Lord, do I desire), No. 150 (*BG*, v. 30, p. 303; *CMA*, 425).

7.　Other cantatas to texts by **Salomon Franck** include No. 31 (*BG*, v. 7, p. 3); No. 152 (*BG*, v. 32, p. 19); No. 132 (*BG*, v. 28, p. 35); No. 155 (*BG*, v. 32, p. 85); No. 162 (*BG*, v. 33, p. 31); No. 163 (*BG*, v. 33, p. 49); No. 185 (*BG*, v. 37, p. 103); and No. 208 (*BG*, v. 29, p. 3).

F.　Cöthen (1717-1723)

1.　The court at Cöthen belonged to the Reformed or Calvinistic Church, and **Bach** was not required to provide either church or organ music for the simple chapel Services.

2.　The cantata *Jesus nahm zu sich die Zwölfe* (Jesus took to himself the twelve), No. 22, 1723, was performed by **Bach** at St. Thomas Church, February 7, 1723, as a test piece for the post of Cantor for which he had applied (*BG*, v. 5^1, p. 67).

3.　The very few cantatas written during the Cöthen period also include No. 23 (*BG*, v. 5^1, p. 95); No. 47 (*BG*, v. 10, p. 241); No. 92 (*BG*, v. 22, p. 35; *BM*, 209); No. 134a (*BG*, v. 29, p. 209; *NB*, Ser. 1, v. 10, p. 11); No. 173a (*BG*, v. 34, p. 3; *NB*, Ser. 1, v. 35, p. 97); No. 141 (*BG*, v. 30, p. 3); and the secular cantata No. 202 (*BG*, v. 11^2, p. 75; *NB*, Ser. 1, v. 40, p. 3).

G.　Leipzig (1723-1750)

1.　Between 1723 and 1745 (the last dated cantata) **Bach** composed about 165 cantatas. Other choral works of the Leipzig period include the motets, Masses, Magnificat, Passions, and oratorios.

　a.　The cantatas, as do the other choral works, reveal **Bach's** mastery of old and new techniques and their complete integration, the perfect balance between contrapuntal and harmonic writing, vivid pictorial passages, and the skillful use of symbolism.

　　1)　*Herr, gehe nicht ins Gericht* (Lord, enter not into judgment), No. 105, written in Leipzig between 1723 and 1727, illustrates these characteristics (*BG*, v. 23, p. 119).

b.   **Bach's** normal choir in Leipzig consisted of 15 to 20 men and boys (5 S – 2 A – 3 T – 7 B), accompanied by about the same number of instrumentalists. His preference was four on a part (*BR*, 121).

c.   The typical cantata was made up of a series of varied movements. These included an instrumental introduction, a chorus in fugal style (often based on a chorale), two or three recitatives and arias (for each of the solo voices, or possibly the entire section), a concluding chorale (always accompanied).

d.   The cantata texts of the Leipzig period, most of whose authors are unknown, cover a wide range of subjects and theology.

    1)   **Friedrich Henrici** (1700-1764), a postmaster in Leipzig whose pen name was **Picander**, wrote free texts, and paraphrased a number of Bible and chorale texts, particularly for **Bach's** later chorale cantatas and the *St. Matthew Passion*.

2.   Chorale cantatas

a.   **Bach** began to show an increasing interest in chorale cantatas about 1735. In these cantatas the chorale melody was used in a wide variety of ways and forms, including instrumental forms.

    1)   There is, however, only one example of a cantata which uses the original text and melody throughout (No. 4, *BG*, v. 1, p. 97).

b.   The opening chorus was usually a fantasia on the sermon chorale, using the text of the first stanza. The texts of the recitatives and arias which followed might be free paraphrases of the hymn (chorale) text, or free poetry. The cantata concluded with the last stanza of the chorale in four-part harmony, accompanied by instruments.

c.   Soloistic settings of chorale melodies include the vocal solo with continuo (No. 44); vocal solo with instrument and continuo (Nos. 4, 6, 95, 113, 137, 140); vocal solo with two instruments and continuo (Nos. 36, 85, 92, 178); vocal solo with several instruments and continuo (No. 13); aria with chorale sung by another voice (Nos. 49, 58, 106); aria with chorale played by an instrument (Nos. 12, 31, 106, 137); duet with chorale sung by another voice (No. 122); duet with chorale played by an instrument (Nos. 10, 93, 172); free contrapuntal setting of chorale for soloists and instruments (Nos. 36, pt. 2; 37, pt. 3); vocal recitative with chorale played by instruments (Nos. 5, pt. 4; 23, pt. 2; 70, pt. 9); chorale with recitative (Nos. 83, pt. 2; 91, pt. 2; 92, pt. 2; 113, pt. 4).

    1)   There are not more than 10 cantatas in any one of the above classifications.

d.   Chorus settings of chorale melodies include chorus with the chorale played by instruments (Nos. 14, pt, 1; 25, pt. 1; 48, pt. 1); chorale fantasia with chorale melody sung (Nos 1, pt. 1; 2, pt. 1; 3, pt. 1; 4, pt. 1; and 73 others); simple chorale with accompaniment doubling voice (Nos. 2, 3, 4, 5, 6, 7, 8, 9, 10, and 112 others); simple chorale with obbligato instruments (Nos. 1, 12, 19, 29, 31, and 22 others); simple chorale with instrumental interludes (Nos. 15, 41, 46, 76, 79, 105, 171 only); simple chorale with recitative (Nos. 3, 18, 92, 178, 190 only). There is one chorale setting for instruments (No. 75).

e.   There are only 21 church cantatas which do not use a chorale (Nos. 34, 35, 50, 53, 54, 63, 82, 134, 141, 150, 152, 160, 170, 173, 181, 189, 191, 193, 196, 198, 200).

f.   *Christ lag in Todesbanden* (Christ lay in the bonds of death), No. 4, Easter, 1724, probably revised from a Weimar cantata (*BG*, v. 1, p. 97)

    1)   This outstanding cantata consists of seven movements, preceded by a sinfonia and each movement uses one stanza of **Luther's** chorale text.

        a)   The text speaks of the sacrifice of Christ on the Cross, His Resurrection, and His Saving Grace.

    2)   The chorale melody, based on a 12th-century tune *Christ ist erstanden*, is divided into eight sections, with the first section repeated (a(2)–a(2)–b(4)). The

various movements are in the style of the organ chorale.

3) The introductory *Sinfonia,* with its poignant harmonies and gradual increase in contrapuntal complexity, reaches an intensification near the end. This is resolved by a single melodic line, a device that is also used at the end of the fifth movement.

4) The opening chorus, scored for 2 violins, 2 violas, *cornetto,* 3 trombones, and continuo, is of the **Pachelbel** type. The chorale is in the soprano, and each line of the chorale is preceded by a fughetta in the three lower voices. This fughetta is based on the next line of the chorale melody in diminution.

5) The second movement is a duet for soprano (doubled by a *cornetto*) and alto (doubled by a trombone) with continuo. The quasi-ostinato bass and instrumental ritornellos emphasize the power of Death.

6) The following solo for tenor (2 violins in unison), also with ritornellos, expresses joy in Christ's victory over Death.

7) The fourth movement, for chorus, is without orchestral accompaniment and repeats a number of sections, in contrast to the first movement. There are a number of pictorial illustrations, especially for the sixth line "how one death (Christ's) devoured the other." This is illustrated by canonic imitations which seem to struggle until one voice finally "devours" the other. With the final "Hallelujah," the conflicts are resolved – Christ's Resurrection has brought Salvation to mankind.

8) The fifth movement, for bass solo (2 violins, 2 violas, continuo), is in triple meter and there are also melodic changes in the chorale melody. The first violin imitates the chorale melody as sung by the bass voice. The descending chromatic line of the continuo is almost identical with the chaconne bass in the *Crucifixus* of **Bach's** *Mass in B Minor.* The text and music return to the expression of great sorrow over Christ's death on the Cross.

9) The sixth movement, for soprano, tenor, and continuo, emphasizes the first line of the text, "Thus we celebrate the Holy Feast," with the dance-like rhythm of dotted eighths and sixteenths and joyful melismas.

10) The last stanza of the hymn is set as a simple chorale, **Bach's** customary procedure.

g. *Ein feste Burg* (A mighty fortress), No. 80, Reformation Festival, 1730 (*BG,* v. 18, p. 319; *MSO,* v. 1, p. 152). A revision, with additions, of a cantata written in 1716 to a text by **Franck,** which was based on **Luther's** hymn. It is possible that **Friedemann Bach** added trumpets and timpani to the first and fifth choruses.

1) Four of the eight movements use the chorale melody (1, 2, 5, 8). The opening chorus, a large-scale chorale fantasie in fugal style, is in seven sections. Each section is based on a line of the chorale melody, and the chorale melody is also stated in strict canon between the highest and lowest instrumental parts. The second chorus in the cantata has an unusual and powerful effect—the chorale is sung in unison, and the orchestra plays independent parts.

h. *Wachet auf* (Sleepers, wake!), No. 140, Trinity, 1731 (*BG,* v. 28, p. 251; *NB,* Ser. 1, v. 27, p. 151; *NS,* 219)

1) The chorale text and melody are sung in the first, fourth, and seventh movements. The text, based on the hymn by **Philipp Nicolai** (1599), tells the parable of the wise and foolish virgins and then describes the heavenly Zion, all portrayed by **Bach** pictorially and symbolically.

i. A few other Leipzig cantatas of special interest include No. 1, *Wie schön leuchtet der Morgenstern* (How brightly shines the morning star) (*BG,* v. 1, p. 1); No. 78 *Jesu, der du meine Seele* (Jesus, by Thy Cross and Passion) (*BG,* v. 18, p. 257; *NB,* Ser. 1, v. 21, p. 117) in which the opening chorale fantasie is built on the chaconne bass **Bach** used in the *Crucifixus (Mass in B Minor)* and Cantata No. 12, *Weinen, Klagen, Sorgen, Zagen* (Weeping, sighing, sorrowing, fearing) (*BG,* v. 2, p. 61); No. 7, *Christ unser Herr* (Christ our Lord) (*BG,* v. 1, p. 179); No. 92,

Ich hab in Gottes Herz und Sinn (To God I give my heart and soul) (*BG*, v. 22, p. 35); and No. 116, *Du Friedensfürst* (Thou Prince of Peace) (*BG*, v. 24, p. 135; *NB*, Ser. 1, v. 27, p. 81).

3.   Solo cantatas

a.   **Bach** began to write church cantatas for solo voice, or voices, about 1730, possibly because of the difficulty he was having at that time in maintaining an adequate choir (*BR*, 120).

b.   Many of the solo church cantatas have a concluding chorale, probably intended to be sung by the congregation.   In the following list the numbers in italics have a concluding chorale.

Soprano: Nos. 51, *52*, *84*, 199   Tenor: Nos. *55*, 160, 189

Alto: Nos. 35, 53, 54, *169*, 170   Bass: Nos. *56*, 82

Soprano and Bass: Nos. *32*, 49, *57*, 58, *59*, 152

Alto and Bass: Nos. *197a*   Tenor and Bass: No. *157*

Soprano, Alto, and Bass: No. *89*

Alto, Tenor, and Bass (all with concluding chorale): Nos. *60, 81, 83, 87, 90, 153, 154, 156, 159, 166, 174, 175*

Soprano, Alto, Tenor, and Bass (all with concluding chorale): Nos. *13, 15, 42, 85, 86, 88, 132, 151, 155, 162, 163, 164, 165, 167, 168, 183, 185, 188*

IX.   Secular Cantatas

A.   The secular cantatas were written for special occasions, including birthdays, civic and University ceremonies, weddings, and functions in honor of royalty.

1.   They were performed in various places: the home, at the *Collegium Musicum*, coffee houses, and at outdoor concerts.

2.   Those intended for indoor performance are scored for strings and woodwinds, and those for use outdoors usually include trumpets and timpani.

3.   The music from many of the secular cantatas was used in later church music. The Baroque composers did not differentiate in quality between secular and church music, and operatic and concertato styles were used in church music. The substitution of a religious text for a secular text was usually not difficult, especially as the two texts generally had a smiliar feeling and the quality of the music was high. Both church and secular cantatas were also arranged as instrumental pieces.

4.   Coffee Cantata: *Schweigt stille, plaudert nicht* (Be silent, do not speak), No. 211 (*BG*, v. 29, p. 114; *NB*, Ser. 1, v. 40, p. 195), Leipzig, 1732. Strings, flute, continuo.

a.   This comic operetta was first performed at the *Collegium Musicum* and probably also in **Bach's** own home. The amusing text by **Picander** tells of the effort of the stubborn father (*Schlendrian*) to make his daughter (*Lieschen*) give up the new fad of coffee drinking. She finally outwits her father by winning a husband who agrees in the marriage contract to let her have coffee whenever she wishes. A narrator (tenor) opens and closes the cantata, explaining the plot and joining in the singing of a final trio. His recitatives are very much in the style of the Evangelist in the Passions.

5.   Peasant Cantata: *Mer hahn en neue Oberkeet* (The chamberlain is now our squire), No. 212 (*BG*, v. 29, p. 175; *NB*, Ser. 1, v. 39, p. 153), Leipzig, 1742.

a.   A burlesque cantata, written in Saxon dialect for a rustic celebration. The text, also by **Picander**, is similar to the Coffee Cantata in its comic operetta style. A number of the arias are based on folk songs, and the overture includes material from folk dances.

b.   The burlesque is written for one soprano and one bass, with an accompaniment of flute, 2 violins, viola, corno, and continuo with viola da gamba. Most of the accompaniments are provided by a "rustic" orchestra of violin, viola, and continuo.

6.   Other secular cantatas include Nos. 201, 202, 203 (Italian text), 204, 205, 206, 207, 207a, 208, 209 (Italian text), 210, 210a, 213, 214, 215, 216, 217.

    a.   The well-known aria for two recorders and soprano, "Sheep may safely graze," is from Cantata No. 208, part 9 (*BG,* v. 29, p. 3; *NB,* Ser. 1, v, 35, p. 17).

    b.   Cantatas No. 201, 205, 206, 207, 207a, 213, 214, 215 were designated as "Dramma per musica," and many of these were performed at outdoor concerts, possibly with costumes and some action.

X.   Oratorios

A.   **Bach** gave the title "Oratorium" to the cantatas which make up the Christmas (6 cantatas); Easter (1 cantata, *S.* 249; *BG,* v. 21³, p. 3; *NB,* Ser. 2, v. 7); and Ascension (1 cantata, *S.* 11; *BG,* v. 2, p. 1; *NB,* Ser. 2, v. 8) Oratorios.

    1.   Eleven of the 64 numbers in the Christmas Oratorio were borrowed from **Bach's** secular cantatas (*contrafacta*). The Easter Oratorio is unusual in having the entire text in rhyme. The music comes, in part, from a secular cantata (No. 249a). The Ascension Oratorio is church cantata No. 11.

B.   *Weihnachts-Oratorium* (*S.* 248) (*BG,* v. 5², p. 3; *NB,* Ser. 2, v. 6), 1734

    1.   A series of six cantatas which were performed for the days of the Christmas Festival. These were the Christmas Days (December 25, 26, 27), New Year's Day, the Sunday following, and Epiphany.

    2.   The cantatas of the oratorio that are in pastoral style (Nos. 2, 4, 5) are scored for flutes, oboes, strings, and continuo. The brilliant cantatas (Nos. 1, 3, 6), all in D major, are scored for the "festival orchestra" which includes trumpets and timpani.

    3.   The text, from St. Luke and St. Matthew, is sung by an Evangelist, with soloists singing the parts of individuals as in the Passions. Chorales, arias, duets, and trios are generally reflective. A few choruses represent the "*turba*" (crowd).

    4.   The second cantata begins with a Pastoral Symphony in which the song of the angels (flutes, strings) is contrasted with the shepherds' song (oboes).

        a.   The chorale *Vom Himmel hoch*, at the end of the second cantata, is combined with the theme of the Pastoral Symphony.

    5.   The Passion chorale "O Sacred Head" is sung as the first chorale and the last chorale of the entire oratorio. **Bach** thus brings out the thought that the birth of Jesus foreshadows His death for the Salvation of mankind.

    6.   Church cantata No. 213 is used in the Christmas Oratorio for Nos. 30, 19, 39, 41, 4, 29; Cantata No. 214 in Nos. 1, 15, 8, 24; Cantata No. 215 for No. 47, and No. 45 is from the lost St. Mark Passion.

XI. Passion Music

A.   **Bach's** Obituary (*BR,* 215) states that he wrote five Passions (*BR,* 2 21), one to each of the four gospels and one to a text by **Picander**. Only two Passions survive: St. John and St. Matthew, and parts of St. Mark.

B.   The history of Passion music

    1.   The musical setting of the Passion story (the suffering and death of Christ) began in the 12th century with the text sung in plainsong.

    2.   During the 16th century, parts for the crowd (*turba*) from the Passions were generally set in polyphonic style, with the plainsong in the tenor. Among the composers who set the Latin text were **Lassus, Vittoria,** and **Byrd.**

    3.   During the 16th and 17th centuries in Germany, texts in the vernacular were set for the *turba* in a more homophonic style by **Walther, Scandello, Mencken, Vulpius,** and others. Settings of the complete Passion text in polyphonic style (sometimes with a plainsong tenor) were also made during the 16th century by **de Rore** and others.

4. The 17th century saw the addition of dramatic elements of the Baroque, the recitatives, arias, instruments, chorales, and poetic additions to the Bible texts (**Sebastiani, Theile**).

   a. The three late Passions of **Schütz** (1585-1672) are unique in that instruments, including a continuo, are lacking, and the style is archaic and austere. They include unaccompanied recitatives (possibly with an improvised organ accompaniment) in a free Gregorian reciting style and *a cappella* choruses.

5. Poetic settings of the Bible text, particularly those of **Brockes**, became popular in the 18th century. Some of these texts were of doubtful artistic value, and musical settings were not always in the best taste.

C. The Passion According to St. John (*S.* 245) (*BG*, v. 12[1], p. 3; *NB*, Ser. 2, v. 4)

1. **Bach** wrote this work, his first Passion, in 1722/23 while at Cöthen, and it is said to have been performed for the first time on Good Friday, 1723, at the Thomaskirche in Leipzig. However, a notice at the time states that **Bach** produced his first music there on the first Sunday after Trinity, May 1, "with great success."

   a. The work was revised at least four times before reaching its present form. Among the changes was the replacing of the first chorale fantasia, "O man, bemoan thy grievous sin," with another chorus and placing the chorale fantasia at the end of the first half of the St. Matthew Passion.

2. The instrumentation includes 2 flutes, 2 oboes, oboe d'amore, 2 oboi da caccia, strings, 2 viole d'amore, lute (**Bach** designated "Organo ó cembalo" instead of lute in one of the parts), and continuo (organ).

3. The Biblical text is taken from the Gospel of St. John xvii, xviii, xix, with three additional verses from St. Matthew. **Bach** selected the chorales and adapted texts by **Picander** for the arias.

4. The music of the St. John Passion is often forceful and has great dramatic power, with considerable use of pictorial realism. The work is concise and requires only one four-part chorus in contrast to the two choruses of the larger-scaled St. Matthew Passion. In a number of the shorter choruses, **Bach** used the same music with a different text.

5. The words of the Evangelist are sung by a tenor in *recitativo secco*, the individual characters (Jesus, Pilate, Peter, the Maids) by soloists and the crowd (Priests, Pharisees, soldiers) by the chorus.

6. The texts of the arias represent the feelings of the individual as the dramatic story unfolds, and the chorales, probably sung by the congregation, represent the feelings of the worshippers.

D. The Passion According to St. Matthew (*S.* 244) (*BG*, v. 4, p. 1; *NB*, Ser. 2, v. 5; *MSO*, 117) (*BR*, facing page 384)

1. The St. Matthew Passion, often referred to as "one of the greatest expressions of devotional feelings in the history of music," was first performed on Good Friday, 1729. **Bach** subsequently revised and extended the Passion into its present form and copied out a complete score about 1740.

   a. An interesting feature of this beautiful score is the use of red ink for the words of the Gospel as sung by the Evangelist, and in the chorale melody in the first chorus.

   b. As in many works which he valued highly, **Bach** inscribed the letters J. J. (*Jesu, Juva*: "Jesus, Help me") at the top of the first page of the score and the letters S. D. G. (*Soli Deo Gloria*: "To God alone the glory") at the end of the last page.

2. This Passion is one of **Bach's** most extensive works. It is in two parts with a total of 78 numbers and requires two choruses, each with its own orchestra. The chorale melody "O Innocent Lamb of God," without the words of the chorale which were well-known, is usually sung by a boy choir or sometimes played on an instrument.

   a. The instrumentation includes 2 transverse flutes, 2 recorders, 2 oboes, 2 oboi d'amore, 2 oboi da caccia, strings, organ, and continuo (organ).

3. The work as a whole is well unified and somewhat more lyrical and reflective than

the St. John Passion. The dramatic qualities become more apparent, however, as the drama unfolds with increasing intensity in the second part of the Passion.

4.   The Biblical text is taken from the Gospel of St. Matthew xxvi, xxvii; the poetic texts are by **Picander**. These texts, in the nature of commentaries on the Gospel text, are of considerably higher quality than usual and were possibly partly by **Bach**.

    a.   The words of the Evangelist, as in the St. John Passion, are sung by a tenor in *recitativo secco*. After the death of Jesus the rending of the temple veil and earthquake are vividly portrayed in the organ accompaniment. **Mendelssohn**, in his performance of the Passion in 1829, could not resist the temptation to orchestrate this passage.

    b.   The words of Jesus (bass) are, with one exception, accompanied by strings which surround the voice like a halo. As Jesus sings the words "My God, why hast Thou forsaken me?" (No. 71) the strings are silent, and the organ supplies the accompaniment. In one notable instance, the words of Jesus are set in arioso form (No. 17). Short ariosos of only a few measures frequently concluded the recitatives sung by Jesus (Nos. 20, 24).

    c.   The parts of Peter, Judas, Pilate, the Maids and others are assigned to individual singers as in the St. John Passion.

5.   **Bach** has indicated which of the two choirs is to sing the individual numbers and when they are to sing together.

    a.   The choruses vary from the wild shouting of the mob "Let Him be crucified" (Nos. 54, 59) and the overwhelming effect of the word "Barrabas" (No. 54) to the gentle, peaceful ariosos and chorus (No. 77) just before the final chorus of the Passion.

    b.   The first chorus is a monumental chorale fantasia for double chorus in eight parts with two orchestras, and the chorale "O Innocent Lamb of God" (see above D 2). In this prologue to the Passion story, the allegorical Zion and her daughters call to the crowd of believers to behold Christ who is going to His death. They ask "whom? how? where?" in dramatic outbursts as the solemn procession continues.

    c.   Throughout the Passion the chorus takes part in the dramatic action at one moment and at another reflects the feelings of the worshippers who are longing for Redemption and contemplating the supreme sacrifice of Jesus.

    d.   There are many examples of pictorialism and symbolism in the choruses as well as in the parts for solo voices. The chorus "Lord, is it I?" (No. 15), for example, has 11 entries of the theme with its question (Judas was not present), and the gentle rocking motion of the chorus "So all our sins have gone to sleep" (No. 26) alternates 10 times with the tenor solo sung by Peter (again Judas is absent). Also the dramatic interruptions by the chorus in the duet (No. 33), the lightning and thunder in No. 33, and the concluding movement——a noble double chorus with strong descending and ascending bass line and an extraordinary ending on an ascending appoggiatura.

    e.   There is extensive use of chorales, which were probably sung by the congregation and reflected their feelings as the dramatic story unfolded. The Passion chorale, "O Sacred Head," (*CMA*, 454) is used five times (Nos. 21, 23, 53, 63, 72) with texts which comment on the event that has just taken place, and varied harmonizations (except No. 23) which are singularly appropriate in feeling.

6.   Ariosos, arias, and recitatives also offer many striking examples of pictorialism and symbolism.

    a.   The accompanied recitatives (ariosos), among them Nos. 9, 18, 20, 25 (with a chorale), 28, 60, 65, 74, and 77 (with chorus), portray in tone the underlying thought of the text.

    b.   The arias are accompanied by instruments and continuo, and also reflect, sometimes very realistically, the text. This is often accomplished by the melodic figures used in the instrumental accompaniment and the tonal characteristics of the accompanying instruments.

       1)   Among the outstanding arias are No. 12 (soprano), No. 26 (tenor), No. 47 (alto), and No. 71 (bass).

XII.   Six Motets

A.   **Bach** wrote six motets to German texts, one for New Year, four for funerals, one for an unnamed occasion (*Lobet den Herrn*). Motets were sometimes sung at the beginning of the early Sunday morning service (Matins) and also Vespers.

    1.   There are four motets for double chorus, one for four voices (*Lobet den Herrn*), and one for five voices (*Jesu, meine Freude*).

    2.   The motets are written without accompaniment, except for the indication of a continuo in *Lobet den Herrn* and a set of orchestral parts doubling the voices and a continuo part for *Der Geist hilft*.

        a.   All of the motets were undoubtedly accompanied by the harpsichord, organ, or instruments, in performance.

    3.   The texts for the motets are taken from the Bible and chorales.

B.   *Singet dem Herrn* (Sing to the Lord), Leipzig, 1746? (*S.* 225) (*BG*, v. 39, p. 5; *NB*, Ser. 3, v. 1, p. 3)

    1.   A motet for double chorus, probably written for a New Year's celebration at the end of the second Silesian War.

    2.   The structure is based on the larger organ forms. The first movement is a prelude and fugue, the second is a chorale fantasia for alternating double chorus. The chorale *Nun lobe mein Seel* (Now praise my soul) is also introduced. The final movement is a prelude for antiphonal double chorus and a fugue for four-part chorus.

C.   *Der Geist hilft* (The Spirit also helpeth us), 1729. (*S.* 226) (*BG*, v. 39, p. 41; *NB*, Ser. 3, v. 1, p. 39; *AM*, v. 45, p. 108)

    1.   A motet for double chorus in four sections, closing with the chorale *Komm, heiliger Geist* (Come, Holy Spirit).

D.   *Jesu, meine Freude* (Jesu, priceless treasure), 1723. (*S.* 227) (*BG*, v. 39, p. 61; *NB*, Ser. 3, v. 1, p. 77; *CMA*, 395) Chorale text by **Johann Franck**, 1653.

    1.   The chorale is used in Nos. 1, 3, 5, 7, 11, giving the effect of a rondo. The even numbers are free choruses, based on a Biblical text from Romans viii. There are five choruses in five parts (Nos. 2, 3, 5, 6, 10), four in four parts (Nos. 1, 7, 9, 11), and two trios (Nos. 4, 8). The concluding number recalls the first chorale.

E.   *Fürchte dich nicht* (Be not afraid), 1734 (*S.* 228) (*BG*, v. 39, p. 87; *NB*, Ser. 3, v. 1, p. 107)

    1.   This motet, to a text from Isaiah xli:vs. 9, 34 is for two four-part choruses. The two choruses unite in the second half in a fugue, during which the sopranos sing the melody of the chorale *Warum sollt ich mich denn grämen* (Why must I grieve?).

F.   *Komm, Jesu, komm!* (Come, Jesus, come!), 1723/34. (*S.* 229) (*BG*, v. 39, p. 109; *NB*, Ser. 3, v. 1, p. 127)

    1.   There are six divisions in this motet for double chorus. Each division is based on one line of the first stanza of the hymn. The motet concludes with an original chorale by **Bach** on the second stanza of the hymn.

G.   *Lobet den Herrn* (Praise ye the Lord), 1723/34. (*S.* 230) (*BG*, v. 39, p. 129; *NB*, Ser. 3, v. 1, p. 149)

    1.   This is the only motet for four voices and the only one without a chorale.

XIII.   Magnificat in D Major, 1723, revised 1730 (*S.* 243) (*BG*, v. 11[1], p. 3; *NB*, Ser. 2, v. 3, p. 67)

A.   The words of the *Magnificat* (St. Luke i:vs. 46-55) are spoken by the Virgin Mary to Elizabeth, the mother of St. John the Baptist, after the Archangel Gabriel had announced to the Virgin: "Thou shalt conceive in thy womb, and bring forth a Son and shall call his name Jesus."

1. The twelve short movements include the 10 verses of the text and the concluding *Gloria Patri.* The third movement, for soprano solo, is interrupted by the chorus which sings the fourth movement, based entirely on the last two words of the verse, *omnes generationes.*

B. The *Magnificat* is for five-part chorus, soloists, and **Bach's** "festival orchestra" with trumpets and timpani added to the flutes, oboes, bassoon, strings, and organ continuo.

1. **Bach** used the typical Baroque type of orchestration, with instrumental groups (flutes, oboes, strings, trumpets) set against each other (No. 1).
2. There are five choruses (SSATB), five arias (SSATB), one duet (AT), and one trio (SSA).
3. Instrumental introductions are frequently repeated in whole or part at the end of a movement (Nos. 1, 2, 5, 6, 8, 9). Instrumental ritornellos are used between sections (Nos. 6, 8, 9).
4. The motives, usually heard at the beginning of a movement, are used over and over in various ways throughout the movement.

C. Symbolism is sometimes used, either to underline single words, or the basic thought.

1. Descending curves on the word *"humilitatum"* (No. 3). The constant repetition of the rhythmic theme in *"omnes generationes"* (all generations) (No. 4). The treatment of the repeated notes on *"timentibus"* (fear) (No. 6). The word *"dispersit"* (scatter) (No. 7).

D. The *concerto grosso* style is used in No. 7.

1. No. 10 introduces the *Tonus peregrinus* in the oboes. This chant was used with the old German Magnificat, *"Meine Seel' erhebt den Herren."*
2. No. 11 is a choral fugue, accompanied only by the bass instrument and continuo.
3. No. 12, at the words *"Sicut erat"* (As it was in the beginning), uses music from the first movement.

XIV. **Mass in B Minor** (*S.* 232) (*BG,* v. 6, p. 3; *NB,* Ser. 2, v. 1; *SS,* 440)

A. The German Lutherans originally used the Office of Holy Communion, often called the Mass (*Missa*), on the principal Sunday Service and on festival days.

1. The *Kyrie, Gloria, Credo, Sanctus,* and *Agnus Dei* were said or sung in Latin (except the *Kyrie,* which is in Greek).
2. In the time of **Bach,** however, the word "Missa" came to mean the *Kyrie* and *Gloria.*
   a. **Bach** composed (c. 1737/38) four of these Masses (*Kyrie* and *Gloria*) (*S.* 233-236) (*BG,* v. 8; *NB,* Ser. 2, v. 2) which were sometimes incorrectly called "short Masses." There are also five settings of the *Sanctus* (*S.* 237, 238) (*BG,* v. 11, pp. 69, 81; *NB,* Ser. 2, v. 2, pp. 313, 327), at least three of which are probably arrangements of works of other composers.

B. **Bach** composed his "Missa," consisting of the *Kyrie* and *Gloria,* and sent it to Frederick Augustus II at the Catholic court in Dresden. In the letter, dated July 27, 1733, which accompanied the manuscript, **Bach** wrote that he was submitting "the present slight labor of that knowledge" which he had "achieved in *musique.*" He continued with a "humble prayer" that Augustus II (Elector of Saxony) would grant him a court title (*BR,* 128). **Bach** received the title three years later.

1. The second part of the *Mass* (*Credo, Sanctus, Agnus Dei*) was completed by **Bach** at a later date, but probably before 1738.

C. The *Mass in B Minor* is a work of stupendous proportions, requiring nearly three hours for its performance. It represents **Bach's** Christian idealism and is, strictly speaking, neither a Catholic (the Catholic liturgical text is slightly varied) nor a Lutheran Mass. Its extreme length also would preclude performance in a liturgical Service.

1. **Bach** divided the *Mass* into four sections which include 24 (25 if the *Confiteor* is

divided) numbers. These are the *Kyrie* (3); *Gloria* (8); *Credo* (*Symbolum Nicenum*) (8); *Sanctus* (1); and *Osanna* (1); *Benedictus* (1); *Agnus Dei* (2).

2.   Separate movements were frequently sung in church under **Bach's** direction, especially the *Sanctus* and parts of the *Gloria*.

D.   The Mass, as a whole, is made up of a wide variety of styles and forms and, as with all Baroque composers' works, includes some pictorialism and symbolism. The da capo form is used in arias, duets, and even in choruses. The Mass begins in B minor and concludes in D major, a key which is used in about half of the numbers. B minor is the prevailing key in only five numbers. The key relationships between movements are especially effective.

1.   The instrumentation includes 2 flutes, 3 oboes, 2 oboi d'amore, 2 fagotti, 3 trumpets, corno da caccia, timpani, strings, and continuo. The instrumental vocal style predominates in much of the music. The voice and an instrument often "compete" in arias (No. 9), and the voices are required to adopt an instrumental idiom.

2.   **Bach** borrowed and adapted over one third of the Mass from his church cantatas, and one movement (No. 21) from a secular cantata. The Mass, as might be expected, has somewhat the effect of a series of cantatas.

No. 6 (*Gratias agimus*) and No. 24 (*Dona nobis*) use the same music, borrowed from Cantata No. 29, part 2.

No. 4 (*Gloria*), No. 7 (*Domine Deus*), and No. 11 (*Cum sancto*) are from Cantata No. 191, parts 1, 2, 3.

No. 8 (*Qui tollis*) from Cantata No. 46, part 1.

No. 13 (*Patrem*) from Cantata No. 171, part 1.

No. 16 (*Crucifixus*) from Cantata No. 12, part 2.

No. 19 (*Et expecto*) from Cantata No. 120, part 2.

No. 21 (*Osanna*) from secular Cantata No. 215, part 1.

No. 23 (*Agnus Dei*) from Cantata No. 11, part 4.

3.   The original choruses are all in five parts, except the *Sanctus* (No. 20) which is in six parts, and the *Kyrie* (No. 3) which is in four parts. The *Osanna* is the only double chorus.

4.   The *Kyrie* begins immediately with a dramatic four-measure introduction for chorus and orchestra, followed by a fugal exposition of the main theme for orchestra. The five-part chorus then continues with a massive fugue on the same theme, a theme suggesting mental grief and torment.

a.   The *Christe eleison*, a duet for two sopranos, is written in a more tender and personal style, which is characteristic of **Bach's** treatment of the text when it refers to Christ (also Nos. 8 and 15).

5.   Gregorian melodies are used as *cantus firmi* at the beginning of the *Credo* (No. 12) and after the exposition of the two main themes in the *Confiteor* near the end of the *Credo* (No. 19, meas. 73).

a.   In the *Confiteor* **Bach** introduces the Gregorian theme in canon and in augmentation, combined with the other two themes. The change of mood (marked *Adagio* by **Bach** and recalling the *Crucifixus*) at the words "*et expecto resurrectionem mortuorum*" heightens the sense of anticipation as the words are repeated *vivace ed allegro* in a joyful shout joined by the trumpets and timpani.

1)   This final section of the *Confiteor* is sometimes listed as a separate number (No. 20).

6.   The *Crucifixus* (No. 16) (*NS*, 274), borrowed from the chaconne of Cantata No. 12, makes use of the descending chromatic motif, often associated with the thought of grief. The constantly reiterated bass line (it occurs 13 times), the rich and varied harmony, the four independent contrapuntal voice parts, and **Bach's** genius have produced a supreme example of religious music.

a.   During the last statement of the chaconne theme, **Bach** has omitted the orchestral accompaniment. The extraordinary use of a German sixth at the final cadence, modulating to G major, produces an almost overpowering sense of awe, relief, and triumph.

7.   The arias and duets are mostly written in the "modern" florid style and, as usual, there

are examples of symbolism in both solo and chorus numbers.

  a.   The ornate aria, *Laudamus te* (No. 5) has an elaborate violin obbligato, recalling the alto aria in the St. Matthew Passion (No. 47).

  b.   The duet *Et in unum Dominum, Jesum Christum* (And in one Lord, Jesus Christ) (No. 14), for soprano and alto, symbolizes the relation between God the Father and God the Son in canonic imitations at various intervals.

      1)   In the duet *Domine Deus* (No. 7), for soprano and tenor, canonic imitation is also used in a symbolic way. The voices unite in the last measures at the expression of the unity of the Father and the Son.

  c.   The *Credo* (No. 12) symbolizes the unshakable faith of the Church by the steadfast progression of the bass throughout the entire movement.

XV.   **Spiritual Songs** (*BG,* v. 39)

  A.   **Bach** contributed a few original melodies, and figured many basses to melodies by other composers in **Georg Christian Schemelli's** *Musicalisches Gesangbuch,* Leipzig, 1736, which included "954 Spiritual Songs and Arias Old as well as New." These songs, many in chorale style, were intended to be sung by a single voice or voices in unison. Songs in this style are also found in **Anna Magdalena's** *Notenbuch,* 1725 (*Bist du bei mir*).

    1.   Original melodies by **Bach** included in **Schemelli's** Song Book are *Dir, Dir, Jehovah* (also in **Anna Magdalena Bach's** *Notenbuch*) (*S.* 452), *Komm, süsser Tod* (Come, sweet death) (*S.* 478), and *Vergiss mein nicht* (*S.* 505).

SELECTED BIBLIOGRAPHY

Books

1.   Barbour, J. Murray. *Tuning and Temperament.* East Lansing: Michigan State College Press, 1951.

2.   Blume, Friedrich. *Two Centuries of Bach: An Account of Changing Taste,* tr. S. Godman. New York: Oxford University Press, 1950.

3.   Burney, Charles. *A General History of Music.* London: 1776-1789. (Reprint, 2 vols., ed. Frank Mercer. New York: Harcourt, Brace & Co., 1935).

4.   Carrell, Norman. *Bach the Borrower.* London: Allen & Unwin, 1967.

5.   Chiappusso, Jan. *Bach's World.* Bloomington: Indiana University Press, 1969.

6.   David, Hans. *J. S. Bach's Musical Offering.* New York: G. Schirmer, 1945.

7.   David, Hans, and Arthur Mendel, eds. *The Bach Reader.* New York: W. W. Norton, 1945. Revised with a supplement, New York: W. W. Norton, 1966.

8.   Dickinson, A. E. F. *Bach's Fugal Works.* London: Pitman Publishing Co., 1956.

9.   Geiringer, Karl. *The Bach Family: Seven Generations of Creative Genius.* New York: Oxford University Press, 1954.

10. ––––––*Johann Sebastian Bach. The Culmination of an Era.* New York: Oxford University Press, 1966.

11. Hindemith, Paul. *J. S. Bach: Heritage and Obligation.* New Haven: Yale University Press, 1952.

12. Keller, Hermann. *The Organ Works of Bach,* tr. Helen Hewitt. New York: C. F. Peters, 1967.

13. Kinsky, Georg. *Die Originalausgabe der Werke Johann Sebastian Bachs.* Vienna, 1937.

14. Pirro, André. *J. S. Bach,* tr. Mervyn Savill. New York: Orion Press, 1957.

15. Schmieder, Wolfgang. *Thematisch-systematisches Verzeichnis der Musikalischen Werke von Johann Sebastian Bach (Bach-Werke Verzeichnis).* Leipzig: Breitkopf & Härtel, 1950.

16. Schrade, Leo. *Bach, the Conflict between the Sacred and the Secular. Journal of the History of Ideas,* v. 7, No. 2.

17. Schwendowius, Barbara, and Wolfgang Dömling, eds. *Johann Sebastian Bach, Life, Times, Influence.* Kassel: Bärenreiter, 1977.
18. Schweitzer, Albert. *J. S. Bach,* 2 vols., tr. Ernest Newman. London: Breitkopf & Härtel, 1911. Revised, 1952.
19. Smallman, Basil. *The Background of Passion Music; J. S. Bach and His Predecessors.* New York: Dover Publications, 1970.
20. Spitta, Philipp. *Johann Sebastian Bach,* 3 vols., tr. Clara Bell and J. A. Fuller-Maitland. London: Novello, 1884-1885. Reprint, 1951.
21. Tangeman, Robert S. "The Ritornello Forms in Bach's Catechism Chorale Preludes," in *Essays on Music in Honor of Archibald Thompson Davison.* Cambridge: Department of Music, Harvard University, 1957.
22. Terry, Charles Sanford. *Bach: A Biography.* London: Oxford University Press, 1933.
23. –––––––*Bach's Orchestra.* London: Oxford University Press, 1932.
24. –––––––*Bach: The Cantatas and Oratorios.* New York: Oxford University Press, 1925.
25. –––––––*Johann Sebastian Bach: Cantata Texts, Sacred and Secular.* London: Constable and Co., 1926.
26. –––––––*The Music of Bach: An Introduction.* London: Oxford University Press, 1933. Reprint, New York: Dover Publications, 1963.
27. –––––––*The Origin of the Family of Bach Musicians.* London: Oxford University Press, 1933.
28. –––––––*Bach's Chorales,* 3 vols. Cambridge: Cambridge University Press, 1915-1921.
29. –––––––*Bach: The Mass in B Minor.* London: Oxford University Press, 1924.
30. –––––––*Bach: The Passions.* London: Oxford University Press, 1926.
31. Tovey, Sir Donald F. *A Companion to 'Art of Fugue' of J. S. Bach.* London: Oxford University Press, 1931.
32. –––––––*Essays in Musical Analysis,* v. 2. London: Oxford University Press, 1935.
33. Tusler, Robert L. *The Style of J. S. Bach's Chorale Preludes.* New York: Da Capo Press, 1968.

Articles

1. Aldrich, Putnam. "Bach's Technique of Transcription and Improvised Ornamentation," *MQ* 35 (1949), p. 26.
2. Babitz, Sol. "The Problem of Rhythm in Baroque Music," *MQ* 38 (1952), p. 533.
3. Barbour, J. Murray. "Bach and the Art of Temperament," *MQ* 33 (1947), p. 64.
4. Boyden, David D. "The Violin and Its Technique in the 18th Century," *MQ* 36 (1950), p. 9.
5. Chiappusso, Jan. "Bach's Attitude Toward History," *MQ* 39 (1953), p. 396.
6. David, Hans T. "Bach's Musical Offering," *MQ* 23 (1937), p. 314.
7. Geiringer, Karl. "The Artistic Interrelations of the Bach's," *MQ* 36 (1950), p. 363.
8. Harris, Roy, and M. D. H. Norton. "The Art of the Fugue," *MQ* 21 (1935), p. 166.
9. Haydon, Glen. "On the Problem of Expression in Baroque Music," *JAMS* 3 (1950), p. 113.
10. Herz, G. "A 'New' Bach Portrait," *MQ* 29 (1943), p. 225.
11. Lang, Paul Henry. "On the Bach Bicentenary," *MQ* 36 (1950), p. 574.
12. Lippman, E. A. "Symbolism in Music," *MQ* 39 (1953), p. 554.
13. Mansfield, Orlando A. "J. S. Bach's First English Apostles," *MQ* 21 (1935), p. 143.
14. Mendel, Arthur. "More for the Bach Reader," *MQ* 36 (1950), p. 485.
15. –––––––"On the Pitches in Use in Bach's Time," *MQ* 41 (1955), pp. 332, 466.
16. –––––––"On the Keyboard Accompaniments to Bach's Leipzig Church Music," *MQ* 36 (1950), p. 339.
17. –––––––"Pitch in the 16th and Early 17th Centuries," *MQ* 34 (1948), pp. 28, 199, 336, 575.
18. Ratner, L. G. "Eighteenth-Century Theories of Musical Period Structure," *MQ* 42 (1956),

p. 439.

19. Sachs, Curt. "Bach and Blavet," *MQ* 30 (1944), p. 84.

20. Scheide, W. H. "Luther and Bach's *Cantata 50*," *JAMS* 4 (1951), p. 36.

21. Shanet, H. "Why Did J. S. Bach Transpose His Arrangements?" *MQ* 36 (1950), p. 180.

22. Terry, Charles Sanford. "Bach's Swan Song," *MQ* 14 (1933), p. 233.

23. Wolff, Christoph. "Bach's *Handexemplar* of the Goldberg Variations: A New Source," *JAMS* 29 (1976), p. 224.

Music

There is a large number of editions of Bach's works available from publishers in Europe and the United States. Some of the editions are over-edited and should be avoided.

1. Bach, Johann Sebastian. *Neue Ausgabe Sämtlicher Werke.* Kassel: Bärenreiter, 1954-

2. ———————*Werke*, 46 vols. Leipzig: Breitkopf & Härtel, 1851-1900.

3. Geiringer, Karl. *Music of the Bach Family: An Anthology.* Cambridge: Harvard University Press, 1955.

4. Mainous, Frank D. and Robert W. Ottman. *The 371 Chorales by Johann Sebastian Bach.* New York: Holt, Rinehart and Winston, 1966.

15.   A page from the first edition of **Bach's** *Canonic Variations* for organ on *Vom Himmel hoch* (1748). Only the beginning of the canonic voice is engraved.

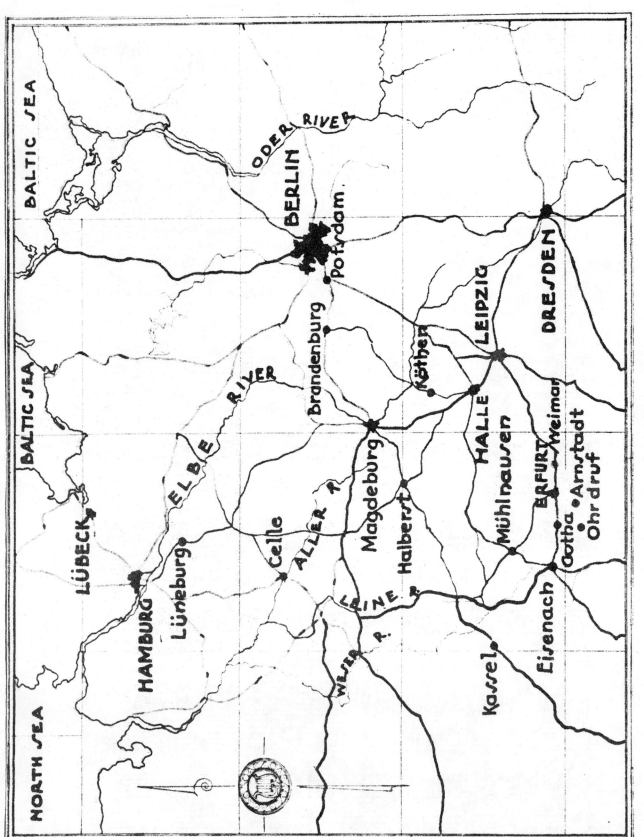

16.   Map of the "Bach Country."

17.   The first page of **Bach's** MS of the full score of his
Passion According to St. Matthew (1739).

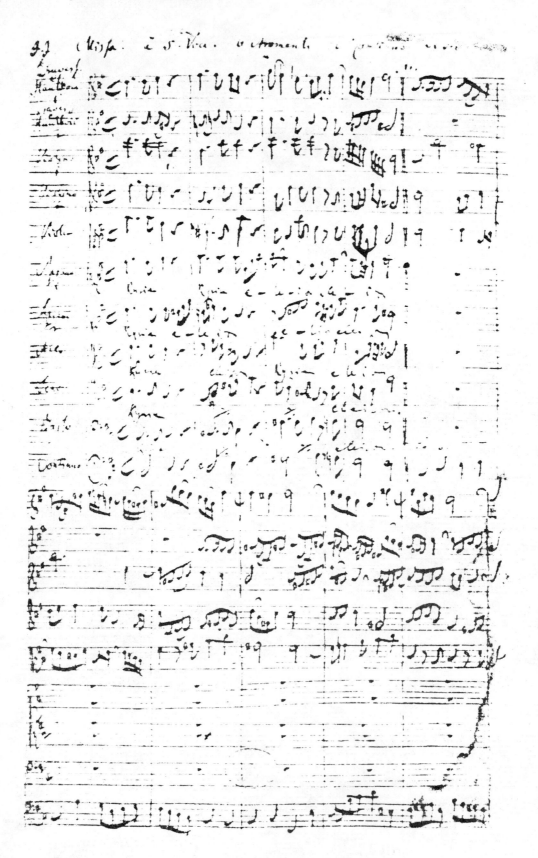

18.   The first page of **Bach**'s MS of his
Mass in B Minor (1733).

19.   *Aria* from the first edition of **Bach**'s
Goldberg Variations Clavierübung, Part IV (1742)

OUTLINE XII

GEORGE FRIDERIC HANDEL (1685-1759)

Life of Handel
Chamber Cantatas — Operas — Church Music — Serenatas
Odes — Oratorios — Instrumental Music — Bach and Handel
Bibliography of Books — Articles — Music

I.   **Life of Handel** (1685-1759)

  A.   Germany (1685-1706)
    1.   **Georg Friedrich Händel** was born in Halle, February 23, the son of the barber-surgeon Georg Händel. He studied keyboard instruments, oboe and violin, and for three years was a pupil of **F. W. Zachow (Zachau)** in counterpoint. He learned composition by copying music of German and Italian composers. Although a Lutheran, he became organist at the Calvinist *Domkirche* in Halle, a Reformed church, in 1702. He went to Hamburg in 1703 as a violinist, and later a harpsichordist, at the opera under **Keiser**. He composed operas there and was strongly influenced by **Keiser's** Italian style.
  B.   Italy (1706-1710)
    1.   **Handel** visited Florence, Rome, Venice, and Naples. In Rome he met with the "Arcadians" **Alessandro** and **Domenico Scarlatti, Corelli, Marcello, Lotti, Pasquini, Steffani,** and others. He composed secular cantatas, some Catholic church music, and a few oratorios and operas. Here he developed his Italian *bel canto* style and became known as a performer on the harpsichord and organ.
  C.   Germany (1710-1712)
    1.   He succeeded **Steffani** as *Kapellmeister* to the Elector of Hanover who became King George I of England in 1714. **Handel** made his first visit to London when *Rinaldo* was produced there in 1711 and then returned briefly to Hanover.
  D.   England (1712-1759)
    1.   In 1712 **Handel** returned to England to live and later changed the spelling of his name. He visited Hanover in 1716 and Italy and Germany again in 1729. He became composer to the Duke of Chandos in 1717 and remained in his service until 1720. In 1721 he purchased a house in London, and on February 20, 1727, became a British subject.
    2.   **Handel** was one of the conductors and composers of the Royal Academy of Music, organized for the performance of opera at the Haymarket in 1719. After the failure of the Academy in 1728, he formed a partnership with Heidegger in the New Royal Academy, 1729-1733. This partnership was dissolved in 1733 but **Handel** continued to produce operas, with artistic success and some financial failures, until 1741.
    3.   With the composition of *Messiah* in 1741, **Handel** devoted himself to oratorio for the remainder of his life. He became blind in later years, but with the help of his pupil, **John Christopher Smith**, he continued to compose. **Handel** conducted *Messiah* for the last time on April 6, 1759, at Covent Garden and died a week later on April 14. He was buried, according to his wishes, in Westminster Abbey. The choirs from the Chapels Royal, St. Paul's Cathedral, and Westminster Abbey sang a Funeral Anthem by **Dr. Croft**, and "there was almost the greatest Concourse of People of all Ranks ever seen upon such, or indeed upon any other Occasion."
  E.   The edition of music referred to is the complete edition of **Handel's** works, *Georg Friedrich Handels Werke,* called "Handel-Gesellschaft" edition (*HG*). Pertinent references in Otto Erich Deutsch, *Handel: a Documentary Biography* (*DH*) and Paul Henry Lang, *George Frideric Handel* (*LH*) are included.

II. **Chamber Cantatas**

  A. **Handel** mastered the Italian *bel canto* style under **Alessandro Scarlatti** and others, and developed his lyric and dramatic powers in his secular chamber cantatas. Most of the cantatas were composed in Italy (1706-1710), and they represent some of his finest and often most difficult music.

  B. Solo cantatas with continuo (*HG*, vols. 50-51)

   1. There are 72 solo cantatas (51 for soprano, 19 for alto, 2 for bass), all composed to Italian texts (8 have the same text). These cantatas usually consist of two or three da capo arias and recitatives.

   2. *O Numi eterni* (*La Lucretia*, No. 46)   (*HG*, v. 51, p. 32)

  C. Cantatas with instrumental accompaniments (*HG*, v. 52a-b)

   1. The instrumentation, not always indicated, includes strings, and sometimes an oboe is added. The recitatives are with continuo. Some cantatas begin with an Overture or Sinfonia. All but six of the 28 cantatas are for one solo voice (17 soprano, 2 alto, 2 bass, 1 tenor). No. 8, for tenor, has an English text, and No. 18, for soprano, has a Spanish text with guitar accompaniment.

   2. *Armida abbandonata*, No. 13, for soprano, has an unusual recitative for two violins with continuo. The recitative with "furioso" accompaniment is characteristic of **Handel's** early period.

   3. *Delirio amoroso*, No. 12, for soprano, shows the influence of the *concerto grosso* style in the arias.

   4. There are two trios, 1712 (*HG*, v. 32), each for two sopranos and bass.

  D. Duets (*HG*, v. 32)

   1. Thirteen duets with Italian texts were written at Hanover in 1712. They are for two sopranos, soprano and alto, and soprano and bass. The accompaniments are for figured bass with an independent "basso" part.

III. **Operas**

  A. **Handel** wrote his first opera in Hamburg in 1705 (*Almira*) and his last one in London in 1741, the masterpiece, *Deidamia*.

   1. He used the operatic forms of Neapolitan *opera seria* and, although his operas follow a general pattern, there is great variety in each opera.

   2. The operas consist principally of recitatives with continuo (rarely accompanied by instruments), some arioso passages, da capo arias, duets, ensembles (often at the end of acts) and, exceptionally, choruses. The use of a ballet is rare.

    a. The dramatic action usually occurs in the recitatives and large scenes, and the arias are often reflective.

    b. The leading male parts were usually sung by soprano or alto castrati, especially after 1720. Basses were also given important parts. The leading female parts were sung by women, and tenors and baritones were allotted subordinate parts.

     1) Among the leading castrati were **Farinelli** (**Carlo Broschi**), **Senesino** (**Francesco Bernardi**), and **Giovanni Carestini**. Most of **Handel's** famous songs for bass were written for **Giuseppe Boschi**.

     2) Women singers included **Susanna Cibber** (**Arne**), **Faustina**, the wife of the composer **Hasse**, and her rival, **Francesca Cuzzoni**.

    c. There is much use of tone painting and musical symbolism throughout the operas.

   3. **Handel's** principal librettists were **Nicola Haym** (*Giulio Cesare*) and **Paolo Rolli** (*Scipione*). Three librettos were by **Pietro Metastasio**, one of the most distinguished librettists of the time (*Siroe*).

   4. The orchestra was used for the overture (usually the French type with added movements (*Rinaldo*, *HG*, v. 58), to introduce scenes and acts, for some stage business, and to

provide accompaniments, introductions, and interludes for arias.

    a.   The basis of **Handel's** opera orchestra was the harpsichord, from which he conducted, and the string bass. Individual instruments of various types were added to this combination. The full string section was used for large effects, with the occasional addition of flutes, oboes, bassoons, horns, and trumpets.

    b.   The instruments were often divided into three groups, as in the *concerti grossi* of **Corelli.** These consisted of the *concertino* of two violins and cello with harpsichord or large lute playing the continuo, the *tutti* group of strings, and an added group of *ripieno* strings with another harpsichord.

B.   Hamburg

    1.   *Almira,* 1705 *(HG,* v. 55)

        a.   **Handel** wrote three operas in Hamburg, but only *Almira* has survived. The music of *Almira* is heavily indebted to **Keiser's** operas. The recitatives are in German and many of the arias are in Italian.

        b.   The *Saraband (HG,* v. 55, p. 81) in Act III, an "Asiatic's" dance, became famous in *Rinaldo* as the aria, *"Lascia ch'io pianga."*

C.   Italy

    1.   *Agrippina,* Venice, 1709 *(HG,* v. 57)

        a.   This was one of **Handel's** first important operas, and it was immediately successful. It was borrowed in part from *Acis et Galatea, Rodrigo,* and other works.

        b.   **Handel** used both old and new devices of Italian opera. These include the repetition of short phrases, extension of the melody to avoid the cadence, alternation of meter *(HG,* v. 57, p. 121), *bel canto* arias, and "unison arias" with the melody doubled by the violins without continuo, or by all the strings, sometimes with continuo.

D.   England (1711-1741)

    1.   A few unsuccessful attempts had been made to establish English opera after the death of **Purcell** in 1695. Italian operas were given English translations, and some had mixed Italian and English texts.

        a.   Italian opera was being heard in London when **Handel** arrived in 1711 to produce *Rinaldo (HG,* v. 58). The opera was a success, but **Handel** was severely criticized by Addison and Steele in the *Spectator (DH,* 35).

    2.   1711-1715

        a.   *Rinaldo,* 1711 *(HG,* v. 58) *(LH,* 119-123), borrowed freely from earlier operas, oratorios, and cantatas.

        b.   *Teseo,* 1713 *(HG,* v. 60), with its famous aria, *"Vieni, torna, idolo mio."* (p. 56)

        c.   *Amadigi,* 1715 *(HG,* v. 62)

    3.   1719-1728

        a.   The Royal Academy of Music was founded in 1719 with **Heidegger** as manager and **Handel, Bononcini,** and **Ariosti** as composers and conductors. In spite of the rivalry which developed and the quarrels of the prima donnas, **Faustina** and **Cuzzoni, Handel** wrote a large number of successful operas before the collapse of the Royal Academy in bankruptcy in 1728.

        b.   *Muzio Scevola,* 1721 *(HG,* v. 64), is a composite work of little value. It was designed to test the comparative ability of **Handel** and rival composers. Act I was composed by **Mattei** or **Ariosti,** Act II by **Bononcini,** and Act III by **Handel.**

        c.   *Ottone,* 1723 *(HG,* v. 66) was one of **Handel's** most successful operas of this period.

        d.   *Giulio Cesare,* 1724 *(HG,* v. 68); *Tamerlano,* 1724 *(HG,* v. 69); *Rodelinda,* 1725 *(HG,* v. 70); and *Admento,* 1727 *(HG,* v. 73) were equally successful and of high musical quality.

    4.   1729-1733

        a.   The New Royal Academy, founded by **Handel** in partnership with **Heidegger,** lasted until 1733. At the end of this period **Handel** wrote one of his most powerful and striking operas, *Orlando,* 1732 *(HG,* v. 82).

5. 1733-1737
   a. The "Opera of the Nobility" was founded in 1733 in rivalry with **Handel**. **Nicola Porpora** and later **Johann Adolf Hasse** were assigned as conductors and composers. The famous castrati **Senesino** and **Farinelli** were among the singers.
   b. During this period **Handel** wrote two operas, *Ariodante* (*HG*, v. 85) and *Alcina*, 1735 (*HG*, v. 86). These unusual operas were influenced by French opera and are light, graceful, and less dramatic than his usual style.
6. 1737-1741
   a. *Serse*, 1738 (*HG*, v. 92), a comic opera, was not a success when first performed, but is known today for the famous song about the shade of a plane tree, *"Ombra mai fu"* (*"Largo"*) (*HG*, v. 92, p. 6).
   b. *Deidamia*, 1741 (*HG*, v. 94), also a failure, was the last of **Handel's** 40 London operas.
E. **Handel** developed the large dramatic scene which combined recitatives, arias or parts of arias, and sometimes orchestral preludes, in one unified whole.
   1. A dramatic scene in *Orlando* (*HG*, v. 82, pp. 64-72) includes an accompanied recitative, partly in 5/8 meter (pp. 65-66), a rondo-like section with a recurring gavotte (pp. 67, 69, 71) and a chaconne used as an intermediate section.
   2. In *Giulio Cesare*, 1724 (*HG*, v. 68), the scene beginning *"Dall' ondoso"* (p. 102) forms a musical picture. This consists of an orchestral prelude, an accompanied recitative, the recitative with figured bass, and a concluding da capo aria.
F. Arias
   1. Arias usually follow the Italian da capo aria form: A—B—A.
      a. The first section (A) begins with two announcements of the opening part of the theme (called a "motto" beginning), first by the orchestra and then by the solo voice. A complete statement of the theme by the voice then follows.
      b. The middle section (B) is often in the relative key and its dominant. It may be for continuo or, in more dramatic arias, accompanied by instruments. It usually contains different, but not greatly contrasting, material.
      c. The final section (A) is a repetition of the first section.
   2. Other types of arias.
      a. Arias in two parts with highly contrasting sections: *Ah! crudel!* sung by Rinaldo, a castrato (*Rinaldo*, *HG*, v. 58, p. 72)
      b. Through-composed arias: *Ombra mai fu* (*Serse*, *HG*, v. 92, p. 6)
      c. Arias in rondo form: *Verdi prati* (*Alcina*, *HG*, v. 86, p. 94)
      d. Influence of the rhythms of dance music: Siciliano, *Affani des pensier* (*Ottone*, *HG*, v. 66, p. 39); Saraband, *Lascia, ch'io pianga* (*Rinaldo*, *HG*, v. 58, p. 61); Gavotte, *Gia lo stringo* (*Orlando*, *HG*, v. 82, p. 79); slow dance-like rhythms, *Cara sposa* (*Rinaldo*, *HG*, v. 58, p. 39)
      e. The *concerto grosso* style is used in some bravura arias.
   3. Ensembles for two, three, four voices are frequently on a large scale and often conclude an act.
      a. Duet (*Orlando*, *HG*, v. 82, p. 93)
      b. Trios (*Tamerlano*, *HG*, v. 69, p. 79; *Alcina*, *HG*, v. 86, p. 140)
   4. Choruses are comparatively few in number and usually occur at the end of an act (*Giulio Cesare*, *HG*, v. 68, pp. 81, 130; *Alcina*, *HG*, v. 86, pp. 132, 145). There is very little choral polyphony, and the choral style is distinct from the oratorio chorus.
G. The failure of **Handel's** operas was due to the lack of support of the nobility for whom they were intended, and of the middle class who were not interested in opera in a language which they could not understand. The criticisms, which began in 1711, by Joseph Addison and Richard Steele in the *Spectator*, and the success of the *Beggar's Opera*, 1728, by **John Gay** and **John Christopher Pepusch**, supported the feeling of the middle class.
   1. The *Beggar's Opera* was a ballad opera satirizing political figures and parodying Italian opera. Ballad opera consists of spoken English dialogue with music borrowed from

folk songs, well-known tunes by contemporary composers, and dances.
2.   The *Beggar's Opera* included some French melodies and adaptations of music by **Giovanni Bononcini, Henry Carey, Handel, Purcell,** and others. **Gay** wrote the libretto and **Pepusch** composed the French overture and arranged the tunes. Criticism and the popular success of the *Beggar's Opera* did not discourage **Handel** from continuing to write operas, however, and after that time he composed many of his greatest works.

H.   **Handel** borrowed extensively from his own music as well as from the music of **Carissimi, Kerll, Keiser, G. Muffat, Corelli, Graun,** and others. Sometimes he would borrow only a theme or a phrase; at other times he would borrow an entire movement. He used this material in a great variety of ways, transcribing both vocal and instrumental music for various combinations.
1.   **Mattheson** in *Der Vollkommene Capellmeister,* 1739, said that "borrowing is allowable, but one must pay interest, *i. e.,* one must so contrive and work out the imitations that they take on a fine and better appearance than the things from which they are borrowed."

IV. Church Music

A.   **Handel** composed comparatively little music for use in church, and most of it was written for a special occasion or purpose. The oratorios were not designed for use in church.
1.   *St. John Passion,* 1704 (*HG,* v. 9)
   a.   This Passion-oratorio was written in Hamburg to a "reform" text by Christian Postel. It is in operatic style without chorales and includes *secco* recitatives, ariosos, ensembles, arias, and choruses in concerto style.
2.   Catholic church music (1706-1710) (*HG,* v. 38)
   a.   Two Psalms, *Laudati pueri,* first setting, 1701-1703, and *Dixit Dominus* for solo, chorus, and orchestra, were written in Rome, 1703.
3.   *Brockes Passion,* 1716 (*HG,* v. 15)
   a.   **Handel** set the German text by **Barthold Heinrich Brockes** during a visit to Germany in 1716. The music includes a fugal overture, accompanied recitatives, arias, choruses (action and reflective), and a number of chorales. **Keiser, Telemann,** and **Mattheson** also made settings of the Brockes Passion text, and **Bach** copied out parts of **Handel's** score.
4.   *Utrecht Te Deum* and *Jubilate,* 1713 (*HG,* v. 31)
   a.   The *Te Deum* is set to an English text. It includes chorus, parts for solo voices, and orchestra. It was written to celebrate the Peace of Utrecht, and shows the influence of **Purcell's** choral style. The *Jubilate,* in six sections, also features the chorus, with a solo, duet, and trio.
5.   *Chandos Anthems, c.* 1718-1720 (*HG,* vols. 34, 35)
   a.   These 12 anthems were composed while **Handel** was composer to the Duke of Chandos at Cannons, 1717-1720. They are set to texts taken from the Psalms.
   b.   The anthems are in cantata style and include instruments and three- and four-part choruses (a few five- and six-part) separated by solos and duets. The choruses frequently alternate fugal and homophonic writing.
   c.   No. 6, "As Pants the Hart," is based on the chorale *Christ lag in Todesbanden* (*HG,* v. 34, p. 212).
      1)   The use of the chorale is rare in works of **Handel.** Other examples may be found in the *Funeral Anthem, L'Allegro, Occasional Oratorio, Brockes Passion,* and in the *Foundling Hospital Anthem.*
6.   Coronation Anthems, 1727 (*HG,* v. 14)
   a.   *Zadok the Priest* (*HG,* v. 14, p. 1)
      1)   This is the first of the four texts which **Handel** set for the coronation of George II in 1727. This magnificent work has been performed at coronations ever since.
   b.   The text of the third anthem, *My Heart is Inditing,* was set by **Purcell** for the

coronation of James II.

    c.   The coronation anthems include choruses in four, five, six, and seven parts and a large orchestra of trumpets, timpani, oboes, strings, and organ. Handel himself selected the fifty singers for the chorus which sang at the coronation.

  7. Other large scale anthems featuring choruses

    a.   *Wedding Anthem*, 1736 (*HG*, v. 36). Written for the marriage of Frederick, Prince of Wales, to Princess Augusta of Saxe-Gotha.

    b.   *Funeral Anthem*, 1738 (*HG*, v. 11). This anthem, *The Ways of Zion Do Mourn*, was occasioned by the death of Handel's former patron, Queen Caroline.

    c.   *Dettingen Te Deum*, 1743 (*HG*, v. 25) and *Dettingen Anthem*, 1743 (*HG*, v. 36). Written to celebrate the victory of Hanoverian and English armies over the French at Dettingen, near Frankfurt.

    d.   *Foundling Hospital Anthem*, 1749 (*HG*, v. 36, p. 151). Written for a benefit performance for the Hospital, one of Handel's charities. It uses the chorale *Aus tiefer Noth* (*HG*, v. 36, p. 164).

V.   Serenatas, Odes, Masques, Pastorales

  A. These were short choral works in the nature of cantatas and without action.

    1. The early dramatic cantata (Serenata), *Aci, Galatea, e Polifemo* (*HG*, v. 95), was written in Naples, 1708. The music was used later in an English version by Gay (*Acis and Galatea, c.* 1720, *HG*, v. 3). New music was added to a third version in Italian, 1732 (*HG*, v. 95).

    2. Odes were free cantatas for soloists, chorus, and orchestra and were usually in several sections.

      a.   *Birthday Ode for Queen Anne*, 1714 (*HG*, v. 46); *Ode for St. Cecilia's Day*, 1739 (*HG*, v. 23).

    3. Masques included choruses and arias with scenery and costumes, but were without action.

      a.   *Haman and Mordecai* (*HG*, v. 40), with music largely taken from the *Brockes Passion*, was later revised and became Handel's first English oratorio, 1732.

      b.   *Haman and Mordecai: a Masque*, 1720 (*HG*, v. 40) and other works emphasizing chorus mark the transition to oratorio.

VI.   Oratorios

  A. Handel's oratorios were designed as entertainment and were generally performed in the theatre, especially during Lent when theatrical presentations were forbidden by law. Some of the texts which Handel set were decidedly inferior, but most of his greatest oratorios were inspired by texts from the Bible and the poets Dryden (*Alexander's Feast*), Milton (*Samson*), and Congreve (*Semele*).

  B. The oratorio, as developed by Handel, consisted of a libretto based on a religious, mythological, allegorical, or contemplative subject, set to music for solo voices, chorus, and orchestra, and performed without costumes, scenery, or action.

    1. There is no difference in style between oratorios on religious or secular subjects. The majority of the oratorios are great choral dramas based on Old Testament stories. They are in three sections or acts and, in contrast to the operas, the chorus is featured and there are fewer da capo arias.

  C. The following oratorios with allegorical subjects show the influence of the ode.

    1. *Alexander's Feast*, 1736 (*HG*, v. 12). Text by Dryden.

    2. *L'Allegro ed il Penseroso*, 1740 (*HG*, v. 6). Libretto by Charles Jennens. The first two acts are based on Milton's poems, the third is by Jennens.

    3. *Occasional Oratorio*, 1746 (*HG*, v. 43). Written for the occasion of national rejoicing

over the failure of the rebellion of the Young Pretender, Charles Stuart.   The text of the first two acts was adapted from the Psalms, and the third act was borrowed largely from *Israel in Egypt.* The four-movement *Overture,* ending with a *March,* is outstanding.

    4. *Triumph of Time and Truth,* 1757 (*HG,* v. 20). **Handel's** last secular oratorio is based almost entirely on his earlier works.

D.   Oratorios with strong operatic influence and emphasis on the aria.

    1. *Semele,* 1743 (*HG,* v. 7), is an opera without action. Text by **Congreve.**

    2. *Hercules,* 1744 (*HG,* v. 4) was called a "New musical drama."

    3. *Susanna,* 1748 (*HG,* v. 1) is a Biblical drama with the individual characters clearly delineated.

    4. *Alexander Balus,* 1747 (*HG,* v. 33) is based on the story of the love of Alexander, King of Syria, for Cleopatra, daughter of Ptolemy.

E.   Choral dramas based on Old Testament stories and conceived on a monumental scale. In these works the chorus plays a most important part, sometimes even taking the place of soloists (*Israel in Egypt,* 1738, *HG,* v. 16).

    1. *Deborah,* 1733 (*HG,* v. 29). The overture uses melodies from two of the choruses.

    2. *Saul,* 1739 (*HG,* v. 13) is known for the "Dead March" and the lengthy overture for organ and orchestra.

    3. *Judas Maccabaeus,* 1746 (*HG,* v. 22), one of **Handel's** finest oratorios, relates the exploits of the great Jewish military leader, *c.* 160 B. C.

    4. *Joshua,* 1747 (*HG,* v. 17) contains the well-known "See the conquering Hero comes."

    5. *Jephtha,* 1751 (*HG,* v. 44) is **Handel's** last oratorio on a religious subject.

F.   *Messiah,* 1741 (*HG,* v. 45) (*LH,* 332-356)

    1. *Messiah,* **Handel's** best known work, is unique among his oratorios. The text, selected by **Charles Jennens** (possibly with the help of **Handel**), was taken from the Bible. It is a "representation of the fulfillment of redemption through the Redeemer, Messiah." The three parts deal with I) The prophecy and God's plan of redemption through the coming of the Messiah; II) Redemption through the sacrifice of the Messiah; III) The conquest of Death.

    2. The oratorio was completed in 24 days and first performed in Dublin, April 13, 1742, after a public rehearsal on April 8 in the "New Musick Hall in Fishamble-street." The work met with great success and over 700 persons were present. During the intervals between the three parts of the oratorio, **Handel** played one of his organ concertos as was his custom.

G.   **Handel's** oratorio orchestra was similar to his opera orchestra, but the organ instead of the harpsichord was used for the continuo. Occasionally he uses unusual instruments for special effects, as in the aria "Hark! he strikes the golden lyre" from *Alexander Balus* (*HG,* v. 33, p. 27).   Here he uses two flutes antiphonally with two solo cellos, harp, and mandolin.

    1. **Mozart** was commissioned by Baron van Swieten, about 1788, to write additional wind parts, to take the place of the organ, for performances of several of **Handel's** works, including *Messiah.*

H.   Arias and ensembles

    1. Oratorio arias were in operatic style (many were borrowed from operas) and in a variety of forms.

    2. Types of arias

       a. *Bel canto*, without da capo ("I know that my Redeemer liveth," *Messiah*)

       b. Unison aria ("The people that walked in darkness," *Messiah*)

       c. Da capo aria ("Why do the nations," *Messiah)*

       d. Aria concluded (da capo) with the orchestral introduction ("O had I Jubal's lyre," *Joshua, HG,* v. 17, p. 188)

       e. Aria in concerto style ("Hark, he strikes the golden lyre," *Alexander Balus,*

HG, v. 33, p. 27). The accompaniment includes harp, mandolin, organ, flutes, and strings.

    f.   Strophic aria ("Ask, if yon damask rose be sweet," (*Susanna, HG,* v. 1, p. 110)

  3.   Solo ensembles were infrequently used. They are usually more contrapuntal than operatic ensembles.

    a.   The quartet in *Semele* (*HG,* v. 7, p. 40) begins with the typical short statement of the theme by the orchestra, then by one voice, then by the complete statement of the theme.

    b.   *Solomon* (*HG,* v. 26, p. 153) has a trio with simple accompaniment for violin and continuo.

    c.   The quartet in *Jephtha* (*HG,* v. 44, p. 160) is one of **Handel's** most dramatic ensembles.

    d.   *Hercules* (*HG,* v. 4, p. 207) has ariosos and accompanied recitatives similar to the dramatic scenes found in the operas.

I.   Choruses

  1.   **Handel's** choral technique was derived from Italian opera, **Purcell's** choruses, the German cantata, and the **Carissimi** oratorio. His contrapuntal technique is free, and contrapuntal and harmonic writing frequently alternate (*Judas Maccabaeus, HG,* v. 22, p. 88). Fugal movements often have only an exposition, followed by chordal passages (*Hallelujah, Amen* choruses).

  2.   Forms and styles used in choral writing

    a.   Motet style

    b.   Double chorus with *a cappella* sections contrasted with accompanied sections

    c.   Madrigal style (*Saul, HG,* v. 13, p. 100, and *Triumph of Time, HG,* v. 24, p. 68)

    d.   The *cantus firmus* was sometimes based on a chorale, but was usually an original melody (*L'Allegro, HG,* v. 6, p. 168)

    e.   Dance rhythms (*Joshua, HG,* v. 17, p. 82)

    f.   Chaconne and ground bass (*Saul, HG,* v. 13, p. 17)

    g.   Choral recitative (*Israel in Egypt, HG,* v. 18, p. 55)

    h.   Concerto style ("His yoke is easy," *Messiah*)

    i.   Da capo chorus (*Judas Maccabaeus, HG,* v. 22, p. 210; *Triumph of Time, HG,* v. 24)

    j.   Solo and chorus alternating (*Israel in Egypt, HG,* v. 16, p. 258)

    k.   Quadruple fugue (*Alexander's Feast, HG,* v. 12)

J.   Tone-painting (pictorialism)

  1.   Tone-painting on a broad scale is frequent in the oratorios as well as in the operas.

  2.   In the famous chorus, "And there came all manner of flies and lice" (*Israel in Egypt, HG,* v. 16, p. 27), both chorus and orchestra illustrate the text. The two scenes picturing the night are also remarkable descriptive passages (*CMA,* 354).

  3.   "The people that walked in darkness" and "All we like sheep" (*Messiah*) are other examples of tone-painting.

  4.   The orchestral *Sinfonia* (*Hercules, HG,* v. 4, p. 192), alternating between *Largo* and *Furioso e forte,* pictures the agony of the hero.

VII.   **Instrumental Music**

A.   **Handel's** instrumental works are comparatively few in number. They consist of keyboard music, chamber music, and orchestral music. As in his other works, he was influenced by all the forms and styles of his time, French, German, and especially Italian.

B.   Harpsichord music (*HG,* vols. 2, 48)

  1.   The music for harpsichord consists of suites ("lessons"), fugues (for harpsichord or organ) and miscellaneous pieces. Many of these compositions were written for his pupils and are relatively simple. Those that he wrote for his own use are often only skeletons on which he elaborated in a free improvisatory manner.

2.   Handel's harpsichord music cannot be compared to that of his contemporaries, **Bach**, **Scarlatti**, or **Couperin**, but it often reveals his gift for melody, rhythmic interest, and the expression of the *affetti* (mood, emotion, or passion).

3.   Collections of suites

    a.   *Suites de pièces pour le clavecin*, 1720, 1733, 1742 (*HG*, v. 2)

       1)   The three suites contain a variety of movements (from 3 to 7) including, in addition to the usual dance movements (allemande, courante, sarabande, gigue), the **Scarlatti**-type sonata, French overture, chaconne, passacaglia, air, gavotte, siciliano, prelude, fugue, variation, minuet, and "lesson."

       2)   The suites are in one key throughout (except for two), with a preference for the minor mode. Many of the suites are unified by using the same thematic material in two or more movements.

       3)   The first collection in 1720 contains eight suites, **Handel's** first instrumental music to be published. The fifth suite includes one of **Handel's** best known works, the so-called "Harmonious Blacksmith" variations.

       4)   The second collection of 1733 contains seven suites and two chaconnes, one with 21 and one with 62 variations. The air from the first suite in B-flat was used by **Brahms** for his "Handel Variations."

       5)   The third collection of 1742 includes two suites and two capriccios, a fantasia, a sonatina, and other pieces.

       6)   A number of early clavier pieces are included in *HG*, v. 48 and *Six Fugues faciles*, published in 1776, said to be by **Handel**.

4.   *Six Fugues or Voluntarys*, Op. 3, 1735 (*HG*, v. 2)

    a.   These works, for organ or harpsichord, are written on two staves with optional pedal part. The organs in England, with very few exceptions, did not have pedals until after **Handel's** time. They were generally small instruments with light tone and were often portable.

C.   Chamber music

  1.   **Handel's** principal chamber works include sonatas for one instrument and continuo, Op. 1, and two sets of trio sonatas, Op. 2, and 5.

    a.   These works show the influence of **Corelli** and are rarely technically or formally advanced. They are mostly in the form of the church sonata and some have dance movements added (*HG*, v. 27, p. 19). Dance-like movements are sometimes designated "Allegro" (*HG*, v. 27, p. 41).

    b.   Many of the movements were arranged from earlier vocal and instrumental compositions and some were used in later works.

  2.   "XV Solos for a German Flute, Hoboy, or Violin, with a Thorough Bass for the Harpsichord or Bass Violin, Opera Prima," 1724 (*HG*, v. 27)

    a.   This collection of 15 sonatas is based on 12 sonatas originally published in Amsterdam and then by Walsh in London. The instrumentation is not always indicated, but Nos. 3, 10, 12, 13, 14, 15, are known as the "violin sonatas." Nos. 1, 2, 4, 5, 7, 9, 11 are for the German flute (transverse flute), although Nos. 2, 4, 7, 11 are also suited to the recorder. Nos. 6, and 8 are for oboe (No 6 may have been originally for gamba).

  3.   "IX Sonatas or Trios for Two Violins, Flutes, or Hoboys with a Thorough Bass for the Harpsichord or Violoncello, Opera Seconda," 1733 (*HG*, v. 27)

  4.   "VII Sonatas or Trios for Two Violins or German Flutes with a Thorough Bass for the Harpsichord or Violoncello, Opera Quinta," 1739 (*HG*, v. 27)

  5.   "VI Sonatas for Two Hoboys with a Thorough Bass for the Harpsichord," c. 1696? (*HG*, v. 27; *MSO*, v. 1, p. 188)

  6.   "Sonata di Viola da Gamba e Cembalo concertato," c. 1705 (*HG*, v. 48, p. 102)

D.   Orchestral music

  1.   **Handel's** works for instrumental ensembles are usually in *concerto grosso* form. They include the *concerti grossi*, Op. 3 & 6; organ concertos, Op. 4 & 7; *Water Music*, and *Royal Fireworks Music*.

  2.   *Six Oboe Concertoes*, Op. 3, 1729 (*HG*, v. 21)

    a.   The six so-called "oboe" concertos include flutes (Nos. 1, 3) and bassoons (Nos. 1, 6) with oboes, strings, and continuo. The oboe usually doubles the strings and is used as a solo instrument only in the slow movement of Nos. 2, and 3. There are, however, three solo concertos for oboe and strings (*HG,* v. 27, p. 85).

  3.   *Twelve Grand Concertos,* Op. 6, 1740 (*HG,* v. 30)

    a.   This set includes examples of the orchestral concerto (No. 5, 5th movement, and No. 7), solo concerto (No. 6, 4th movement), and also the typical *concerto grosso.*

    b.   There are four to six varied movements including, in addition to church-sonata movements, the French Overture, Polonaise, Siciliana, Menuet, Hornpipe, Musette, and Gigue.

    c.   The concertos are all scored for strings, and the *concertino* consists of the usual **Corelli** trio sonata (2 violins, cello, and continuo).

E.   Organ concertos (*HG,* vols. 28, 48)

  1.   **Handel** wrote three sets of six organ concertos each: 1) Op. 4, 1738; 2) 1740; 3) Op. 7, published in 1760. They were all published by Walsh as "Concertos for the Harpsichord or Organ."

    a.   Many of the concertos were arranged from other compositions, principally *concerti grossi* and chamber works. The original concertos are Op. 4, Nos. 1, 2, 4, 6, and most of Op. 7, with certain movements borrowed.

    b.   **Handel,** who was considered one of the greatest keyboard players of his time, intended the concertos for his own use and played them between the acts of his oratorios. In fact, it is related that some came to hear the concertos and only tolerated the oratorios.

  2.   The small organs on which **Handel** played his concertos were probably similar to the one which he recommended in 1749 for the residence of **Charles Jennens.** This chamber organ, built by **Richard Bridge,** consisted of only one keyboard, no pedal, with a compass from G up to d'''. All of the stops were to be "whole," not divided into two parts, one playable in the treble and one in the bass. The stops included an Open Diapason, 8'; "Stopt" Diapason, 8'; Principal, 4'; Twelfth, 2 2/3'; Fifteenth, 2'; Great Tierce, 1 3/5'; and a Flute, probably a soft 8'. **Handel** suggested that reed stops be omitted, because of the difficulty of keeping them in tune.

    a.   Music for organ was very slow in developing in England and was never in any way comparable to that in France and especially Germany where good-sized organs, with independent pedal organs, were known as early as the 16th century.

  3.   The original organ score of the concertos consisted of the upper part and figured bass, and the performance was improvised on this outline. Modern editions of the concertos vary a great deal as regards the editors realizations of the two lines of music. The organ played with the orchestra in the tuttis, except when the score was marked "*senza organo.*" Sometimes an entire slow movement was missing and was intended to be improvised by the performer (Op. 7, Nos. 2, 4, 6).

    a.   The orchestra usually consisted of two oboes or flutes, and strings, and was used in a variety of ways. It often played only at the beginning and end of the sections, framing a long solo section for the organ in *concerto grosso* style. The harpsichord was probably used with the continuo.

    b.   *Concerto,* Op. 4, No. 6 was published for "*Harpa o Organo*" and includes two recorders and strings.

  4.   No. 1 of the Second Set (there is no opus number) is borrowed from the *Trio Sonata,* Op. 5, No. 6, and Nos. 2, 3, 4, 5, are arrangements of Nos. 11, 10, 1, 5, 6, from the *Concerti Grossi,* Op. 6.

  5.   The first concerto in the Third Set, Op. 7, has a pedal part indicated for the first and only time in the concertos. Possibly **Handel** performed the concerto in 1724 at the opening of the enlarged organ in St. Paul's Cathedral which was equipped with pedals at that time.

F.   *Water Music* (*HG*, v. 47)
   1.   Walsh published "The Celebrated Water Musick," *c.* 1732-33, which consisted of 21 movements. A second publication, "Handel's Celebrated Water Musick Compleat," 1743, was "set for the harpsichord" and contained 41 movements.
   2.   Parts of the *Water Music* were composed as early as 1715 and may have been performed at that time at one of the water parties given by George I. An augmented version of the 1715 *Water Music*, with trumpets, horns, flutes, oboes, bassoons, and strings, was played, twice before supper and once after, at a royal water party on the Thames in 1717 (*DH*, 76, 77).
   3.   The separate numbers include an overture, popular airs, dances, adagios, allegros, and andantes (*AM*, v. 45, p. 116).
G.   *Royal Fireworks Music* (*HG*, v. 47)
   1.   Handel was commissioned in 1749 to compose music for a fireworks display in Green Park to celebrate the signing of the Treaty of Aix-la-Chapelle, 1748.
      a.   The music was a success, but the large "temple" erected for the fireworks display caught fire and burned to the ground (*DH*, 667).
   2.   The original orchestra (strings were added at later performances) included 24 oboes, 12 bassoons, 1 of the new double bassoons, 1 serpent, 9 horns, 9 trumpets, and 3 timpani.
   3.   The music, published by Walsh in 1749, is in five movements: 1) "A Grand Overture of Warlike instruments," 2) Bourrée, 3) "La Paix," (*AM*, v. 34, p. 54), 4) "La Rejouissance," 5) Menuet I, II. It was followed by a "Royal Salute" of 101 cannons.

VIII.   Bach and Handel

A.   **Bach** and **Handel**, two exceptional geniuses, were born in the same year, 26 days apart, and in the same general environment.
   1.   They were, however, far apart in their artistic achievements, personalities, and lives. They both represent fundamental characteristics of the Baroque style which they emphasized in their individual ways.
   2.   **Bach**, a family man, spent all of his life in Germany and only became known to the general public in the 19th century. **Handel**, who never married, was also born in Germany, but spent some time in Italy, and lived most of his life in England. While there he made occasional visits to Germany, France, and especially Italy. He became a national celebrity and was well known on the continent as well as in Great Britain.
   3.   **Bach** was not a man of his age and composed for himself, his pupils, and for the needs of his position. **Handel** was an active and successful man of his times and numbered among his friends all strata of society.
      a.   **Bach** and **Handel** both had their roots in German music, but were influenced in various ways and in varying degrees by Italian and French styles. **Handel**, in addition, was influenced by the choral writing of **Purcell**.
   4.   **Bach's** eminence lies in his religious and instrumental music, **Handel's** in his operas and oratorios.
   5.   **Bach** and **Handel** both drew inspiration from the Bible. **Bach**, however, was primarily interested in the ideas of Death and Redemption. **Handel** almost always chose stories dealing with the strong characters of the Old Testament.
   6.   **Bach** composed with great attention to detail, seeking to make every part a work of art. He was not concerned with the world about him and reached emotional heights far beyond the remarkable polyphonic intricacy of his music. **Handel** was inspired by the world about him. He painted large scenes without regard for details. His writing is idiomatic, direct, and easily understood. The differences between **Bach** and **Handel** only serve to emphasize the fact that both men were supreme artists and that each complements the other.

SELECTED BIBLIOGRAPHY

Books

1. Abraham, Gerald, ed. *Handel: A Symposium.* London: Oxford University Press, 1954.
2. Burney, Charles. *A General History of Music, from the Earliest Ages to the Present Period.* 4 vols. London: 1776-1789. (Reprint in 2 vols., ed. Frank Mercer. New York: Harcourt, Brace Co., 1936.
3. Chrysander, Friedrich. *G. F. Händel,* 3 vols. Leipzig: Breitkopf & Härtel, 1856-1867.
4. Cannon, Beekman. *Johann Mattheson, Spectator in Music.* New Haven: Yale University Press, 1947.
5. Carse, Adam. *The Orchestra of the XVIIIth Century.* Cambridge: W. Heffer and Sons, 1940.
6. Dean, Winton. *Handel's Dramatic Oratorios and Masques.* New York: Oxford University Press, 1959. Reprint, 1966.
7. Dent, Edward J. *Foundations of English Opera.* Cambridge: The University Press,1928. Reprint, New York: Da Capo Press, 1965.
8. ――――――*Handel.* London: Duckworth, 1934.
9. Deutsch, Otto Erich. *Handel: A Documentary Biography.* New York: W. W. Norton, 1955.
10. Hall, J. S. *G. F. Handel, the Story of His Life and Work.* London: Boosey & Hawkes, 1960.
11. Hawkins, Sir John. *A General History of the Science and Practice of Music,* 5. vols., 1776. Reprint, London: Novello, 1853. Reprint, 2 vols., New York: Dover Publications, 1963.
12. Kidson, Frank. *The Beggar's Opera: Its Predecessors and Successors.* Cambridge: The University Press, 1922.
13. Lang, Paul Henry. *George Frideric Handel.* New York: W. W. Norton, 1966.
14. Langley, H. *Doctor Arne.* Cambridge: The University Press, 1938.
15. Larsen, Jens Peter. *Handel's Messiah, Origins, Compositions, Sources.* New York: 1948.
16. Mainwaring, John. *Memoirs of the Life of the Late George Frederic Handel.* London: R. and J. Dodsley, 1760.
17. Myers, Robert Manson. *Handel's Messiah: A Touchstone of Taste.* New York: Macmillan Co., 1947.
18. Rolland, Romain. *Handel,* tr. A. E. Hull. London: Paul, Trench, Trubner & Co., 1916.
19. Schultz, W. E. *Gay's Beggar's Opera: Its Content, History and Influence.* New Haven: Yale University Press, 1923.
20. Smith, William C. *Concerning Handel.* London: 1948.
21. Streatfield, R. A. *Handel.* New York: J. Lane Co., 1909.
22. Taylor, Sedley. *The Indebtedness of Handel to Works by Other Composers.* Cambridge: The University Press, 1906.
23. Young, Percy M. *Handel.* London: 1947.
24. ――――――*The Oratorios of Handel.* New York: Roy Publishers, 1950.

Articles

1. Burt, N. "Opera in Arcadia," *MQ* 41 (1955), p. 145.
2. Coopersmith, Jacob Maurice. "Handel Lacunae: A Project," *MQ* 21 (1935), p. 224.
3. Deutsch, Otto Erich. "Burney, Handel and the Barrel Organ," *MT* 90 (1949), p. 227.
4. ――――――"Handel's Hunting Song," *MT* 83 (1942), p. 362.
5. Edwards, Frederick George. "The Foundling Hospital and its Music," *MT* 43 (1902), pp. 304, 377.

6. Hughes, C. "John Christopher Pepusch," *MQ* 31 (1945), p. 45.
7. James, Robert Rutson. "Handel's Blindness," *ML* 13 (1932).
8. Kidson, Frank. "Handel's Publisher, John Walsh, his Successors and Contemporaries," *MQ* 6 (1920), p. 430.
9. Lam, Basil. "Authenticity and the St John Passion," *Early Music* 5 (1977), p. 45.
10. Larson, Jens Peter. "The Text of Handel's *Messiah*," *MQ* 40 (1954), p. 21.
11. Lawrence, William John. "Early Irish Ballad Opera and Comic Opera," *MQ* 8 (1922), p. 397.
12. ————"The Early Years of the First English Opera House," *MQ* 7 (1921), p. 104.
13. Leichtentritt, Hugo. "Handel's Harmonic Art," *MQ* 21 (1935), p. 208.
14. Mansfield, Orlando A. "The Minuet in Handel's *Messiah*," *MQ* 5 (1919), p. 90.
15. Myers, Robert M. "Mrs. Delany: An 18th Century Handelian," *MQ* 32 (1946), p. 12.
16. ————"Samuel Butler: Handelian," *MQ* 34 (1948), p. 177.
17. Redway, N. L. "Handel in Colonial and Post-Colonial America," *MQ* 21 (1935), p. 190.
18. Robinson, Percy. "Handel up to 1720: A New Chronology," *ML* 20 (1939), p. 55.
19. Rogers, Francis. "Handel and Five Prima Donnas," *MQ* 29 (1943), p. 214.
20. Schuller, Herbert M. "Imitation and Expression in British Music Criticism in the 18th Century," *MQ* 34 (1948), p. 544.
21. Smith, William C. "Earliest Editions of Handel's *Messiah*," *MT* 66 (1925), p. 985.
22. ————"The Earliest Editions of Handel's *Water Music*," *MQ* 25 (1939), p. 60.
23. Squire, William B. "Handel's *Clock Music*," *MQ* 5 (1919), p. 538.
24. Wolff, Hellmuth Christian. "Mendelssohn and Handel," *MQ* 45 (1959), p. 175.

Music

1. *Hallische Handel-Ausgabe.* Kassel: Bärenreiter, 1955-   (in progress)
2. Handel, Georg Friedrich. *Werke*, 96 vols., ed. Friedrich Chrysander. Leipzig: Breitkopf & Härtel, 1859-1895. Reprint, Gregg Press, *c.* 1965. (This edition called "Handel Gesellschaft edition" and "Chrysander edition.")

20. *Siciliana* and the beginning of the *Presto* movement from Handel's *Organ Concerto*, Op. 4, No. 5.

21.   The first page of **Handel's MS** of the
Hallelujah Chorus, from *Messiah*.

ABBREVIATIONS

Acta Mus – *Acta Musicologia*

AIM – *Anthology of Instrumental Music,*
ed. Wasielewski

AM – *Anthology of Music,* ed. Fellerer

AMI – *L'Arte Musicale in Italia,* ed. Torchi

AMO – *Archives des Maîtres de l'Orgue,*
ed. Guilmant & Pirro

B – Book

BACH – *Bach, The Quarterly Journal of
the Riemenschneider Bach Institute*

BG – Bach-Gesellschaft

BM – *Baroque Music,* Palisca

BMB – *Bibliotheca Musica Bononiensis:
Musica Pratica*

BR – *The Bach Reader,* ed. David &
Mendel

c. – circa (about)

CE – Complete or Collected Edition

CEKM – *Corpus of Early Keyboard
Music,* ed. Apel

CMA – *Choral Music, a Norton Historical
Anthology,* ed. Robinson

CO – *Cantantibus organis,* ed. Krauss

COF – *Chefs d'oeuvre Classiques de
l'Opéra Français,* ed. Weckerlin

CS – *Cantio Sacra,* ed. Ewerhart

CW – *Das Chrowerk,* ed. Blume

DdT – *Denkmäler deutscher Tonkunst*

DH – Deutsch, *Handel*

DRM – *Denkmäler Rheinischer Musik*

DTB – *Denkmäler der Tonkunst in
Bayern,* ed. Sandberger

DTÖ – *Denkmäler der Tonkunst in
Österreich,* ed. Adler

ed. – editor, edition

EDM – *Das Erbe deutscher Musik*

Facs. – Facsimile

Fasc. – Fascicle

F – Fanna (Vivaldi)

GMB – *Geschichte der Musik in
Beispielen,* ed. Schering

GS – G. Schirmer

HAM – *Historical Anthology of Music,*
ed. Davison & Apel

HG – Handel-Gesellschaft, ed. Chrysander

HM – *Hortus Musicus*

ICDMI – *I Classici della Musica Italiani,*
ed. d'Annunzio

ICMI – *I Classici Musicali Italiani*

JAMS – *Journal of the American
Musicological Society*

K – Kirkpatrick (D. Scarlatti)

L – Longo (D. Scarlatti)

LO – *Liber Organi,* ed. Kaller

LP – *Le Pupitre,* ed. Lesure

LU – *Liber Usualis*

M – Music

MB – *Musica Britannica*

MD – *Musica Divina,* ed. Stablein

ML – *Music and Letters*

MM – *Masterpieces of Music,* ed. Parrish & Ohl

MMA – *Monuments de la Musique Ancienne*

MMF – *Monuments of Music and Music Literature
in Facsimile*

MQ – *Musical Quarterly*

MR – *Music Review*

MSO – *Music Scores Omnibus,* ed. Starr & Devine

MT – *Musical Times*

NagMA – *Musik-Archiv,* ed. Nagel

NASW – *Neue Ausgabe sämtliche Werke* (Schütz)

NAW – *Neue Ausgabe sämtliche Werke,* ed. Adrio
(Schein)

NB – *Neue Ausgabe sämtliche Werke* (Bach)

n.d. – no date

NOH – *New Oxford History of Music*

NS – *Norton Scores,* ed. Kamien

Op. – Opus

P – Pincherle (Vivaldi)

p. – page (pp. – pages)

PAM – *Publikationen älterer praktischer und
theoretischer Musikwerke,* ed. Eitner

PE – Peters Edition

PMA – *Proceedings of the Royal Musical
Association*

rev. ed. – revised edition

RGO – *Zur Geschichte des Orgelspiels,* ed. Ritter

RRMB – *Recent Researches in the Music of the
Baroque Era*

S – *Bach-Werke Verzeichnis,* ed. Schmieder

SCMA – *Smith College Music Archives*

Ser. – Series

SHO – *A Short History of Opera,* Grout

SR – *Source Readings in Music History,*
ed. Strunk

SS – *Schirmer Scores,* ed. Godwin

SWV – *Schütz-Werke Verzeichnis*

TEM – *Treasury of Early Music,* ed. Parrish

v. – volume (vols. – volumes)

WE – *The Wellesley Edition,* ed. La Rue

Z – Zimmermann (Purcell)

INDEX OF NAMES AND FORMS